Antiquities and Classical Traditions in Latin America

T0287834

The *Bulletin of Latin American Research* Book Series
BLAR/SLAS

The *Bulletin of Latin American Research* publishes original research of current interest on Latin America, the Caribbean, inter-American relations and the Latin American Diaspora from all academic disciplines within the social sciences, history and cultural studies. The BLAR/SLAS book series was launched in 2008 with the aim of publishing research monographs and edited collections that compliment the wide scope of the Bulletin itself. It is published and distributed in association with Wiley-Blackwell. We aim to make the series the home of some of the most exciting, innovatory work currently being undertaken on Latin America and we welcome outlines or manuscripts of interdisciplinary, single-authored, jointly-authored or edited volumes. If you would like to discuss a possible submission to the series, please contact the editors at blar@liverpool.ac.uk

Antiquities and Classical Traditions in Latin America

EDITED BY ANDREW LAIRD
AND NICOLA MILLER

Contents

Preface

Antiquities and classical traditions in Latin America are not confined to those of Greece and Rome. Several sites now deemed to be of archaeological interest, such as Teotihuacan in Mexico or Tiwanaku in present-day Bolivia, were revered for their ancient standing as well as for their sacred significance, long before the first European incursions; and the *Popol Vuh*, a Mayan text with origins in pre-Columbian tradition, is often referred to as a classic.

But Greek and Roman legacies have also been prominent in the Caribbean, Mesoamerica and South America. They have played a crucial role in the history, thought and politics of the entire region, just as they have been an important element in its literature, art and architecture. In the mid-1500s, the Controversy of the Indies turned on the significance of Aristotle's notion of natural slavery and the precedent of the Roman Empire. The eighteenth-century Dispute of the Americas was rooted in the conflicting responses of Renaissance humanists to ancient geography in the light of new discoveries. Throughout the colonial period, images and evocations of Greece and Rome abounded in theatrical productions, public ceremonies and patriotic orations. Several insurgents and liberators were inspired by specific antiquarian interests as much as by more general classical ideals. Following independence, Greco-Roman precedents and *exempla* were invoked on all sides in debates about how to build civilised nations. Recent appropriations of Greek tragedy for contemporary representations of racial conflict and drug wars are evidence of the continuing appeal of classical paradigms to those seeking to portray or influence current social realities.

It has been some time since John Elliott, Anthony Pagden and other historians began to identify different ways in which early modern views of antiquity shaped European responses to the New World. Yet there is still little systematic study of the significance of classical traditions that emerged from *within* the Americas. Our purpose is to consider the significance of those traditions, not purely for their own sake, but for their importance in Latin American history. By highlighting their ambivalent role and by focusing on how they have been transformed, we hope to integrate 'Hispanic' or 'Latin American' legacies into the humanities more generally, so that those legacies are no longer marginalised in language-specific or area studies disciplines. The region's contributions to global intellectual history might then become more evident. The present endeavour is offered as an opening salvo, which we hope will be a stimulus for investigations in future. To that end, the bibliographical references for each contribution and especially for the introductory chapter serve as a guide to further reading in the reception of Greece and Rome and the ramifications of classical learning in the Americas.

Preface

This publication is the result of a colloquium entitled *Classical Traditions in Latin American History*, hosted by the Warburg Institute in London on 19–20 May 2016. It is a pleasure to acknowledge the generous support of the Warburg, the Institute of Classical Studies, the Society of Latin American Studies, the History Department of University College London, the Royal Historical Society and the Classics Departments of Brown University and Warwick University for this event, for which Jane Ferguson provided invaluable administrative and practical assistance. Nicola Miller carried out most of the research for her paper as part of a larger project on the history of knowledge in Latin America, generously funded by a Leverhulme Trust Major Research Fellowship. All of the papers presented at the Warburg have been revised for this volume; in addition, Rebecca Earle, Avi Lifschitz and Felipe Fernández-Armesto made important contributions as discussants. We are deeply grateful to Greg Woolf and to Peter Mack for making possible the Warburg Colloquium which led to this collection, and to Matthew Brown, Jo Crow, Nelissa Duarte, Jasmine Gideon and especially Ken Lestrange for the work involved in bringing it to publication.

Andrew Laird
Nicola Miller

1

Introduction: Classical Traditions and Controversies in Latin American History

ANDREW LAIRD

In 1896, Aby Warburg, the art historian whose pioneering researches gave rise to the modern study of the Greek and Roman classical tradition, travelled to the *pueblos* of New Mexico where he spent six months living among the Hopi. The German scholar came to believe that his observations of this Amerindian people, still unadulterated by external contacts, enabled him better to appreciate the alien nature of religious beliefs and practices in ancient Greece (Warburg, 1939: 288; Saxl 1957, 1: 325). Yet Warburg apparently had no idea of how early or of how deeply knowledge of Greece and Rome had taken root in Spanish America and Brazil (Leonard, 1992; Gruzinski, 2002: 2). Nor was any mention made of Latin America in the foundational studies of the classical heritage which would be produced in Warburg's wake during the mid-twentieth century (Highet, 1949; Bolgar, 1954; Weiss, 1964).[1]

Historians in more recent decades have amply demonstrated the extent to which Renaissance views of European antiquity and early perceptions of the New World interacted with and shaped each other, but classical traditions generated *within* the Americas, at least those outside the United States, continue to be overlooked.[2] Out of several recent volumes in English aspiring to provide universal coverage of the influence or reception of Greece and Rome, only one includes a designated discussion of Latin America (Kallendorf, 2007: 222–236).[3] While the vast amount of Latin writing produced in the region during the colonial era has received some attention from specialists, wider

---

1 Highet (1953:147), however, contrasted the Mexico City of the mid-twentieth century to its Aztec antecedent without considering the intervening eras.

2 Pagden (1982), Todorov (1984), Brading (1991), Greenblatt (1991), Grafton, Shelford and Siraisi (1992), Haase and Reinhold (1994), Kupperman (1995) showed how classical antiquity influenced understanding of the New World and its peoples. Conversely, Elliott (1970, 1992), Chiappelli (1976) accentuated the effects of knowledge of the Americas on classical conceptions of nature, geography and history.

3 Martindale and Thomas (2003), Hardwick and Stray (2008), and Silk, Gildenhard and Barrow (2013) do not mention the region and it is not covered in Grafton, Most and Settis (2010). Collections in Spanish devoted to Latin America's classical

appropriations of Greco-Roman culture – which reach to the present day – have generally been ignored.[4] David Lupher's study of classical models in sixteenth-century Spanish America and Sabine MacCormack's work on the prominence of ancient Rome in the political and intellectual life of viceregal Peru are among some outstanding exceptions (González, 1981; MacCormack, 1995, 2007; Lupher, 2003; Pohl and Lyons, 2010, 2016).

The principal aim of this collection has been to consider, from a variety of perspectives, the significance of Greek and Roman antiquity and classical traditions for Latin American history. The idea is to highlight the role those traditions have played in shaping beliefs or influencing events – and to suggest that some crucial developments in thought, hitherto conceived as 'Latin American', might be integrated into mainstream currents of the humanities. The contributions Latin America has made to global intellectual history, or rather to intellectual history *tout court*, may then be more apparent. The discussions in this book are therefore not typical studies in classical reception – which all too often presuppose the centrality of classics even as they seek to affirm it (Brockliss, Chaudhuri, Lushkov and Wasdin, 2012: 7). The impetus for the present volume comes rather from recognition that conceptions of European antiquity have proved a foundational and enduring element in many phases of historical change.

The fact that classical legacies in the history of the Americas have tended to be most evident in conflicts and controversies is a sobering reminder of the social and ethnic divisions that those legacies reflected and sometimes helped to actualise. The celebrated remark of the philosopher Walter Benjamin (1969: 256) that 'there is no document of civilization which is not at the same time a document of barbarism' could certainly be applied to the countless documents from all over Latin America which show evidence of classical learning. Literary works or scientific treatises cannot be considered in isolation from politics, race, gender or class any more than tracts on the rights of Indians and 'moral histories' or ethnographies. Their creation routinely depended on the economic exploitation of peoples who gained little from the scholarly advances made within universities and other institutions. Just as classicising motifs or tendencies in visual art are often redolent of high culture, classical references or *exempla* in modern or contemporary writing generally indicate a privileged provenance, however critical of inequity and the status quo such writing might be (Taboada, 2012).

---

traditions have emerged only recently: Grammatico, Arbea and Edwards (2003), Bocchetti (2010), and Cruz Barros and Huidobro (2018). See also Osorio Romero et al. (1983, 1991) on Mexico, and Hampe Martínez (1999) on Peru.

4   Ijsewijn (1996, 1: 296–307) and Laird (2014, 2015) are surveys of Ibero-American Latin.

Nonetheless, invocations of Greece and Rome can illuminate historical realities. The present collection of essays can only hint at the range of examples over the course of five centuries. Prior to giving a brief overview of the individual contributions, this Introduction will attempt to contextualise them by identifying three major fields of Greco-Roman influence which had a pivotal bearing on Latin American history. These fields of influence were roughly successive: the classical idea of the Golden Age, which was prevalent in the wake of the discovery and conquest; the role of Aristotle which endured in education and intellectual life from the early colonial period until at least the end of the eighteenth century; and aspects of both Ciceronian republicanism and Romantic Hellenism which acquired more political momentum with the onset of independence.

In his *Decades de orbe novo* (Decades on the New World), which were widely read in the early 1500s, the Italian humanist Peter Martyr described how the native inhabitants Columbus found in the Caribbean held their property in common, with little conception of 'mine' and 'yours'. 'It is their *Golden Age*', Martyr wrote, '[…] without laws, without books, without judges; they *revere what is right* naturally and automatically' (Martyr, *Decades* 1.3.10; Mazzacane and Magioncalda, 2005, 1: 272). Those words echoed the ancient Roman poet Ovid's narrative of the mythical 'first *Golden Age* which, with no coercion and *automatically without any law, revered* trust and *what is right*' (*Metamorphoses* 1.189–190). Various descriptions of the New World, including Thomas More's fictional *Utopia* (1516), were inspired by Peter Martyr.

The *Utopia*, in turn, is supposed to have prompted Vasco de Quiroga to establish residential communities for native Mexicans in the 1530s (Zavala, 1998). Lucian's *Saturnalia*, a Greek text popularised by More's Latin translation, was another notable influence on the Spanish judge: the god Saturn promises the return of his former reign, in which men did not have to sow or till the earth, there were no masters and slaves, and wine, milk and honey flowed in abundance. That led Quiroga to conclude that the people of the Indies lived in such a Golden Age while the Spaniards were in an Age of Iron; and he also envisioned the formation of two 'republics', one for the Spaniards, and another on a communitarian model for the Indians (Martínez Baracs, 2005: 248–250). Oddly enough another pagan classical text, Virgil's fourth *Eclogue*, legitimised this political pluralism in Christian terms: Virgil's poem, which also predicted the restoration of Saturn's kingdom, was believed to refer to the coming of Christ. All these connections were made in Vasco de Quiroga's *Información en derecho* – not a literary work, but a legal brief sent to the Spanish crown in 1535 (Torres de Mendoza, 1868: 333–513).

The mythical Golden Age served the first generations of missionaries as a convenient allegory, but later utopian authors in the Americas would rely on other classical authorities to construct more elaborate theories. The story of

Atlantis which originated in Plato's *Timaeus* and *Critias*, the political prescriptions of his *Republic* and *Laws*, and a range of neo-Platonic doctrines, mostly mediated by Marsilio Ficino's Latin translations and commentaries, were of recurrent interest to creole scholars in the Indies and even to some indigenous authors, from the sixteenth century onwards (Tord, 1999; Vidal-Naquet, 2007). As in Europe, the Greek works of Plutarch, Josephus and Eusebius were largely known in Latin. Several classical poets, especially Virgil and Ovid, were popular in vernacular translation, as well as studied in the original.

Aristotle had even more traction. The philosopher's pervasive impact on colonial history was determined simply by his central place in school curricula. The Valladolid Controversies of 1550–1551, about the justifications for the conquest of the New World and about the rights of the Indians, hinged on interpretation of Aristotle's *Politics*. That text was first invoked to substantiate the claim that Indians were natural slaves – a claim made by John Mair of the University of Paris in 1510 and later supported by Juan Ginés de Sepúlveda. His 1545 dialogue in manuscript, *Democrates secundus*, quoted many passages from his then unpublished Latin translation of the *Politics* (1548). Sepúlveda attributed those quotations to the speaker Democrates, who argued that an uncivilised people should yield to a people who can subordinate their passions to reason.

Bartolomé de las Casas opposed this interpretation of Aristotle in his *Argumentum apologiae* (1552), to affirm that all humans were equally rational. Challenging the application of the term 'barbarian' to the Indians, he insisted that war and slavery should not be imposed upon them, and confronted head-on his adversary's invocation of the *Politics*. Las Casas went so far as to question Aristotle's foundational authority altogether: 'although the Philosopher, in his ignorance of Christian truth and love, wrote that advanced people can hunt barbarians like wild animals, let no one conclude that barbarians are to be killed or oppressed with excessive toils […] Goodbye Aristotle! From Christ, the Eternal Truth, we are told: Love your neighbour as yourself' (Las Casas, 1992: 39–40).

Aristotle's philosophy informed another controversy in the mid-sixteenth century – less well known, but just as far-reaching for American history. Julius Caesar Scaliger, a renowned physician and philologist, maintained in his *Exotericae exercitationes* (1557) that the Indies were barren and uninhabitable. This was part of his ferocious defence of traditional Aristotelian physics and cosmology against the scientific observations advanced in an encyclopedic work of natural philosophy by Gerolamo Cardano (Maclean, 1984; Sakamoto, 2016). The Jesuit historian and missionary José de Acosta took on Scaliger in his *Historia natural y moral de las Indias* (Natural and Social History of the Indies), published in 1590, and Juan de Solórzano y Pereira, an eminent jurist and judge in the *Audiencia* of Lima, also countered Scaliger's *Exercitationes* in his

De indianorum jure disputatio (Disputation on Law in the Indies), originally published in 1629 (translated into Spanish in 1647 as *Política indiana*). On the basis of their classical education as well as their experience of the Americas, Acosta and Solórzano y Pereira rejected the view that the Indies represented unwelcome extremes of climate.

The seminal role of the quarrel between the Aristotelian Scaliger and Cardano in the eighteenth-century 'Dispute of the New World' has almost gone unnoticed (Cañizares-Esguerra, 1999). The French naturalist George Louis Leclerc Buffon was following in Scaliger's footsteps when he argued that America's climate was deficient and that all the forms of life it sustained were inferior to those in Europe – and Buffon also confessed how much he found himself agreeing with the ancient philosopher: 'I open Aristotle and what do I find but all my ideas in this wretched Aristotle' (Séchelles, 1829: 38). Cornelius de Pauw, who drew on Buffon's work to hold that indigenous Americans were a degenerate species of humanity, even maintained that Spaniards had fabricated their reports of the calendars, magnificent buildings and other achievements of pre-Columbian peoples. Similar opinions were expressed by other Enlightenment historians in Europe, notably Guillaume Thomas Raynal and William Robertson (Gerbi, 2010).

Spanish American Jesuit scholars were far more prone than their Brazilian counterparts to rebut these European polemics. They did so by presenting the history, geography and indigenous peoples of the Americas in a classical frame. Francisco Javier Clavijero's decision to call the history of Mexico he published in Italian in 1780 an *'ancient* history' (*Storia Antica del Messico*) is very pertinent, and his associate Rafael Landívar celebrated the flora and fauna of Mesoamerica in the *Rusticatio Mexicana* (1782), a Latin poem modelled on Virgil's *Georgics* (Laird, 2006). José Manuel Peramás' comparison of the social organisation of the Guarani Indians in Paraguay to Plato's ideal republic was a thinly veiled response to the conjectural histories of De Pauw and Raynal, as Desiree Arbo's chapter will show below. The fact that a controversy initiated in the Italian Renaissance could continue until the end of eighteenth century attests to the longevity of Aristotle's grip on early modern thought and education.

This was the case on both sides of the Atlantic: the Aristotelianism of the Iberian scholastic revival in the sixteeenth century had a long run in American universities, even after the expulsion of the Jesuits from all the territories of Portugal in 1759 and from Spain's dominions in 1767. There had been some significant achievements: Fray Alonso de la Vera Cruz's ontological theory of relations is held to have anticipated positions advanced by Frege and Peirce in the twentieth century (Redmond, 1990). Antonio Rubio's Aristotelian *Logica mexicana* was printed all over Europe in the early 1600s and influential commentaries on Aristotle's *Logic* and *Metaphysics* were also published in

Lima (Osorio Romero, 1988; Rivara de Tuesta, 1999; Hampe Martínez, 1999: 69–100). But in the mid-1700s, José Rafael Campoy, a Jesuit professor in New Spain, formed a new impression of Aristotle from reading texts which were not in the scholastic curriculum (Navarro, 1948: 128). A generation later, Miguel Hidalgo y Costilla wrote a dissertation challenging the standard theological methods of exegesis by calling for sources to be read critically in their historical contexts – the same Hidalgo who would lead the Mexican War of Independence in the early 1800s (Hidalgo, 1998; Varela Chávez, 2011).

If Aristotelianism had informed and largely delimited scientific thought and philosophical speculation, Cicero shaped not just education in the humanities but conceptions of humanity itself. His recognition that that there was no difference of definition between the nations of mankind (*De legibus* 1.10.28–30) was crucial to the conception of natural law held by Bartolomé de las Casas in the *Apologética historia sumaria* 2.48 (1992a, 7: 536–537). Cicero's illustrative story, in *De inventione* 1.2, about how a wise man in pre-historic times used eloquence to bring the 'savage people of old' ('ferales antiquos homines') into civilised communities was cited or echoed by many of the missionaries in the Americas, including the Dominican Las Casas in Hispaniola, the Franciscan Cristóbal Cabrera in New Spain, and the Jesuit José de Anchieta in Brazil – and Cicero's illustration was also a model for the Inca Garcilaso de la Vega's account of the origin of civilisation in Peru (Laird, 2016: 124–128).

The association Cicero had made between *ratio*, reason, and *oratio*, persuasive speech, was paralleled by the connections between pedagogy, rhetoric and political theology in the writings of Erasmus of Rotterdam which so enthralled the first churchmen in the New World (Bataillon, 1932, 1937). But while Erasmus' mockery of corrupt institutions appeared to lead to schisms and heresy, Cicero's advocation of citizens' unanimous devotion to the *Patria* must have had its attractions for educated members of colonial elites living in societies rendered unstable, and sometimes violent, by harsh economic and ethnic divisions. In his *Theatro de virtudes políticas*, Theatre of Political Virtues (1680), the most celebrated intellectual of seventeenth-century New Spain, Carlos de Sigüenza y Góngora (1984: 167–240), endorsed the view that 'a citizen lives not for himself but his *patria*'. It is telling that Sigüenza (1984: 95–135) later wrote his *Alboroto y motín de los Indios*, a memoir of a 1692 uprising in which a mob of natives and mixed-race *castas* attempted to burn down the viceregal palace in Mexico City.

Cicero's works were accorded pride of place in the Jesuit curriculum known as the 'ratio studiorum', 'system of study'. Latin and latinate eloquence had both a practical and symbolic value for the Jesuits in seventeenth-century New Spain – and this obtained all over the Americas. Cicero's emphasis on probability in moral philosophy had also led

Jesuits to the view that in difficult matters of conscience one can follow a probable opinion about an ethical course of action. In the New World that historically controversial position had a palpable consequence: the energetic production of confessional manuals in Spanish and in Amerindian indigenous languages (Maryks, 2008). Such manuals are a potentially valuable resource for ethnohistorians because the topics and questions they cover throw light on assumptions and expectations about native beliefs, customs and conduct.

The Aristotelian Dispute of the Americas, discussed above, intersected with another controversy in which Cicero had a major part to play (Laird, 2012: 243–251). The quarrel was provoked by the Dean of Alicante in Spain who was one of the most eminent classical scholars of his age. Manuel Martí was a formidable Greek and Roman antiquarian, but he was especially devoted to Cicero whom he emulated by writing to his acquaintances in Latin. Martí's collected letters were first published in the year of his death in 1737: in one of them he described the Indies as lying 'in a deserted intellectual wilderness', without books, libraries, or teachers (Martí, 1738 2: 38–39). These casual remarks caused a furore in American centres of learning because the Dean had hitherto been revered throughout the Hispanic world for bringing to publication in 1696 the *Bibliotheca Hispana Vetus* (The Old Spanish Library), a bibliography in Latin of every pre-modern Iberian author, from earliest antiquity to the end of the fifteenth century (Antonio, 1996b).[5]

It was thus in a spirit of antagonism that a Jesuit in Mexico City sought to emulate Martí's best known achievement by producing a catalogue – also in Latin – of authors from New Spain and other Spanish colonies: Juan José de Eguiara y Eguren's *Bibliotheca Mexicana* (The Mexican Library), is now better known than the work which gave rise to it, even though only the first of its several projected volumes appeared in 1755. Other rebuttals of Martí's claims were made in a patently Ciceronian style because of his fondness for the Roman statesman: in an *Oratio apologetica* (Defence Speech), Juan Gregorio de Campos y Martínez (1746: 1) personified the Mexican *Patria*, having her call on her citizens to save her name and honour, in exactly the same way as Cicero had brought the Roman *Patria* to life in the first of his speeches against the mutinous conspirator Catiline (*In Catilinam* 1.1, 1.19–26).

The creole Jesuits' *Patria* had always been their own Society, but after that was dissolved in 1773, they increasingly applied the notion of *Patria* to their one-time provinces in Spanish America. One former Jesuit even urged his

---

5   Nicolás Antonio, the original editor, died in 1684 having completed only the *Bibliotheca Hispana Nova* (Antonio, 1996a) on authors of the sixteenth and seventeenth centuries.

younger countrymen to master Ciceronian Latin as a patriotic duty (Fabri, 1780). Such an exhortation might now appear ridiculous, but classical references abounded in the orations that were very prominent in the painful struggles and conflicts over independence in American countries over the century to follow. As Republicans and monarchists clashed in Mexico during the 1830s, the patriotic soldier and historian Carlos María de Bustamante felt impelled to produce the first translation into Spanish of the previously lost parts of Cicero's *De republica*, only a few years after they had been rediscovered in the Vatican Library (Buelna Serrano, 1976).

The generation of liberators active earlier in the 1800s also derived their conceptions of republicanism from classical authorities as well as from modern thinkers such as Hobbes and Rousseau (Aguilar and Rojas, 2002: 13–56, 86–117, 313–350; Miller 2016). Francisco de Miranda, founder of the ill-fated First Republic of Venezuela, had travelled to Italy and Greece – numerous mentions of ancient history or quotations from Greek or Roman authors adorned his writings (Castillo Didier, 1995). Simón Bolívar's republicanism, perhaps more classicising than classical (Bolívar, 1976; Briceño Perozo, 1992), was symbolised by an oath he allegedly swore in 1805 on the Monte Sacro in Rome, vowing not to rest until the chains of Spanish oppression were broken (Bartosik-Vélez, 2016). The attested location for this declaration has been deemed appropriate: the same *Mons sacer* had been the site of a plebeian secession in 494 BC after which the people of Rome were granted new rights and the power to elect their own tribunes (Mignone, 2016: 17–47, 196–202).

Orators of independence and nation-building over the course of the nineteenth century made frequent, if often specious, references to ancient Greece and Rome, sometimes affirming that the pre-Columbian civilisations matched or surpassed those of European antiquity (Gierich-Carvajal, 2005: 223–305; Earle, 2007). Several political leaders, though, had availed themselves of a thorough classical education. Andrés Bello for a brief period had acted as Bolívar's tutor and his best known poem, *Silva a la agricultura de la zona tórrida* (Poetic Medley on Farming in the Torrid Zone), which was closely modelled on Virgil's *Georgics*, had a decisive role in shaping South American educational and constitutional thought (Jaksic, 2006). Others applied their erudition in more overt and concrete ways. José Gaspar Rodríguez de Francia instituted a system of consulship for Paraguay in 1813, before establishing himself as the 'Perpetual Dictator of the Republic' three years later (Williams, 1979: 43–62). The title recalled Julius Caesar's appointment in 45 BC as 'dictator perpetuo rei publicae constituendae causa' (Lintott, 1999: 113). Miguel Antonio Caro, the president of Colombia from 1892 until 1896, was an enthusiastic scholar of Latin literature and a poet who translated Virgil (Rivas Sacconi, 1949). Caro's programme of conservative reform may have been modelled on Augustus' social legislation (Laird, 2007: 224–226). The president set such great store by philological learning that his opponent General Rafael Uribe Uribe report-edly took Latin lessons before confronting him in the Senate. In any event, the determination that knowledge of grammar and literature should be a pre-requisite for political power endured in Colombia into the 1930s (Deas, 1993: 28–29).

Such strongly conservative tendencies were at odds with a progressive Hel-lenism which percolated into the Americas as part of a broader current of Romantic thought at the end of the nineteenth century. While Carlos Manuel de Céspedes, who declared independence for Cuba in 1868, had also trans-lated Virgil into Spanish verse, the 'apostle of Cuban independence', José Martí, discerned a parallel between the Greek struggle for freedom in his own time and the predicament of his homeland. Elina Miranda Cancela will argue in her chapter that Martí believed Greek culture had the potential to shape a common future for America. Only a few years after Martí's death, the Uruguayan José Enrique Rodó would urge the youth of Latin America, in his *Ariel* (1900), to unite in embracing an antique ideal in contrast to 'Puritan asceticisms' (Rodó, 1967: 46). Both writers have had a longstanding influence on Latin American thought (Fernández Retamar, 1989). Praising Plato and Athens, Rodó affirmed that 'the perfection of human morality should consist in pouring the spirit of charity into the mould of Greek elegance' (Franco, 1999: 452).

Rodó's thinking was mediated by Pedro Henríquez Ureña to an intellec-tual coterie established in Mexico City in 1909 as the *Ateneo de la Juventud* or 'Young People's Athenaeum' (Laird, 2010: 172–180). Henríquez Ureña would become president of the Dominican Republic: his philhellenism is explored in Rosa Andújar's chapter to follow. The devotion to Greece shared by the *Ateneo*'s other leading members inspired or at least reflected their opposition to a political establishment which endorsed the social Darwinism of Herbert Spencer. For instance José Vasconcelos, an activist before the Mexican Revolu-tion of 1910 who would have a long political career, remarked that Spencer's own system of evolution, even after two thousand years had not made him a match for the fifth-century BC sophist Gorgias of Leontini (Vasconcelos, 2000: 311–312). Vasconcelos' first two books published in 1916, an essay entitled 'Pythagoras', and *Prometeo vencedor* (Prometheus the Conqueror), an attempt at a Greek tragedy, celebrated the people of Latin America as 'a new human-ity with the best of all cultures, harmonized and ennobled within the Spanish mould'. That view would be reaffirmed in his best known work, *La raza cós-mica* (The Cosmic Race), first published in 1925. A later preface argued that Rome and Hellenistic Egypt were precedents for the success of Latin Amer-ica's *mestizo* or multicultural civilisation (Vasconcelos, 1997: 3–7).

Alfonso Reyes, the greatest literary scholar of Latin America in the first half of the twentieth century, was another co-founder of the *Ateneo*. Though he had no political ambition, his abundant writing on Greek literature and history in the 1930s and 1940s had an ideological motivation, as Robert Conn's chapter will make clear below. In 1930 the bimillennium of Virgil's birth was celebrated in Mexico as well as in Ecuador, prompting topical interpretations of the expropriation of land which the poet had addressed in the *Eclogues*: concerns about policies of land reform were current in both countries (Ziolkowski, 1993: 21–22). In his own contribution to that commemoration, *Discurso por Virgilio* (Discourse through Virgil), Reyes affirmed that he 'wanted Latin for the left' and argued that to abandon the colonial inheritance of Latin was tantamount to prescribing the abolition of human knowledge (Reyes, 1955: 160–161). But his comparison of the autochthonous elements of Mexican culture with 'red clay destined to be washed in Latin waters' suggests that the masses are subject to a kind of processing by those who see themselves as the heirs of European tradition (Franco, 1999: 452).

At the very time that the nation state was becoming the fundamental political, cultural and economic unit of the modern age, twentieth-century intellectuals from the Caribbean, Mexico and the Southern Cone were espousing visions of pan-Americanism. Such visions – the inclusiveness of Martí's *Nuestra América*, Rodó's aesthetic idealism, Henríquez Ureña's supranational *Patria*, Vasconcelos' ambitious multiculturalism – all invoked precedents from the Greco-Roman past. Yet Latin America's emergence as a civilisation has long been overlooked by global historians and poorly explained by political scientists outside the region. In the earlier twentieth century, Oswald Spengler (1939) and Arnold Toynbee (1953) bypassed it altogether in their equations of civilisation with a 'unified culture' (Birkenmaier, 2013). Latin America was much later identified by Samuel Huntington as one of nine global civilisations – but one which was problematically distinguished from Western civilisation (Huntington, 1996).

Despite any vestigial evocations of Latin or even of Latin culture in the region's name, Latin America's classical legacies are now less likely than ever to bear on the vexed question of its identity.[6] Statesmen may continue to use illustrations from Greco-Roman myth or history: among many recent instances are the designation of capitalism as a 'hydra' by Subcomandante Galeano (formerly known as Subcomandante Marcos), and Fidel Castro's remark that President Obama's rhetorical craft surpassed that of Cicero's Catilinarian speeches (EZLN, 2016; Castro, 2014). But from the mid-twentieth century onwards, classical models ceased to determine political agenda, although they have continued to supply analogies for writers seeking to

---

6   Gruzinski (1997) cited in Quijada (1998: 19–21), Habinek (1998: 31, 176) and Pym (2000: 191) discuss origins and implications of the nomenclature.

represent or reflect on historical developments. The story of Palinurus in Virgil's *Aeneid* was a matrix for Fernando del Paso's oblique commentary on the 1968 massacre at Tlatelolco in his novel *Palinuro de México* (1974); the Minotaur and his labyrinth symbolised the cunning and menace of military dictatorship for the contemporary Salvadorean poet Álvaro Darío Lara, and countless stagings or renovations of classical Greek tragedies have addressed contemporary social or political themes (Paso, 1977; Darío Lara, 1998; Nikoloutsos, 2011).

The essays below are arranged roughly in the chronological order of the subjects they address. Natalia Maillard Álvarez shows how classical texts were first conveyed to New Spain and Peru in the 1500s, giving an indication of the ancient authors which were in circulation and of the kind of readership they reached. Colleges and convents were the principal sites for the dissemination of texts and ideas in the early colonial period: a Latin herbal produced at the College of Santa Cruz de Tlatelolco is discussed by Alejandra Rojas, who argues that its authors and painters strategically aligned Mexican legend with Greco-Roman myth as well as biblical narrative. A contrasting relation between ancient Mediterranean and Mexican traditions emerges in another mid-sixteenth century pictorial manuscript surveyed by Byron Hamann. There, an illustration which is markedly pre-Hispanic in style and content, incorporates a recognisable European detail, charging it with a very different set of meanings.

The Inca Garcilaso de la Vega combined classical learning and native memory in his histories of Peru. Erika Valdivieso presents the Inca's less well known *Diálogos de amor* in the context of Renaissance Neoplatonic translation and interpretation to show how he held his own in a European milieu. It is seldom acknowledged that native Mexican chroniclers also made use of Greco-Roman authors, incorporating numerous references to classical antiquity in their writings: Andrew Laird argues that they did so in order to claim universal significance for their own history and for the Nahuatl language as a literary medium. Conversely, indigenous legacies were appropriated by American-born Spaniards or 'creoles'. Stuart McManus illuminates the use of models drawn from pre-Hispanic antiquity in Sigüenza y Góngora's *Theatro de virtudes políticas* by comparing them to the Greco-Roman *exempla* regularly deployed in the ceremonial oratory of New Spain's Jesuit elites. The implications of the specific analogies José Manuel Peramás drew between native communities in the Jesuit missions of Paraguay and the ideal society of Plato's *Republic* will then be considered by Desiree Arbo.

A panorama of the emergence of a classicism in modern Latin American history and culture is offered by Robert Conn, before the particular achievements of Jose Martí and of Pedro Henríquez Ureña are explored by Elina Miranda Cancela and Rosa Andújar respectively. But the use of classical references in connection with nation-building was not always confined to intellectual elites: in her chapter Nicola Miller brings to light remarkable evidence of such references in popular poetry, sayings and songs from the later nineteenth century. Eric Cullhed identifies an alternative to the prevalent constructions of the classical in modern Latin America by focusing on the recurrent and varied invocations of Byzantium in poetry and other discourses.

Finally, in the *Envoi* to this book Jorge Cañizares-Esguerra calls attention to a number of colonial thinkers whose contributions to scholarship and intellectual history have been ignored or forgotten outside Latin America. Even if classical traditions once had their ultimate origin in the ancient Mediterranean, they soon ceased to belong to Europe alone. That is in accord with an observation made more than 50 years ago by the Cuban essayist Roberto Fernández Retamar which is a suitable epigraph for the discussions to follow:

> Mientras el 'occidental' es un mero intruso en la mayor parte de las colonias que ha asolado, en el Nuevo Mundo es, además, uno de los componentes, y no el menos importante, que dará lugar al mestizo (no sólo el mestizo racial, por supuesto). Si la 'tradición occidental' no es toda la tradición de este, es también su tradición. (Fernández Retamar, 1965: 55)

> Whereas the 'Westerner' is a mere intruder in most of the cultures he has devastated, in the New World he is also a component – and an important one – in the person of mixed identity (mixed not just in the racial sense of course). The 'Western Tradition' is not the entire tradition of the New World, but it is its tradition as well.

References and further reading

Aguilar, J. A. and Rojas, R. (eds.) (2002) *El republicanismo en Hispanoamérica. Ensayos de historia intelectual y política*. Fondo de Cultura Económica: Mexico City.

Antonio, N. [1672] (1996a) *Bibliotheca Hispana nova*. (2 vols.). Visor Libros: Madrid.

Antonio, N. [1696] (1996b) *Bibliotheca Hispana vetus*. (2 vols.). Visor Libros: Madrid.

Bartosik-Vélez, E. (2016) 'Simón Bolívar's Rome', *International Journal of the Classical Tradition*. [WWW document]. URL https://link.springer.com/article/10.1007/s12138-016-0428-0 [accessed 23 June 2018].

Bataillon, M. (1932) 'Érasme au Mexique', *Actes du 2e Congrès national des Sciences historiques, Alger, 14-16 avril 1930*. Societé historique algérienne: Algiers, 31–44.

Bataillon, M. (1937) *Erasme et l'Espagne: recherches sur l'histoire spirituelle du XVIe siècle*. Geneva.

Benjamin, W. (1969) 'Theses on the Philosophy of History' in *Illuminations* (ed. H. Arendt; trans. H. Zorn). Schocken: New York, 253–264.

Birkenmaier, A. (2013) 'Scenarios of Colonialism and Culture: Oswald Spengler's Latin America'. *MLN* **128**(2): 256–276.

Bocchetti, C. (ed.) (2010) *La influencia clásica en América Latina*. Universidad Nacional de Colombia: Bogotá.

Bolgar, R. R. (1954) *The Classical Heritage and its Beneficiaries*. Cambridge University Press: Cambridge.

Bolívar, S. (1976) *Bolívar, Doctrina del Libertador* (ed. M. Pérez Vila). Biblioteca Ayacucho: Caracas.

Brading, D. A. (1991) *The First America: The Spanish Monarchy, Creole Patriots and the Liberal State 1492–1867*. Cambridge University Press: Cambridge.

Briceño Perozo, M. (1992) *Reminiscencias griegas y latinas en las obras del Libertador*. Editorial Texto: Caracas.

Brockliss, W., Chaudhuri, P., Lushkov, A. H. and Wasdin, K. (eds.) (2012) *Reception and the Classics*. Cambridge University Press: Cambridge.

Buelna Serrano, M. E. (1976) *Carlos María de Bustamente, traductor del De re república de M. T. Cicerón*. UNAM Licenciatura thesis: Mexico City.

Campos y Martínez, J. G (1746) *Oratio Apologetica Quae Velut Supplex Libellus Potentissimo Hispaniarum Regi Philippo V*. Imprenta de Marin de Rivera: Mexico City.

Cañizares-Esguerra, J. (1999) 'New World, New Stars: Patriotic Astrology and the Invention of Indian and Creole Bodies in Colonial Spanish America, 1600-1650'. *American Historical Review* **104**: 33–68.

Castillo Didier, M. (1995) *Grecia y Francisco de Miranda: precursor héroe y mártir de la independencia hispanoamericana*. Universidad de Chile: Santiago de Chile.

Castro, F. (2014) 'Obama no estaba obligado a un acto cínico'. *Diario Granma*, (Havana) 11 March.

Chiappelli, F. (ed.) (1976) *First Images of America. The Impact of the New World on the Old*. (2 vols.). University of California Press: Berkeley.

Cruz Barros, N. and Huidobro, M. G. (eds.) (2018) *América y lo Clásico; lo Clásico y América*. RIL Editores, Pontificia Universidad Católica de Chile and Universidad Andrés Bello de Chile: Santiago de Chile.

Darío Lara, A. (1998) *Minotauro: 1990*. Impreso Mazatli: San Salvador.

Deas, M. (1993) *Del poder y la gramática y otros ensayos sobre historia, política y literatura colombianas*. Tercer Mundo Editores: Bogotá, 25–60.

Earle, R. (2007) *Return of the Native: Indians and Myth-Making in Spanish America, 1810–1930*. Duke University Press: Durham NC.

Elliott, J. H. (1970) *The Old World and the New, 1492–1650*. Cambridge University Press: Cambridge.

Elliott, J. H. (1989) *Spain and its World*. Yale University Press: New Haven.

EZLN (Ejército Zapatista de Liberación Nacional) (2016) *Critical Thought in the Face of the Capitalist Hydra I: Contributions by the Sixth Commission of the EZLN*. Paperboat Press: Durham.

Fabri, M. (1780) 'Florentissimae Mexicanae Iuventuti', Preface to Diego José Abad, *De Deo Deoque Homine*. G. Blasinius: Cesena.

Fernández Retamar, R. (1965) 'Martí en su (tercer) mundo'. *Cuba Socialista* **41**: 44–49.

Fernández Retamar, R. (1989) *Caliban and Other Essays*. University of Minnesota Press: Minneapolis.

Franco, J. (1999) 'Dominant Ideology and Literature: The Case of Post-Revolutionary Mexico' in M. L. Pratt and K. Newman (eds.) *Critical Passions: Selected Essays*. Duke University Press: Durham NC, 447–460.

Gerbi, A. (2010) *The Dispute of the New World* (trans. J. Moyle). Pittsburgh University Press: Pittsburgh.

Gierich-Carvajal, M. (2005) *Die Rezeption der Antike in Spanisch-Amerika und ihre Bedeutung für die Staatsbildung*. Unpublished doctoral dissertation, University of Eichstätt-Ingolstadt.

González, J. (1981) *La idea de Roma en la historiografía indiana (1492–1550)*. Consejo Superior de Investigaciones Científicas: Madrid.

Grafton, A., Shelford, A. and Siraisi, N. G. (1992) *New World, Ancient Texts: The Power of Tradition and the Shock of Discovery*. Harvard University Press: Cambridge MA.

Grafton, A., Most, G. W. and Settis, S. (eds.) (2010) *The Classical Tradition*. Belknap Press of Harvard University Press: Cambridge MA.

Grammatico, G., Arbea, A. and Edwards, L. M. (eds.) (2003) *América Latina y lo Clásico*. (2 vols.). Universidad Metropolitana de Ciencias de la Educación: Santiago de Chile.

Greenblatt, S. (1991) *Marvelous Possessions: The Wonder of the New World*. University of Chicago Press: Chicago.

Gruzinski, S. (1997) *Usos políticamente incorrectos de la latinidad*. Unpublished lecture, La Caixa de Barcelona, Madrid (March).

Gruzinski, S. (2002) *The Mestizo Mind: The Intellectual Dynamics of Colonization and Globalization*. Routledge: London.

Habinek, T. (1998) *The Politics of Latin Literature: Writing, Identity and Empire in Ancient Rome*. Princeton University Press: Princeton.

Haase, W. and Reinhold, M. (eds.) (1993) *The Classical Tradition and the Americas: European Images of the Americas and the Classical Tradition, Part 1*. De Gruyter: Berlin.

Hampe Martínez, T. (1999) 'Sobre las Escolástica virreinal peruana: el P. Leonardo de Peñafiel, comentarista de Aristóteles' in T. Hampe Martínez (ed.) *La tradición clásica en el Perú virreinal*. Fondo Editorial Universidad Nacional Mayor de San Marcos: Lima, 69–100.

Hampe Martínez, T. (ed.) (1999) *La tradición clásica en el Perú virreinal*. Fondo Editorial Universidad Nacional Mayor de San Marcos: Lima.

Hardwick, L. and Stray, C. (eds.) (2008) *A Companion to Classical Receptions*. Blackwell: Oxford.

Hidalgo Costilla, M. (1998) 'Disertación sobre el verdadero método de estudiar teología escolástica' in M. del C. Rovira (ed.) *Pensamiento filosófico mexicano del siglo XIX y primeros años del XX*. (3 vols.). Universidad Nacional Autónoma de México: Mexico City 1: 165–180.

Highet, G. (1949) *The Classical Tradition: Greek and Roman Influences on Western Literature*. Oxford University Press: New York and London.

Highet, G. (1953) *People, Places, and Books*. Oxford University Press: New York.

Huntington, S. (1996) *The Clash of Civilizations and the Remaking of World Order*. Simon and Shuster: New York.

Ijsewijn, J. (1990) *Companion to Neo-Latin Studies*. (2 vols.). Leuven University Press, Supplementa Humanistica Lovaniensia: Louvain.

Jaksic, I. (2006) *Andrés Bello: Scholarship and Nation-Building in Nineteenth-Century Latin America*. Cambridge University Press: Cambridge.

Kallendorf, C. (ed.) (2007) *A Companion to the Classical Tradition*. Blackwell: Malden, MA.

Kupperman, K. O. (ed.) (1995) *America in European Consciousness, 1493–1750*. Omohundro Institute of Early American History and Culture: Chapel Hill, North Carolina.

Laird, A. (2006) *The Epic of America. An Introduction to Rafael Landívar and the Rusticatio Mexicana*. Duckworth: London.

Laird, A. (2007) 'Latin America' in C. Kallendorf (ed.) *A Companion to the Classical Tradition*. Blackwell: Malden, MA, 222–236.

Laird, A. (2010) 'The Cosmic Race and a Heap of Broken Images: Mexico's Classical Past and the Modern Creole Imagination' in S. A. Stephens and P. Vasunia (eds.) *Classics and National Cultures*. Oxford University Press: Oxford, 163–181.

Laird, A. (2012) 'Patriotism and the Rise of Latin in Eighteenth-Century New Spain: Disputes of the New World and the Jesuit Construction of a Mexican Legacy'. *Renæssanceforum* **8**: 231–262.

Laird, A. (2014) 'Latin America' in: P. Ford, C. Fantazzi and J. Bloemendal (eds.) *Brill's Encyclopaedia of the Neo-Latin World*. (2 vols.). Brill: Leiden and Boston, **1**: 821–832.

Laird, A. (2015) 'Colonial Spanish America and Brazil' in S. Knight and S. Tilg (eds.) *The Oxford Handbook of Neo-Latin*. Oxford University Press: Oxford, 525–540.

Laird, A. (2016) 'Orator, Sage, and Patriot: Cicero in colonial Latin America' in G. Manuwald (ed.) *The Afterlife of Cicero*. Bulletin of the Institute of Classical Studies Supplements: London, 122–143.

Las Casas, B. de (1992a) *Apologética historia* in *Obras completas* ed. V. Abril Castelló (vols. 6–8). Alianza: Madrid.

Las Casas, B. de (1992b) *In Defense of the Indians* (trans. S. Poole). Northern Illinois University Press: DeKalb.

Leonard, I. [1949] (1992) *Books of the Brave: Being an Account of Books and of Men in the Spanish Conquest and Settlement of the Sixteenth-Century New World*. University of California Press: Berkeley, Los Angeles, Oxford.

Lintott, A. (1999) *The Constitution of the Roman Republic*. Oxford University Press: Oxford.

Lupher, D. A. (2003) *Romans in a New World: Classical Models in Sixteenth-Century Spanish America*. University of Michigan Press: Ann Arbor.

MacCormack, S. (1995) 'Limits of Understanding: Perceptions of Greco-Roman and Amerindian Paganism in Early Modern Europe' in K. O. Kupperman (ed.) *America in European Consciousness*. Omohundro Institute of Early American History and Culture: Chapel Hill, North Carolina, 79–129.

MacCormack, S. (2007) *On the Wings of Time: Rome, the Incas, Spain and Peru*. Princeton: Princeton University Press.

MacCormack, S. (2009) 'Classical Traditions in the Andes: Conversations across Time and Space' in J. Pilsbury (ed.) *Guide to Documentary Sources for Andean Studies 1530-1900*. (3 vols.). University of Oklahoma Press: Norman, **1**: 23–64.

Maclean, I. (1984) 'The Interpretation of Natural Signs. Cardano's *De subtilitate* versus Scaliger's *Exercitationes*' in B. Vickers (ed.) *Occult Scientific Mentalities*. Cambridge University Press: Cambridge, 231–252.

Martí, M. (1738) *Emmanuelis Martini, ecclesiae Alonensis decani, epistolarum libri duodecim* (2 vols.). J. Wetstein and G. Smith: Amsterdam.

Martindale, C. and Thomas, R. (eds.) (2006) *Classics and the Uses of Reception*. Blackwell: Oxford.

Martínez Baracs, R. (2005) *Convivencia y utopía: el gobierno indio y español de la 'ciudad de Mechuacan', 1521–1580*. Instituto Nacional de Antropología e Historia: Mexico City.

Maryks, R. A. (2008) *Saint Cicero and the Jesuits: The Influence of the Liberal Arts on the Adoption of Moral Probabilism*. Ashgate: Aldershot.

Mazzacane, R. and Magioncalda, E. (2005) *Pietro Martire d'Anghiera. De orbe novo decades: I–VIII.* (2 vols.). Università di Genova: Genoa.

Mignone, L. (2016) *The Republican Aventine and Rome's Social Order*. University of Michigan Press: Ann Arbor.

Miller, N. (2016) 'Reading Rousseau in Spanish America during the Wars of Independence 1808-1826' in A. Lifschitz (ed.) *Engaging with Rousseau: Reaction and Interpretation from the Eighteenth Century to the Present*. Cambridge University Press: Cambridge, 114–135.

Navarro, B. (1982) *Cultura mexicana moderna en el siglo XVIII*. Universidad Nacional Autónoma de México: Mexico City.

Nikoloutsos, K. P. (ed.) (2012) 'Reception of Greek and Roman Drama in Latin America'. *Romance Quarterly* **59**(1): 1–66.

Osorio Romero, I. (1988) *Antonio Rubio en la filosofía novohispana*. Universidad Nacional Autónoma de México: Mexico City.

Osorio Romero, I. et al. (1991) *La tradición clásica en México*. Universidad Nacional Autónoma de México: Mexico City.

Osorio Romero, I., Moreno, R., Viesca, C. et al. (1983) *Cultura clásica y cultura mexicana*. Universidad Nacional Autónoma de México: Mexico City.

Pagden, A. (1982) *The Fall of Natural Man: The American Indian and the Origins of Comparative Ethnology*. Cambridge University Press: Cambridge.

Paso, Fernando del (1977) *Palinuro de México*. Alfaguara: Madrid.

Pohl, J. M. D. and Lyons, C. L. (2010) *The Aztec Pantheon and the Art of Empire*. J. Paul Getty Museum: Los Angeles.

Pohl, J. M. D. and Lyons, C. L. (eds.) (2016) *Altera Roma: Art and Empire from Mérida to México*. Cotsen Institute of Archaeology Press: Los Angeles.

Pym, A. (2000) *Negotiating the Frontier: Translators and Intercultures in Hispanic History*. St Jerome Press: Manchester.

Quijada, M. (1998) 'Sobre el origen y difusión del nombre "América Latina" (o una variación heterodóxa en torno al tema de la construcción social de la verdad)'. *Revista de Indias* **58**(214): 595–615.

Redmond, W. B. (1972) *Bibliography of the Philosophy in the Iberian Colonies of America*. Nijhof: The Hague.

Redmond, W. B. (1990) 'Relations and 16th-Century Mexican Logic'. *Crítica: Revista Hispanoamericana de Filosofía* **22**(65): 23–41.

Reyes, A. (1955) 'Discurso por Virgilio' in *Obras completas* (vol. 11). Fondo de Cultura Económica: Mexico City: 157–181.

Rivara de Tuesta, M. L. (1999) 'La influencia de los clásicos en la filosofía colonial peruana. Fray Jerónimo de Valera (1568-1625)' in T. Hampe Martínez (ed.) *La tradición clásica en el Perú virreinal*. Fondo Editorial Universidad Nacional Mayor de San Marcos: Lima, 47–68.

Rivas-Sacconi, J. M. (1949) *El latín en Colombia: bosquejo histórico del humanismo colombiano*. Instituto Caro y Cuervo: Bogotá.

Rodó, J. E. (1967) *Ariel*. Cambridge University Press: Cambridge.

Sakamoto, K. (2016) *Julius Caesar Scaliger, Renaissance Reformer of Aristotelianism: A Study of His Exotericae Exercitationes*. Brill: Leiden.

Saxl, F. (1957) *Lectures*. (2 vols.). The Warburg Institute: London.

Séchelles, H. de (1829), *Voyage a Montbard fait en 1785 contenant des détails très-interessans sur le caractère, la personne et les écrits de M. de Buffon*. Audin: Paris.

Sepúlveda, Juan Ginés de (1548) *Aristotelis De republica libri VIII*. Vascosanus: Paris.

Sigüenza y Góngora, C. de (1984) *Seis obras* (ed. W.G. Bryant). Biblioteca Ayacucho: Caracas.

Silk, M. S., Gildenhard, I. and Barrow, R. (2014) *The Classical Tradition: Art, Literature, Thought*. Wiley-Blackwell: Malden, MA, Oxford, Chichester.

Spengler, O. (1939) *The Decline of the West. Complete in One Volume* (trans. C. F. Atkinson). Alfred A. Knopf: New York.

Taboada, H. G. H. (2012) 'Los clásicos entre el vulgo latinoamericano'. *Nova Tellus* **30**(2): 205–219.

Todorov, T. (1984) *The Conquest of America: The Question of the Other* (trans. R. Howard). Harper and Row: New York.

Tord, L. E. (1999) 'Platón, la Atlándida y los cronistas del Perú' in T. Hampe Martínez (ed.) *La tradición clásica en el Perú virreinal*. Fondo Editorial Universidad Nacional Mayor de San Marcos: Lima, 35–46.

Torres de Mendoza, L. (ed.) (1868) *Colección de documentos inéditos relativos al descubrimiento, conquista y organización de las antiguas posesiones españoles de América y Oceania, sacados de los archivos del reino y muy especialmente del de Indias (vol. 10)*. J. M. Pérez: Madrid.

Toynbee, A. (1953) *The World and the West*. Oxford University Press: Oxford.

Varela Chávez, M. del C. (2011) 'Dos documentos relativos a la formación filosófica de Hidalgo'. *Theoría: Revista del Colegio de Filosofía* **24**: 25–35.

Vasconcelos, J. (1997) *The Cosmic Race. La raza cósmica* (trans. D. Tidel Jaén). John Hopkins University Press: Baltimore.

Vasconcelos, J. (1997) *Ulises criollo: edición crítica* (ed. C. Fell). ALLCA XX: Madrid.

Vidal-Naquet, P. (2007) *The Atlantis Story: A Short History of Plato's Myth* (trans. J. Lloyd). University of Exeter Press: Exeter.

Warburg, A. (1939) 'A lecture on serpent ritual'. *Journal of the Warburg Institute* **2**(4): 277–292.

Weiss, R. (1964) *The Spread of Italian Humanism*. Hutchinson: London.

Williams, J. H. (1979) *The Rise and Fall of the Paraguayan Republic, 1800–1870*. University of Texas Press: Austin.

Zavala, S. (1998) *Recuerdo de Vasco de Quiroga*. Porrúa: Mexico City.

Ziolkowski, T. (1993) *Virgil and the Moderns*. Princeton University Press: Princeton.

2

Early Circulation of Classical Books in New Spain and Peru

NATALIA MAILLARD ÁLVAREZ

In August 1575, the cargo of a fleet which had docked in the harbour of San Juan de Ulúa in New Spain underwent an inspection by the Inquisition. No prohibited books were found, but a register was made of the volumes carried by passengers in the different ships. In the vessel *La Candelaria* the inquisitors found a few chivalric romances, some popular devotional titles, a life of Saint Francis and another of Julius Caesar – all in the posssession of a student by the name of San Clemente.[1] The discovery of the two biographies led to their owner being questioned: why did he choose to read the life of Caesar who was in hell, as well as that of a Christian saint? The examination was probably gruelling, and resulted in a report on the soundness of the student's faith. Incidents like this offer insight into attitudes to books and reading in Spain and Latin America during the Counter-Reformation, particularly the circulation of titles on classical subjects and their reading public.

As Irving Leonard made clear some 70 years ago in his renowned study *Books of the Brave*, classical texts played an important role in the conquest and colonisation of the New World (Leonard, 1992). But for a proper idea of how such texts arrived and circulated in the Americas it is important to understand the book trade networks in Europe, especially in Spain, and their interaction with the Latin American market (Rueda Ramírez, 2009). This chapter will first survey the general commerce of European books in the American territories before focusing on the role and distribution of works involving Greco-Roman themes.

International Circulation of Books in the Sixteenth Century

The invention of typography in Germany in the mid-1400s transformed book production and quickly spread throughout Europe. An unprecedented quantity of volumes on the market propelled a complete change in the way books

---

1 The document does not provide enough evidence to identify the exact title or edition, but it could be Suetonius' *Duodecim Caesares*, which appeared in various editions and anthologies in the 1500s.

were bought and sold. Many of the first investments in the new art of printing, by both businessmen and artisans, ended in disaster, in an environment that was increasingly changeable and competitive. Moreover, books were less frequently commissioned: a reading public, which could be taken for granted in the manuscript era, now needed to be identified (Pettegree, 2010: 44; Febvre and Martin, 2005: 264).

In general, the most profitable investment was in 'international books' read for instruction as much as for pleasure. These included Latin works on theology, law and medicine, as well as Greek and Roman classics (Griffin, 1991: 27). Production was mainly concentrated in a few cities, such as Venice, Paris, Lyon and Antwerp. Those centres saw the development of large family publishing firms, which were frequently interconnected by business associations or by marriage, and which functioned very much like international companies. Books were distributed all over Europe, and later on in Latin America, thanks to the networks created by the companies' agents or *factores*. The book fairs facilitated by those networks, such as those of Frankfurt or Lyon, provided ideal opportunities for promotion, buying, selling and redistribution (Myers, Harris and Mandelbrote, 2007).

Printing had reached Spain early on, around 1470, with workshops frequently run by foreign technicians soon being established in major cities, including Barcelona, Salamanca and Seville (Martín Abad, 2003). Yet Spain was never a leading nation in Europe where printing was concerned: lack of proper funding, low quality paper and the difficulties of selling abroad could all be possible explanations for this (Wagner, 1996: 31–42; Moll Roqueta, 1996). In any event, literature during the period of the Golden Age was in a paradoxical position: authors from Spain enjoyed considerable success in Europe at the same time as the output of the Spanish presses had little reach beyond the Iberian borders. As will become clear, the situation for printers in the colonies was no better.

Book production in Spain and its American colonies during the sixteenth century was really a local industry which encountered increasing difficulties as it sought to satisfy demand. Consequently there was a growing dependence on the importation of international titles from Europe. The first legislation on printed books, seeking to guarantee quality and to protect the trade, had been made by Catholic monarchs, Ferdinand and Isabella, at the time of the early voyages to the New World. After 1480, books were exempted from some of the important sales taxes, and from 1548 onwards that exemption was extended to books exported to the Americas, which became a privileged form of merchandise (De los Reyes Gómez, 2000: 771–772).

The need to control books for political and religious reasons was another consideration. In the fifteenth century, the spread of Hebrew, Muslim or pagan books had been a concern for the authorities, but by the 1520s Protestant heresy was perceived as a greater threat (Pinto Crespo, 1983). Regulation of the production and circulation of books in Spain and Latin America originated and developed over the course of the early sixteenth century. After that, responsibility for controlling publications was divided between the Inquisition and the civil authorities – a system that would last with only a few changes until the eighteenth century. This system, and in particular the Inquisition's role in it, has led to a conception of Spain being isolated. According to this idea, 'Spain was not merely cut off from the outside, its citizens were also forbidden to read anything written in the outside world. This effectively destroyed its culture' (Kamen, 2008: 139). The same apparently applied to the Spanish colonies.

But this control and the ensuing isolation only partly affected the spread of classical texts. The Spanish Inquisition prepared its own Indices of prohibited and expurgated books that did not always follow those of Rome. Greek or Roman authors were generally respected, although commentaries on their works by any contemporary scholars deemed heretical were likely to be prohibited (Martínez de Bujanda, 2016). A few ancient authors, notably Lucian and Ovid, were considered dangerous if they were read in modern languages: the Indices thus created a clear division between those readers who could not read Latin, and an elite whose knowledge of Latin and Greek gave them access to a wider collection of texts (Asensio, 1988). Thus a translation of Ovid's controversial verse manual on the art of love, entitled *Ovidio, de Arte Amandi, en romance*, was seized by the Inquisition in Yucatan in 1586 (Fernández del Castillo, 1982: 326).[2] On the other hand, the works of Aristotle confiscated from Francisco Hernández in 1576 (because they had been taken to Cuzco from Lima without authorisation) were duly returned to their owner (Lohmann Villena, 1999: 120).

The first books to arrive in the New World were brought by the early explorers and *conquistadores* as private possessions rather than as merchandise. Early transatlantic readers included soldiers and sailors as well as servants of the Crown and members of religious orders. As the authority of the Spanish monarchy extended over new territories and colonial society started to take shape in the Americas, the demand for books increased, and a new market started to develop, to satisfy Spaniards who wanted to reproduce a European way of life in the New World. But books were also needed for the evangelisation of indigenous people – which was the Spanish Crown's

2   The book belonged to a man called Lorenzo Borrello, who lived in the town of Salamanca. The majority of books seized in Yucatan in 1586 were devotional titles and Bibles, but there was also a copy of the *Gesta Romanorum* owned by one Antonio Arroyo.

justification for the conquest. In order to satisfy these requirements, books were first exported from Spain, and afterwards also produced in America.

In spite of the fact that Spanish printers had only a secondary position in the European market, they were still able to supply a large quantity of the books required in Latin America during the first half of the sixteenth century. In 1503, the Catholic monarchs created in Seville the *Casa de la Contratación*, an institution responsible for control of the trade monopoly with the New World. All the books sent to the Americas had to be shipped from Seville, and printers already established in the city or those with connections to them were naturally the first to benefit from this, although they still encountered obstacles.

The most renowned and important printing dynasty in early modern Seville was that of the Cromberger family. The Crombergers also had the most ambitious business in Latin America, although the real extent of their success has been questioned (Griffin, 1988: 92–93). Jacob Cromberger, who came to Seville from Germany at the end of the fifteenth century, was allowed to trade with the Indies in 1525, despite being a foreigner (Torre Revello, 1991: 100). His son Juan, who was born in Seville, continued the family business in America where he had a wide range of investments from books to mines. Juan's good relationship with the Bishop of Mexico, Fray Juan de Zumárraga, facilitated his business in New Spain. The bishop was aware of the need for books in order to accomplish the evangelisation of indigenous people, and he used Cromberger's shop to provide the first library established in New Spain. The Crombergers produced high quality volumes, mainly in Castilian, which included a few classical texts, but they also imported from outside Seville in order to supply the market there and in America. As nearly all of the classical works that the Crombergers published were in Spanish, they must have been aimed at a non-specialist readership.

Entrusting merchandise to transporters on the trade route to the Indies known as the *Carrera de Indias* must have been the biggest challenge to a transatlantic business and even Juan Cromberger had trouble (Cachero Vinuesa, 2010). A young Sevillian bookseller, Guido de Lavezaris, whom he had despatched to Mexico in 1536 to sell books and other goods, left the trade almost as soon as he got to America.[3] But Cromberger did not give up. In 1539, in response to Bishop Zumárraga's petition, he sent an Italian, Giovanni Paoli (better known as Joannes Paulus or Juan Pablos), to set up a press in Mexico City, the first in the New World. Just as in Spain, many of the first printers were not Spanish but foreigners such as Pedro Ocharte, a

---

3   Guido was the son of Sebastián de Lavezaris. The successful Genoese booksellers, settled in Seville since the fifteenth century, financed editions printed in Seville and in Venice for the Spanish market (Wagner, 1994).

Frenchman, or Antonio Ricardo, an Italian, who led the same itinerant life as their counterparts in the Iberian peninsula.

The printing equipment sent to America was secondhand, but Juan Cromberger's intentions went beyond setting up a successful branch of his printing company in Mexico City. His real aim was to secure the position of his own trade opportunities in New Spain which had hitherto depended too much on entrusting goods to potentially unreliable agents. In exchange for his investment, Juan Cromberger obtained a monopoly on the export of books and textbooks to New Spain in 1539. That prompted complaints from other Sevillian printers who had hoped to profit from the growing opportunities offered by the American market. In South America the commerce of books was not subject to monopoly, but the difficulties involved in pacifying and governing the viceroyalty of Peru probably delayed the arrival of booksellers and printers. A press was finally established in Lima in 1584, thanks to the efforts of Antonio Ricardo.

Prior to the 1540s there had only been a few booksellers in the New World – and those who arrived as part of a second wave of emigration from Europe in the later sixteenth century did not always meet with success (Rojo Vega, 1992; González Sánchez, 1999: 40). It is not easy to establish exactly which titles crossed the Atlantic during this period, not least because books were often sold along with other commodities by non-specialist dealers. For instance, a trader based in Mexico, Fernán Vázquez, together with a future teacher at the Royal University, Blas de Bustamante, purchased 2,142 pesos' worth of goods from a Sevillian, Luis Gómez, in 1547.[4] There were more than 40 books, including the following classical texts:

> *Un libro de Décadas de Tito Libio, 549 maravedíes*
> A volume of Livy's *Decades*, 549 maravedis
>
> *Una docena de Epístolas Familiares de Tulio, a 120 maravedíes*
> Twelve copies of Cicero's *Letters to his Friends*, 120 maravedis
>
> *Seis Epístolas de Ovidio, 510 maravedíes*
> Six *Epistles* by Ovid, 510 maravedis
>
> *Una docena de Terencio a 90 maravedíes, 1080 maravedíes*
> A dozen texts of Terence at 90 maravedis each; 1,080 in total
> *Cuatro Virgilios a 120 maravedíes, 480 maravedíes*
> Four texts of Virgil at 120 maravedis each; 480 in total.

---

4   Francisco Fuentes, 'Obligación de pago', 23rd March 1547. (Mijares, 2014).

The changing situation of the book trade in Spain in the 1550s also affected the Americas: the Cromberger monopoly was over by the beginning of that decade, opening the market to new dealers. At the same time, in Mexico, Juan Pablos hired Antonio de Espinosa, a more skilled employee who gave a new lease of life to his printing workshop, while the inauguration, in 1554, of the Royal University of Mexico increased the demand for books in the colony. In 1560, Espinosa printed the *Túmulo Imperial de la gran ciudad de México* (Imperial Sepulchre for the Great City of Mexico), which contained several original epigrams and prose passages in Latin.[5]

The presence of classical culture in colonial life at that time is not evident from printed publications alone. The celebration of the official entry of the viceroy Don Pedro de la Gasca into Lima in 1548, for instance, involved different towns identifying themselves with Troy in a dance pageant staged to show their loyalty.

> Guánuco y la Chachapoya
> Te besamos pies y manos
> Que por dar al rey la joya
> Despoblamos nuestra Troya
> Trayendo los comarcanos. (Fernández, 1571, 1: 140)

> As Guánaco and Chachapoy,
> We kiss you on the feet and hands.
> Because we want to give the king this gem:
> We depopulated our own Troy.
> Bringing here the dwellers in our lands.

Again, in 1551, the painter Baltasar Grande, together with Miguel Valenciano, hired two residents of Mexico to 'represent Roman antiquities and feats of Hercules for the Easter celebrations' (representar en las fiestas de Pascua a las antiguas romanas y fuerzas de Hércules).[6]

But such popular interest in classical themes could not reverse the decline of the book industry in Spain and the Americas (Griffin, 1991: 157–164). The economic crisis of the later 1550s forced printing workshops to close in a number of Spanish cities, while inflation favoured importation over local production. Political and religious developments also led to closer

---

5   The ceremonies and monuments prepared in Lima after the death of Charles V also included different Latin poems involving ancient models (Lohmann Villena, 1998: 117).

6   Baltasar Díaz, 'Concierto de servicio', 6th July 1551 (Mijares, 2014).

scrutiny by the Inquisition and the civil authorities. When the Crombergers' monopoly ended, no Spanish or Sevillian printers took their place.

Seville's loss was the gain of some northern Castilian cities. A company had already been created in Salamanca in 1530 on the lines of the *Grande Compagnie* of booksellers in Lyon, and biennial fairs in Medina del Campo attracted many foreign sellers who opened stores in the 1530s to import books from Europe (Rojo Vega, 1987: 17–26; De la Mano González, 1998). Large publishing firms, such as Boyer from Lyon, Bellère from Antwerp and the Giunti from Venice, came to control a good part of the Iberian and Latin American market, especially during the later 1500s, drawing large quantities of money from Spain and the Americas to Europe (Moll Roqueta, 1981: 79–84; Rojo Vega, 1985: 22). These international companies expanded into the Americas to satisfy demand, sending their own *factores* as well as books. This is the case of the above-mentioned Antonio Ricardo, who was the first printer in Lima (Tauro, 1996). Born in Turin and trained in Venice and Lyon, he moved to Spain, with his business partner Gaspar Trechsel, to work as a *factor* of the Lyonnais printer Guillame Rouille. In Spain, Antonio married the widow of Melchor Trechsel (Gaspar's brother) and soon after moved to Mexico, where he worked as a bookseller and printer, before travelling to Peru in 1581.

Seville, thanks to its position in the *Carrera de Indias*, held its status as a hub in the trade with the Spanish colonies. Booksellers and printers in the city continued to profit from the American market and the main European companies now established in Spain also sent their representatives to the city or traded through Sevillian agents. The Florentine Andrea Pescioni, for example, who first came to Spain in the 1550s, started his own business as a bookseller, editor and printer in Seville with American booksellers among his main clients (González Sánchez and Maillard Álvarez, 2003; Rojo Vega, 2015). In 1567, he financed the production of Erasmus' popular edition and commentary on Cato's *Distichs* – short sententious verses on moral themes which were used for teaching Latin. There is now only one copy (in the Mexican National Library) of the *Catonis Disticha Moralia cum Scholiis Des. Erasmi* published by Alonso García Escribano in Seville. In their turn, book dealers in the colonies maintained contacts in Spain to supply their stores, and they exchanged letters with printers and exporters in order to keep them informed of the needs of American customers (Sánchez Rubio and Testón Núñez, 1999).

The Role of Classical Texts in the American Book Market

It was only in 1586 that regulations requiring the registration of all books shipped out of Seville were finally put into effect (Rueda Ramírez, 2005). To discover what classical texts circulated in Latin America prior to that, details of purchases (such as the 40 volumes bought by Fernán Vázquez and the university teacher Blas de Bustamante described above), as well as notarial and inquisitorial archives, provide helpful information. Two significant purchases were made by another book dealer based in Mexico, Alonso Losa. In 1545, Alonso, with his brother Juan acting as guarantor, acquired 241 titles from the Sevillian merchant Pedro de Pereyra, to the value of 172,690 maravedis. The majority of the volumes were of a religious nature, but almost 15 per cent of the volumes were classical texts[7]:

— *seis Virgilios pp. en 816 maravedíes*
six Virgils, paper, at 816 maravedis

— *seis Fábulas de Esopo latín, en 714 maravedíes*
six Fables of Aesop in Latin, at 714 maravedis

— *seis Terencios in quarto, en 714 maravedíes*
six Terences, quarto, at 714 maravedis

— *seis Horacios, in quarto, en 714 maravedíes*
six Horaces, quarto, at 714 maravedis

— *12 Catones latin in quarto, en 510 maravedíes*
12 [texts of] Cato in Latin, quarto, at 510 maravedis.

In 1576, Losa received more than a thousand books from a Sevillian dealer, Diego Mexía, including a large number of classical texts. As Irving Leonard observed, a list of this quantity 'reveals a general fashion for the best sellers of the moment' (Leonard, 1992: 205–211; Rueda Ramírez, 1998: 477–496). Again most of the volumes were religious, but about 250 of them, listed in 39 entries, were classical. The ancient author most in demand was Virgil, followed by Cicero, Caesar and Martial, but there were many others. At least one-fifth of these items were written in Spanish, especially in the case of Virgil (44 copies in Spanish and 27 in Latin), Josephus (all twelve texts were in Spanish), Caesar (six in Spanish) and five copies of Homer. The list provides information about the size of the books, which were mainly in folios and in octavos, binding and prices. Costs could range from 2½ reales for a *De officiis* printing in Antwerp by Plantin, to 99 reales for a two-volume edition of Cicero's complete works with Denis Lambin's commentary. In a few cases, the list specifies the city in

---

7   Francisco Valverde, 'Obligación de pago', 16th November 1545 (Mijares, 2014).

which the books were produced. Some of the classical titles from a far longer list of items purchased by Alonso Losa are excerpted in the appendix to this chapter: as the extract shows, the same authors and works are listed more than once because books were mixed randomly in the boxes in which they were transported.

Throughout this period, books were brought to Latin America by individual readers who carried them in their luggage, as well as by professional merchants. On eleven separate occasions the Inquisition registered classical titles in their inspections of the cargo of fleets arriving in New Spain between 1575 and 1585 (Fernández del Castillo, 1982). A copy of Caesar's *Civil Wars*, three of Virgil, two of Homer's *Odyssey*, and single copies of Terence, Ovid and Cicero were listed in addition to the *Life of Julius Caesar* that had been in the possession of the student named San Clemente. No information is given about the owners of the other books or about the use made of them, but they appear to have been largely for recreational reading (Maillard Álvarez, 2011). Classics books were also available, among other items, in lots at public auctions. An inventory of items to be sold in Mexico City in 1608 included more than 80 books belonging to the bachelor Hernando Gutiérrez, who was probably a priest. Nine of them were classical titles, and texts of Horace and Virgil's *Aeneid* were sold a few days later.[8]

Before closing, it remains to draw attention to the ways in which some printers and booksellers disseminated classical culture in Spanish America, which went beyond marketing. The younger son of the Sevillian bookseller Diego Mexía, also named Diego, ran the family business in America. The younger Diego Mexía de Fernangil was also a prominent writer in the viceroyalty of Peru (Gil, 2008). In 1576, during a business trip from Peru to Mexico, he purchased from a student a Latin copy of Ovid's *Heroides*, which he started translating into Spanish to relieve the monotony of the journey. A long stay in Mexico allowed him to complete the endeavour. As noted above, Ovid was not highly regarded by the Inquisition, and still less so when read in modern languages. It was probably to justify his translation that Diego Mexía de Fernangil added some moral reflections of his own, as he explains in his preface:

> Quise traduzirlas en tercetos, por parecerme que corresponden estas rimas con el verso elegíaco latino: limelas lo mejor que a mi pobre talento fue concedido, adornándolas con argumentos en prosa, i moralidades que para su inteligencia i vtilidad d'el lector me parecieron conuenir: pues es cierto que la Poesía que deleita sin aprovechar con su doctrina,

---

8   Archivo Histórico de Notarías de la Ciudad de México (AHNM), Notario José Rodríguez, vol. 3836, fols. 1542r-1543v, 1543bisr-1544v and fols. 1545v-1546r.

no consigue su fin, como lo afirma Horacio en su Arte, i mejor que él, Aristóteles en su Poética. (Mexía de Fernangil, 1608: fol. 3v)

I wanted to translate the poems in tercets, as in my view this rhyme scheme corresponds to Latin elegiac verse. I polished them to the best of my poor ability, embellishing them with prose summaries, and morals that I thought fitting for the reader's understanding and instruction: it is certain that Poetry that gives pleasure without providing the benefit of instruction does not achieve its end, as Horace affirms in his *Art of Poetry*, and better still, Aristotle in his *Poetics*.

Thanks to the mediation of Diego's older brother Fernando, the translation, which was entitled *Párnaso Antártico*, was finally published in Seville in 1608: it was dedicated to Don Juan de Villela, a member of the *Audiencia* or High Court in Lima.[9] Such exceptional and unique accomplishments, as well as the more general trends of production and commerce outlined in this discussion, help to account for the early prominence of classical books in Latin America. Classical texts found their way to the New World and spread widely very early on thanks to professional and non-professional networks. The texts themselves, read in Latin and Spanish, were among a very wide range of literature to reach the Americas, but their availability certainly contributed to the dissemination of classical learning in colonial society.

Acknowledgements

This study has been carried out in connection with the project, *Book Trade Networks between France, the Iberian Peninsula and the Americas*, supported by the EURIAS Fellowship Programme (2015–2016) at the Collegium de Lyon, and with the support of the Research and Development project, *El modelo policéntrico de la soberanía compartida (Siglos XVI-XVIII). Una vía alternativa en*

---

9 *Primera parte del Parnaso Antartico, de obras amatorias. Con las 21 Epistolas de Ovidio, i el In Ibin en terceros [...]. Por Diego Mexia de Fernangil, natural de la ciudad de Sevilla, residente en la de los Reyes, en los riquissimos Reinos del Piru [...] En Sevilla, por Alonso Rodríguez Gamarra*. Probably the publication was also facilitated by the active collaboration of Diego Mexía de Fernangil with the Inquisition, for which he inspected the libraries of Potosí (Guibovich Pérez, 2003: 94).

la construcción del Estado moderno (HAR2013–45357-P), funded by the Projects General Sub-Directorate, MICINN.

Appendix: Classical Titles Excerpted from a List of Items Purchased by Alonso Losa

3 Virgilios en romance, de los largos, pergamino, a 4 reales y medio.
3 [texts of] Virgil in Spanish, full length, parchment, for 4 and a half reals.

1 Opera Aristoteles, de novi, en un tomo, in folio a 33 reales.
1 *Works* of Aristotle, new, in one volume, folio, for 33 reals.

8 Virgilios, en romance, de los largos, en tablas, a 5 reales y medio cada uno.
8 Virgils, in Spanish, full length, in boards, for 5 and a half reals each.

4 Ovidios, Metamorfosis, in octavo, papelones, a 4 reales cada uno.
4 Ovids, *Metamorphoses*, octavo, paperback, for 4 reals each.

1 Julio César historia, in folio, a 28 reales.
1 [text of] Julius Caesar, history, folio at 28 reals each.

Unos Fastos romanorum, in folio a 28 reales.
Fasti of the Romans [Ovid's *Fasti*], in folio for 28 reals.

1 Virgilio en romance, en papelones, en 5 reales.
1 [text of] Virgil in Spanish, in paperback, at 5 reals.

Unas obras de Cicerón, Lanbino [sic], en 2 tomos, de novi, in folio, a 99 reales.
Some works of Cicero, [edited by] Lambin, in 2 volumes, as new, in folio, for 99 reals.

Una Jeroglífica Pievi, de novi, in folio, a 38 reales.
A *Hieroglyphica* [printed at] Pieve [di Sacco], as new, in folio for 38 reals.

5 Virgilios en romance, papelones largos, a 51 reales y medio.
5 Virgils in Spanish, full length paper, for 51 and a half reals.

1 Virgilio en romance, en pergamino, a 4 reales y medio.
1 Virgil in Spanish, in parchment, for 4 and a half reals.

5 Virgilios en romance, largos, en papelones, a 5 reales y medio.
5 Virgils in Spanish, full length, in paper, for 5 and a half reals.

2 *Lucio Apuleyo, en papelones, a 4 reales.*
2 [texts of] Lucius Apuleius, in paper, for 4 reals.

1 *Beroso, en 2 tomos, p., a 6 reales.*
1 Berosus, in 2 volumes, p[aper] for 6 reals.

Unas Obras de Aristóteles, en 7 tomos, p., a 22 reales.
Some Works of Aristotle in 7 volumes, p[aper], for 22 reals.

5 *Ovidios, Metamorfosis, in octavo, a 4 reales y medio.*
5 Ovids, *Metamorphoses*, octavo at 4 and a half reals.

11 *Virgilios, en romance, papelones, a 5 reales.*
11 Virgils, in Spanish, in paper, for 5 reals.

6 *Tulios de Oficis, impreso en Amberes, a 3 reales.*
6 Tullius [Cicero], *De officiis*, printed in Antwerp, for 3 reals.

6 *Virgilios, en latín, in octavo, a 4 reales cada uno.*
6 Virgils, in Latin, octavo, for 4 reals each.

10 *Tulios de Oficis, Plantino, p., a 2 reales y medio.*
10 Tullius [Cicero], *De officiis*, Plantinus [Antwerp printer], paper for 2 and a half reals.

2 *Oraciones de Tulio, en 3 tomos, in octavo a 12 reales.*
2 [texts of] *Orationes* by Tullius [Cicero], in 3 volumes, octavo, for 12 reals.

8 *Tragedias de Séneca, León, p. a 3 reales.*
8 texts of Seneca's Tragedies, León, p[aper] for 3 reals.

1 *Ópera Aristóteles, en un tomo, de novi, in folio a 34 reales.*
1 Works of Aristotle, in one volume, folio, for 34 reals.

2 *Epístolas de Tulio, con comento, París, in folio a 26 reales cada una.*
2 [texts of] Tullius [Cicero], *Epistles*, with commentary, Paris, folio, for 26 reals each.

1 *Virgilio con comento, de novi, in folio, monta 32 reales.*
1 Virgil with commentary, new, folio, totals 32 reals.

12 *Libros de Josepho, en romance, que trata de las guerras de los judíos, in octavo, tablas, a 10 reales.*
12 Books of Josephus, in Spanish, treating the Jewish wars, octavo, hardbound, for 10 reals.

5 Eluxias [sic] de Homero, en romance, in octavo, a 6 reales cada una.
5 *Odysseys* ['Ulyssiads'] of Homer, in Spanish, octavo, for 6 reals each.

25 Marciales, p. a 3 reales cada uno.
25 Martials, p[aper] for 3 reals each.

20 Virgilios en latín, León, p. a 6 reales cada uno.
20 Virgils in Latin, León, p[aper] for 6 reals each.

18 Comentarios de César, en latín, Plantino, a 4 reales.
18 Commentaries on Caesar, in Latin, Plantinus, for 4 reals.

12 Epístolas de Tulio, con anotaciones de Lambino, in octavo, a 4 reales cada una.
12 texts of *Epistles* of Tullius [Cicero], with Lambin's annotations, octavo, for 4 reals each.

6 Epístolas de Tulio, p. León, a 3 reales cada una.
Six [texts of] Tullius [Cicero]'s *Epistles*, p[aper], Leon, for 3 reals each.

6 Comentarios de César, en romance, in octavo, a 7 reales.
Six commentaries on Caesar, in Spanish, octavo, for 7 reals.

23 Salustios, p[aper],. León, a 3 reales.
23 texts of Sallust, p[aper], León, for 3 reals.

Unas Epístolas de Tulio, a 3 reales.
Some *Epistles* of Tullius [Cicero], for 3 reals.

10 Tulios de Oficis, Amberes, in octavo, a 3 reales.
Ten texts of Tullius [Cicero], *De officiis*, octavo, for 3 reals.

6 Virgilios, Amberes, in octavo, a 4 reales cada uno.
6 Virgils, Antwerp, octavo, for 4 reals each.

8 Justinos, Historias, in octavo, a 3 reales cada uno.
14 [texts of] Justinus, *Histories*, octavo, for 3 reals each.

14 Justinos, p. a 3 reales cada uno.
14 [texts of] Justinus, p[aper] for 3 reals each.

References

Asensio, E. (1988) 'Censura inquisitorial de libros en los siglos XVI y XVII. Fluc-
tuaciones. Decadencia' in M. L. López-Vidriero and P. Cátedra (eds.) *El libro
antiguo español: actas del Primer Coloquio Internacional (Madrid, 18 al 20 de diciem-
bre de 1986)*. Universidad de Salamanca: Salamanca, 21–36.

Cachero Vinuesa, M. (2010) *Should We Trust? Explaining Trade Expansion in Early Modern Spain: Seville 1500–1600*. Unpublished doctoral dissertation. European University Institute, Florence.

De la Mano González, M. (1998) *Mercaderes e impresores de libros en la Salamanca del siglo XVI*. Universidad de Salamanca: Salamanca.

De los Reyes Gómez, F. (2000) *El libro en España y América: legislación y censura. Siglos XV-XVIII*. Vol. 2. Arco Libros: Madrid.

Febvre, L. and Martin, H.-J. (2005) *La aparición del libro*. Fondo de Cultura Económica: Mexico City.

Fernández, D. (1571) *Primera y segunda parte de la historia del Perú*. En casa de Hernando Díaz: Seville.

Fernández del Castillo, F. [1914] (1982) *Libros y libreros en el siglo XVI*. Fondo de Cultura Económica: Mexico City.

Gil, J. (2008) 'Diego Mexía de Fernangil, un perulero humanista en los confines del mundo' in J. M. Nieto Ibáñez and R. Manchón Gómez (eds.) *El humanismo español entre el Viejo Mundo y el Nuevo*. Universidad de Jaén: Jaén, 67–142.

González Sánchez, C. A. (1999) *Los mundos del libro. Medios de difusión de la cultura occidental en las Indias de los siglos XVI y XVII*. Universidad de Sevilla: Seville.

González Sánchez, C. A. and Maillard Álvarez, N. (2003) *Orbe tipográfico. El mercado del libro en la Sevilla de la segunda mitad del siglo XVI*. Trea: Gijón.

Griffin, C. (1991) *Los Cromberger. La historia de una imprenta del siglo XVI en Sevilla y Méjico*. Ediciones de Cultura Hispánica: Madrid.

Guibovich Pérez, P. M. (2003) *Censura, libros e Inquisición en el Perú colonial, 1570–1754*. Consejo Superior de Investigaciones Científicas: Seville.

Kamen, H. (2008) *Imagining Spain. Historical Myth and National Identity*. Yale University Press: New Haven.

Leonard, I. [1949] (1992) *Books of the Brave: Being an Account of Books and of Men in the Spanish Conquest and Settlement of the Sixteenth-Century New World*. University of California Press: Berkeley, Los Angeles, Oxford.

Lohmann Villena, G. (1999) 'Huellas renacentistas en la literatura peruana del siglo XVI' in T. Hampe Martínez (ed.) *La tradición clásica en el Perú virreinal*. Universidad Nacional Mayor de San Marcos: Lima, 115–127.

Maillard Álvarez, N. (2011) *Lectores y libros en la ciudad de Sevilla 1550–1600*. Rubeo: Barcelona.

Martín Abad, J. (2003) *Los primeros tiempos de la imprenta en España: c. 1471–1520*. Ediciones Laberinto: Madrid.

Martínez de Bujanda, J. (2016) *Índice de los libros prohibidos y expurgados de la Inquisición española 1551–1589*. Biblioteca de autores cristianos: Madrid.

Mexía de Fernangil, D. de (1608) *Primera parte del Parnaso Antartico, de obras amatorias*. Alonso Rodriguez Gamarra: Seville.

Mijares, I. (2014) (ed.) *Catálogo de protocolos del Archivo General de Notarías de la Ciudad de México, Fondo Siglo XVI*. Seminario de Documentación e Historia Novohispana, UNAM Instituto de Investigaciones Históricas, Mexico. [WWW document]. URL http://cpagncmxvi.historicas.unam.mx/catalogo.jsp (accessed 24 July 2016).

Moll Roqueta, J. (1981) 'Valoración de la industria editorial española del siglo XVI' in M. C. Díaz y Díaz (ed.) *Livre et lecture en Espagne et en France sous l'Ancien Régime*. ADPF: Paris, 79–84.

Moll Roqueta, J. (1996) 'El impresor y el librero en el Siglo de Oro' in F. Asin Remírez de Esparza (ed.) *Mundo del libro antiguo*. Editorial Complutense: Madrid, 27–43.

Myers, R., Harris, M. and Mandelbrote, G. (eds.) (2007) *Fairs, Markets and the Itinerant Book Trade*. Oak Knoll Press: Newcastle; British Library: London.

Pettegree, A. (2010) *The Book in the Renaissance*. Yale University Press: New Haven.

Pinto Crespo, V. (1983) *Inquisición y control ideológico en la España del siglo XVI*. Taurus: Madrid.

Rojo Vega, A. (1985) *Ciencia y cultura en Valladolid. Estudio de las bibliotecas privadas de los siglos XVI y XVII*. Universidad de Valladolid: Valladolid.

Rojo Vega, A. (1987) 'El negocio del libro en Medina del Campo. Siglos XVI y XVII'. *Investigaciones históricas: Época moderna y contemporánea* **7**: 17–26.

Rojo Vega, A. (1992) 'Los grandes libreros españoles del siglo XVI y América'. *Cuadernos Hispanoamericanos* **500**: 115–132.

Rojo Vega, A. (2015) 'Letras Humanas en una de las mejores librerías de la España de Carlos V: Liarcari-Terranova (Salamanca, 1557)' in J. M. Díez Borque (ed.) *Bibliotecas y librerías en la España de Carlos V*. Calambur: Madrid, 251–275.

Rueda Ramírez, P. (1998) 'Los libreros Mexía en el comercio de libros con América en los últimos años del reinado de Felipe II' in J. Martínez Millán (ed.) *Felipe II (1527-1598): Europa y la monarquía Católica*, Vol. 4. Parteluz: Madrid, 477–496.

Rueda Ramírez, P. (2005) *Negocio e intercambio cultural: el comercio de libros con América en la Carrera de Indias. Siglo XVII*. Consejo Superior de Investigaciones Científicas: Seville.

Rueda Ramírez, P. (2009) 'El comercio de libros en Latinoamérica colonial: aproximación al estado de la cuestión (siglos XVI-XVIII)' in I. García Aguilar (ed.) *Complejidad y materialidad: reflexiones del seminario del libro antiguo*. UNAM: Mexico City, 193–279.

Sánchez Rubio, M. R. and Testón Núñez, I. (1999) *El hilo que une: las relaciones epistolares en el Viejo y el Nuevo Mundo. Siglos XVI-XVIII*. Editora Regional: Cáceres.

Tauro, A. (1996) 'Antonio Ricardo. Primer impresor' in I. García Gayoso (ed.) *Incunables peruanos en la Biblioteca Nacional de Perú. 1584–1619*. Biblioteca Nacional del Perú: Lima.

Torre Revello, J. [1940] (1991) *El libro, la imprenta y el periodismo en América durante la dominación española*. UNAM: Mexico City.

Wagner, K. (1994) 'Guido de Lavezaris, genovés (1512-1582), de librero a gobernador de Filipinas' in V. Piergiovanni (ed.) *Tra Siviglia e Genova: notaio, documento e comercio nell'età colombiana: atti del Convegno internazionale di studi storici per le celebrazioni colombiane organizzato dal Consiglio notarile dei distretti riuniti di Genova e Chiavari sotto l'egida del Consiglio Nazionale del Notariato (Genova, 12–14 marzo 1992)*. Giuffrè Editore: Milan, 378–391.

Wagner, K. (1996) 'Les libraires espagnols au XVIe siècle' in F. Barbies, S. Juratic and D. Varry (eds.) *L'Europe et le livre: réseaux et pratiques du négoce de librairie XVIe-XIXe siècles*. Editions Klincksieck: Paris, 31–42.

3

Gardens of Origin and the Golden Age in the Mexican *Libellus de medicinalibus indorum herbis* (1552)

ALEJANDRA ROJAS SILVA

The first school for higher learning founded in the Americas after the Spanish conquest was for native students. The Imperial College of Santa Cruz was established in 1536 in Tlatelolco, adjacent to the city of Mexico (Steck, 1944; Mathes, 1985). The pupils, who were speakers of Nahuatl and Spanish, had a unique formation. Though drawn entirely from the ranks of the indigenous nobility, they were immersed in a European classical curriculum influenced by Erasmus' Christian humanism and pedagogy. Their Franciscan educators taught them Latin grammar, rhetoric and philosophy, with a view to having them lead their people towards the Christian faith and the civilising principles it represented (Kobayashi, 1974; Laird, 2015). Holding positions of privilege in their own culture, the students participated in the highest forms of native communication and some were likely to have become conversant with Mexican pictographic expression. As such, they had the capacity to negotiate at the nexus of the Old World and the New, and they were sensitive to the political implications of their status.

Support for the College of Santa Cruz from the Spanish elite, however, had never been unanimous. The future of the institution was thrown into doubt after the first viceroy of New Spain, Antonio de Mendoza, who had guaranteed his patronage of the school, was transferred to Peru in 1550.[1] In the face of widespread opposition to the rise of an educated native class, teachers and *alumni* of Santa Cruz had a pressing interest in appealing to the Spanish Crown to provide the means required for their college's continued existence. It was this context that led to the preparation of a manuscript to demonstrate the distinctive achievements of the institution and the abilities of its students.

---

[1] The 1545 *matlazahuatl* epidemic had killed many of the college's teachers and pupils, and the Franciscans entrusted the running of the school to its *alumni* in 1546. Its patron, Bishop Juan de Zumárraga, died in 1548 and Spain's royal treasury refused to give the school the 1000 pesos assigned by the Emperor Charles V. Luis Velazco, Mendoza's successor as viceroy, supported the college but it was left destitute after his death in 1564 (Mendieta, 1993: 415–416).

The *Libellus de medicinalibus indorum herbis*, 'A Little Book about the Medicinal Herbs of the Indians', was completed in 1552 (Emmart, 1940: 3–29; Somolinos D'Ardois, 1991).[2] The hastily produced but beautifully illustrated medical herbal, which mingles European and indigenous Mexican conventions, was offered as a gift to Philip II of Spain in the hope of securing royal support.

Medieval European manuscripts were often created in stages: first the line, then the text, and finally the miniatures. But in the *Libellus* the implementation of those elements was more simultaneous. On some of its pages the text was written first, on others the line, and on others again the image came first. That could hint at an indigenous inflection of standard practice – and there is no doubt that the resulting work represents one of the earliest conflations of European and indigenous representational codes (Emmart, 1940: 29–71; Hassig, 1989: 30–53; Fernández, 1991: 101–106; Stols, 1992: 93–100; Zetina *et al.*, 2008: 1). Classical conventions pervade the manuscript: titles, descriptions and recipes are in Latin; the organisation and structure conform to the taxonomy of Dioscorides' herbal which had circulated (in Greek, Latin and Arabic) since the first century AD; and the text presupposes the humoral theory of disease inherited from the Greek physician Galen.

At the same time, the herbs listed are all Mexican and their names are only in the Nahuatl language. Many lack illustrations, giving the herbal a surplus of discursive information, but some plants are painted that do not appear in the recipes below, offering a surfeit of image over text. The hierarchical order of alphabetic writing and illustration typical of European manuscripts is muddled in the *Libellus*, perhaps betraying the legacy of a pre-conquest culture that had relied primarily on pictography for information.

The images of the plants themselves also combine European and indigenous representational codes: while the depiction of individual specimens is in line with European convention, the portrayal of flowers is limited, even formulaic, meaning that few can be identified from the image alone. In contrast, the environments in which the plants grow are rendered with far more particularity: aquatic plants are outlined in blue, have roots surrounded by blue pigment, or emerge from the pictogram for water. Pictograms also indicate whether terrestrial plants grow in rock or soil. Special attention is paid to the latter – perhaps due to the fact that pre-Columbian medicine attributed the curative powers of certain plants to the soil in which they grew.[3]

---

2   The manuscript of the *Libellus*, sometimes known as the *Codex Badiano*, which was discovered in the Vatican Library in 1929, is in the Library of the Museum of Anthropology in Mexico City, after being presented to Mexico by Pope John Paul II in 1992 on the quincentenary of Columbus' 1492 voyage.

3   Maldonado-Koerdel (1964: 294).

The present chapter will argue that aspects of the structure and conception of the *Libellus* suggest a blending of conventions comparable to that seen in its individual images. The focus will be on the visual rhetoric of three illustrated folios at the centre of the manuscript (Figure 1). These colourful illustrations suggest a symbolic connection between the mythical Mesoamerican city of Tollan and the Garden of Eden. They may also tangentially evoke Greco-Roman myths of the 'Golden Age', or Age of Saturn, which were mediated in classical works available in the College of Santa Cruz in Tlatelolco. By implicitly aligning these European and Mexican traditions, the authors of this book likely sought to demonstrate their dual status as civilised Christians, and as inheritors of an indigenous nobility worthy of guiding their people into a new era.

The central folios of the *Libellus*, depicting a brilliant array of plants in a garden, dramatically break with the format of the rest of the manuscript. Such a feature is reminiscent of pre-Columbian screenfolds in which the centre marked the most significant point of meaning. As Byron Hamann has recently argued, some post-conquest artefacts retained the conventions of pre-Columbian art in using the centre as a place of significance to mark a privileged point for elite visual access to the object as an 'instrument of seeing'.[4] Mesoamerican screenfold histories, which were objects analogous to European books, thus placed the most significant narrative moments at their centre. The central break in the structure in the *Libellus* is remarkably in keeping with this indigenous convention, but it is at the same time presented in a typically European form: the three folios constitute a self-contained booklet within the larger herbal manuscript, with folio 38r acting as the cover and the following blanket folios as its contents. The folios are therefore not only significant in terms of Nahua configurations, but also in European terms as a supplementary bound book with its own function or meaning.

Each of the multicoloured plants in these central folios has a name above its image, but no illness or recipe is described underneath, as is the practice throughout the rest of the *Libellus*. Each of these central folios has two rows of three to six plants each, making a total of 28. The break in pagination makes the connection between these plants and the description of the illness that follows appear more remote than it does in the other sections of the book. Nonetheless, some of the plants illustrated are included in the recipe

---

4   Hamann (2013: 518-545) sees the iconography of the *Lienzo de Tlaxcala* as inextricable from its materiality, placing the post-colonial conquest object in conversation with pre-Columbian productions such as screenfolds, mirrors, and mummy bundles: the structural centre holds the most important elements – and the power to communicate between worlds (Hamann, 2004: 68–123; Bakewell and Hamann, 2011: 163–192).

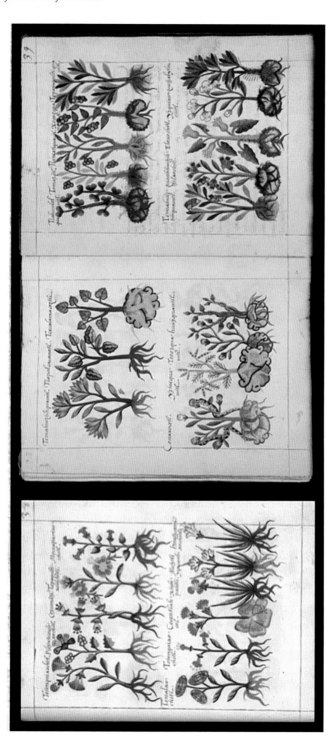

Figure 1.   *Libellus de medicinalibus indorum herbis* (1552), folios 38r–39r

Source: Secretaría de Cultura, INAH, Mexico.

immediately following the break in structure, which is written under this title:

> Contra rempublicam administrantis, et munus publicum gerentis fatigationem Arbores et Flores.

> Trees and flowers to counter the fatigue of one administering the Republic and performing public duty.

In pre-Hispanic Mexico, positions of government had been held by members of noble families. The appearance of this garden immediately preceding an illness limited to the nobility directly links the preceding plants and their symbolic qualities to high-ranking Nahuas. The association of flowering gardens with nobility was common to Europeans and Nahuas.[5] Moctezuma, the last Aztec ruler, himself had pleasure gardens in and around Mexico City in which many of the plants illustrated here were cultivated (Durán, 1967, 2: 247–248; Heyden, 1983: 16–20, 48). Moreover, these folios are some of the most visually compelling pages in the manuscript due to their richness and variety of colour.

Opulently coloured objects and animals were associated with conceptions of paradise as well as with the high ranks in Mesoamerica.[6] The three folios then can be seen as signifying a paradisiacal garden, and – as it remains to argue here – they may allude specifically to the garden of Tollan. For the Nahuas and other groups in Mesoamerica, Tollan was a mythical place of origin. According to early colonial descriptions of Tollan, most of the objects in the city had four or five colours. These central folios of the *Libellus* feature varieties of plants which are supposed to have flourished in the mythical city, and significantly show fruits and flowers growing in four and five different colours. The *xococquauitl* or the *temahuiztiliquauitl*, for instance, are depicted with flowers in which each petal appears in a different colour, creating polychromic patterns at the expense of verisimilitude (Figure 2).

The *Annals of Cuauhtitlan* and the *Florentine Codex* are sources from the early colonial period for the rise and fall of Tollan as well as vivid descriptions of

---

5   In the European Renaissance, air and fire were considered nobler elements than earth, so that vegetables were deemed the food of lower classes and fruit that of the higher (Grieco, 1991: 131–149). Francisco Cervantes de Salazar (1971, 1:317-325) records that Moctezuma forbade the growth of vegetables in his gardens because 'vegetable gardens were for slaves and merchants'.

6   'Flowers, birds, and other iridescent creatures or things reside in the "Flower World", a timeless landscape abounding in beauty, song, and sacrality. This is where the living spirit flourishes and, in death, returns' (Houston, 2009: 13).

Figure 2.   *Libellus de medicinalibus indorum herbis* (1552), folios 38v and 39r

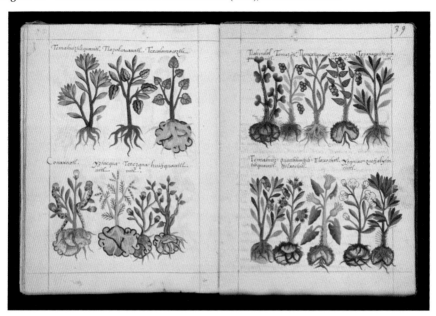

Source: Secretaría de Cultura, INAH, Mexico.

the city. Although their respective narratives differ slightly, they are in accord on the major events. The *Annals of Cuauhtitlan* describe how, until the rise of a brilliant king, a series of rulers had kept their people in a nomadic, uncivilised state:

> [Huacli] had been the ruler of Cuauhtitlan […] who did not know how to plant edible corn. Also his subjects did not know how to make *tilmas*. They still wore hides. Their food was just birds, snakes, rabbits, and deer. As yet they were homeless. They just kept going, kept moving from place to place. (Bierhorst, 1992: 29)

But then Quetzalcoatl, 'Feather-Serpent', who supposedly rose to power in the year 865 (10-House), led his subjects from nomadism to civilisation. According to Sahagún (1577: Book 3, fol. 9r [chapter 3]), Quetzalcoatl 'was esteemed and regarded as a god' ('fue estimado y tenido por dios') and issued new laws to his people. That parallels the classical myth of origins related by the Roman poet Virgil which ascribed a similar role to the divinity Saturn:

> quis neque mos neque cultus erat, nec iungere tauros
> aut componere opes norant aut parcere parto,
> sed rami atque asper victu venatus alebat.
> primus ab aetherio venit Saturnus Olympo

arma Iovis fugiens et regnis exsul ademptis.
is genus indocile ac dispersum montibus altis
composuit legesque dedit […]
aurea quae perhibent illo sub rege fuere
saecula. (Virgil, *Aeneid* 8.316–322, 324–325)

[This race] had no customs or culture, and did not know how to yoke
oxen or accumulate wealth, or save profits, but lived by feeding on
branches and coarse hunting. Saturn was the first to come down from
heavenly Olympus, fleeing Jove's weapons in exile from his lost realm.
He gathered together the untaught race, scattered among the high
mountains, and gave them laws […]. They say that his reign was the
Golden Age.

Quetzalcoatl's reign of civilisation and prosperity was in part characterised
by the multicoloured buildings he constructed: 'his turquoise house of beams,
his house of red-shell, his house of whiteshell, his house of quetzal plumes'
(Bierhorst, 1992: 29). Polychromy continued to signify political authority for
the Nahuas well after the time of the mythical city. Recent excavations suggest
that the Sacred House of the Eagles in the Templo Mayor in Tenochtitlan was
painted in four colours in order to resemble the palaces of Tollan, thus claim-
ing the Aztec capital as the rightful heir to the mythical city and in this way
legitimising its power over other city-states in the valley of Mexico during the
Post-Classic period (López Luján, 2006; López Luján and López Austin, 2007).

In addition, Quetzalcoatl is described as a 'a great craftsman in all his
works: his eating dishes, his drinking vessels, his green-, herb-green, white-,
yellow-, and red-painted pottery' (Bierhorst, 1992: 30). In the *Florentine Codex*
another account of Quetzalcoatl and his city (there called Tulla) and its
people, the Toltecs, expands on this idea, suggesting that all the inhabitants
of Tollan were great artists:

> Y los vasallos que tenia, eran todos oficiales de artes mecanicas, y die-
> stros para labrar las piedras verdes, que se llaman chalchiuites: y tam-
> bien para fundir plata, y hacer otras cosas; y estas artes todas ovieron ori-
> gen, del dicho Quetzalcoatl. (Sahagún, 1577, book 3, chapter 3, fol. 210r)

> And the vassals that he had were all experts in the mechanical arts.
> They were highly skilled in cutting greenstone, which they called
> *chalchiuites*; and also in casting silver and other such things. And all the
> arts proceeded from Quetzalcoatl.

The Nahua association between the ancient Toltecs and great artistry is
such that the word Toltec came to be associated with the idea of an artist or
painter. The *Florentine Codex*'s account of the Toltecs not only includes signs

of Aristotelian ideas of civilisation, such as the knowledge of agriculture and architecture in stone, but also indicators of status within elite Nahua culture – certain bird feathers, precious stones and chocolate drink – much as the multicoloured flowers of the *Libellus* may have been markers of social rank:

> Y mas dizen que en el dicho pueblo de tulla, se criavan muchos, y diversos generos de aves, de pluma rica, y colores diversos, que se llaman xiuhtototl, y quetzaltototl, y çaquan, y tlauhquechol: y otras aves que cantavan dulce, y suavemente. Y mas tenia el dicho que Quetzalcoatl, todas las riquezas del mundo; de oros, y plata, y piedras verdes, que se llaman chalchiuites; y otras cosas preciosas, y mucha abundancia, de arboles, de cacao, de diversas colores, quese llaman xochicacaoatl. (Sahagún, 1577, book 3, chapter 3, fol. 211r)

> And they say that in the city of Tulla many different birds of rich and diverse feathers were bred, which are called *xiuhtototl*, and *quetzaltototl*, and *zacuan*, and *tlauhquechol*. Also other birds that sang sweetly and softly. And said Quetzalcoatl had all the riches in the world: golds and silver, greenstones, which are called *chalchiuites*, and other precious things, and much abundance of cacao trees of different colours that are called *xochicacaoatl*.

Such accounts of abundance in Tollan in this idyllic epoch are in some ways reminiscent of the Golden Age of Saturn as it was described by Greco-Roman authors. In the words of the poet Ovid:

> mulcebant zephyri natos sine semine flores;
> mox etiam fruges tellus inarata ferebat,
> nec renovatus ager gravidis canebat aristis;
> flumina iam lactis, iam flumina nectaris ibant,
> flavaque de viridi stillabant ilice mella.
> (Ovid, *Metamorphoses* 1.108–112)

> The west winds induced flowers to grow without seeds, the unploughed earth promptly yielded crops and, without needing renewal, untended fields turned white with heavy ears of corn; at one moment flowed rivers of milk, at another rivers of nectar, and golden honey seeped out of the green oak.[7]

---

7   Compare the discussion of Ovid, Lucian and Vasco de Quiroga in the introductory chapter to this volume.

Tollan too was such an abundant place that its people did not have to waste their time on agriculture, but could instead dedicate their life to the production of art. The *Florentine Codex* gives this description of conditions in Tollan when the city was at its peak:

> el mahiz era abundantissimo, y las calabaças muy gordas, de una braça en redondo: y las maçorcas de mahiz, eran tan largas, que se llevavan abraçadas, y las cañas de bledos, eran muy largos, y gordos, y que subían por ellas, como por arboles. Y que sembraban, y cogían algodón, de todos colores; que son colorado y encarnado, y amarillo, y morado, blanqueccino, y verde y açul, y prieto, y pardo, y naranjado, y leonado: y estos colores de algodón eran naturales, que asi se nacian.
> (Sahagún, 1577, book 3, chapter 3, fol. 210v)

> The maize was abundant and its ears were so tall that one would have to embrace them in order to carry them. And the amaranth plants were so long and fat that they would climb up them like trees. And they planted and picked cotton of all colours: red and dark red, and yellow, and purple, and white and green and blue, shadowy, brown, orange, and coyote coloured. And these were its natural colours, it grew like this.

That innately coloured cotton recalls a detail in the best known of all the classical accounts of Golden Age – Virgil's fourth *Eclogue* – which heralded the return of Saturn's reign:

> omnis feret omnia tellus […]
> nec varios discet mentiri lana colores,
> ipse sed in pratis aries iam suave rubenti.
> murice, iam croceo mutabit vellera luto,
> sponte sua sandyx pascentis vestiet agnos.
> (Virgil, *Eclogues* 4.39, 4.42–45)

> Every land will bring forth everything […]. Wool will stop learning to fake varied colours. Instead the ram in the meadow will himself change his fleece, now to a sweet blushing purple, now to a saffron yellow: of its own accord scarlet will clothe the grazing lambs.

Sahagún's evocation of this 'messianic' *Eclogue* (so-called because it was often taken to be a pagan prophecy of Christ's birth) is significant. Virgil's poem, which missionaries incorporated into their millenarian thinking, had predicted a new order of things after the voyage of another Argo, captained by another Tiphys, leading to new wars and another Troy.[8] Columbus had explicitly identified himself with the mythological figure of Tiphys; and Sahagún earlier in the *Florentine Codex* had compared the fate of Tollan to that of Troy and Rome (Sahagún, 1982, 1:70; Romm, 1994, 2001).

But while Saturn had been cast out of heaven *before* establishing his Golden Age on earth, Quetzalcoatl's fall from grace was to come after his rule of Tollan. One of the flowers in the 'garden' depicted in the central folios of the *Libellus* makes reference to the ruler's sad fate and strongly hints at further parallels between the myths of Tollan and European traditions. The striking image of the *couaxocotl* flower in folio 38v (Figure 3) of the *Libellus* has a snake flanking either side of the plant, each biting into a round red flower. It has been suggested that these snakes serve to signify the plant's name in Nahuatl which can be translated as 'serpent-fruit'.[9] That might then invite an association with Quetzalcoatl, Feather-Serpent. Although the Tlatelolco students who produced the *Florentine Codex* often used ideograms as phonetic signifiers for the names of the plants they represented, the *Libellus* artist does not, so this would most likely be an exceptional instance. It is remotely possible that serpents were included as an environmental marker: the presence of ants in two illustrations in the *Libellus* indicates that the flowers depicted grew near ant-hills but serpents are less likely to suggest a particular kind of location.[10] Their presence in this image is more likely to be symbolic, and could have any or all of three possible values:

(i) Quetzalcoatl

The *Annals of Cuauhtitlan* mention that the ruler began building his temple by putting up 'serpent columns'. The vertical positioning of the serpents and the degree of symmetry in the way they approximately mirror each other seem to evoke this.

(ii) The Garden of Eden

The image is also suggestive of depictions of a snake in or around a fruit tree in a bountiful garden in iconography of the temptation of Adam and Eve

---

8   Virgil, *Eclogues* 4.34–36. I am grateful to Andrew Laird for drawing my attention to the relevance of these passages of Virgil to this chapter.

9   Emmart (1940: 275) suggests the plant might be *Calocarpum Mammosum*. The first part of the name, *coua-*, could be a form of *cōātl*, the Nahuatl for serpent (and twin), as *xocotl* means fruit (Karttunen, 1992: 36, 329).

10   The expression *ihuan cohuatl izomocayan*, 'where the serpents hiss', however, indicated the site of Tenochtitlan in the late sixteenth-century *Crónica Mexicayotl*.

Figure 3.   Image of *couaxocotl*, *Libellus de medicinalibus indorum herbis*, folio 38v (detail)

Source: Secretaría de Cultura, INAH, Mexico.

in the Garden of Eden prior to their expulsion from Paradise. Although the account in the book of Genesis only included one snake, there are medieval representations showing both Lilith, Adam's earlier wife, and Eve as serpents (Hoffeld, 1967; Sholem, 1971). *Coatl*, the Nahuatl word for serpent, also means 'twin' and in the Spanish text of the *Florentine Codex* (book 1, chapter 6), Fray Bernardino de Sahagún characterised the Aztec goddess Cihuacoatl, 'Snake Woman', as 'our mother Eve, who was tricked by a serpent.' (Laird 2016: 160–161).

(iii) Caduceus

The *caduceus* or staff, an emblem of the classical god Mercury, was conventionally featured upright with snakes encircling each other around it, their heads facing one another at the top. The image (Figure 4) was a common emblem for books produced in the 1500s, adopted in many publications by the Basel printer and associate of Erasmus, Johannes Frobenius (c. 1460–1527). The *caduceus* given to Mercury by Apollo to aid him in his job of guiding souls to the underworld was 'sometimes associated with powers of resurrection – of awakening the dead, and also of curing the severely ill' (Retief and Cilliers, 2006: 194).[11] The reference is also appropriate for a herbal, because of its association with pharmacy (Friedlander, 1992).

There are independent connections between the above significations. For example, the native students at Tlatelolco are likely to have related the symbol to Scripture as well as to science, given that four of Frobenius' editions of Erasmus' New Testament (which was available in New Spain) included the *caduceus* in the frontispiece. More importantly, there are significant correspondences between Tollan and Eden, as sites of abundance in which principal actors fell from grace after being tempted to overindulge.

There are two slightly different accounts of what happened in Tollan, where sorcerers swayed Quetzalcoatl to get drunk on *pulque*, the 'white wine' produced from maguey. In the *Florentine Codex* the saddened Quetzalcoatl is quickly tricked into believing the drink will take away all ailments, when in truth it only heightens his suffering (Sahagún, 1577, book 3, chapter 3, 211v-213r). In the *Annals*, the priest-king is more resistant and it takes longer to persuade him. The sorcerers first attempt to convince him to perform a human sacrifice and, failing that, slowly persuade him to drink *pulque*, which leads him 'to lose his judgment' (Bierhorst, 1992: 31). Although he insists on maintaining his virtue and measure by continuing to fast, they tempt him at least to try the intoxicating drink, eventually inducing him to take five full draughts of *pulque* and getting him and his pages completely drunk. He is then persuaded to destroy his sister's fast by giving her *pulque*. Quetzalcoatl is 'filled with sadness' and chooses to leave the city and all the advances he had introduced into it, bidding his pages to hide all its riches and possessions (Bierhorst, 1992: 35–36). Finally, arriving at the ocean, he cremates himself in despair.

The narrative to be distilled from those two accounts has some similarities to the biblical story of Genesis in which the serpent led Eve into temptation by inciting her to bite into the forbidden fruit. The gendered pairing of Quetzalcoatl and his sister could be seen to correspond to that of Adam and Eve, and the departure of the ruler and his entourage from their abundant city to the

---

11 'With this staff Mercury calls out the pale shades from Orcus, sends others down to sad Tartarus, induces and removes sleep, and closes eyes in death' (Virgil, *Aeneid* 4.242–244). See further Waele (1927).

Figure 4.   Title page of *Novum Instrumentum omne*, Basel 1516, the first edition of Desiderius Erasmus' Greek New Testament

NOVVM IN

ſtrumentũ omne, diligenter ab ERASMO ROTERODAMO
recognitum & emendatum, nõ ſolum ad græcam ueritatem, ue-
rumetiam ad multorum utriuſ g̃ linguæ codicum, eorumq̃ ue-
terum ſimul & emendatorum fidem, poſtremo ad pro-
batiſſimorum autorum citationem, emendationem
& interpretationem præcipue, Origenis, Chry
ſoſtomi, Cyrilli, Vulgarij, Hieronymi, Cy-
priani, Ambroſij, Hilarij, Auguſti-
ni, una cũ Annotationibus, quæ
lectorem doceant, quid qua
ratione mutatum ſit.
Quiſquis igitur
amas ue-
ram
Theolo-
giam, lege, cogno
ſce, ac deinde iudica.
Neq̃ ſtatim offendere, ſi
quid mutatum offenderis, ſed
expende, num in melius mutatum ſit.

APVD   INCLYTAM
GERMANIAE   BASILAEAM.

CVM   PRIVILEGIO
MAXIMILIANI   CAESARIS   AVGVSTI,
NE   QVIS   ALIVS   IN   SACRA   ROMA-
NI   IMPERII   DITIONE, INTRA QVATV
OR   ANNOS   EXCVDAT,   AVT   ALIBI
EXCVSVM   IMPORTET.

expulsion from the Garden of Eden as a consequence of their transgression. The resulting toils and hardships faced by Quetzalcoatl (or even by Adam and Eve) might be pertinent to the 'fatigue of one administering the Republic and performing public duty' – the very ailment which was to be alleviated by the remedy on folio 39v of the *Libellus* – the text following the garden of flowers in the central pages of the volume.

The convergences between Christian and native Mexican traditions in the *Libellus* show how members of the indigenous elite could confer a specific character on their beliefs. The vision of Tollan conveyed by the central folios was consistent with their Catholic faith and perhaps characterised the Nahua authors' ancestors as participants, at least symbolically, in Paradise before the Fall. The affinities between Tollan, Eden and the classical Golden Age might have reflected the preoccupations of their Franciscan instructors: the lack of reference to America in the Bible had led to a variety of eschatological speculation, allowing the continent's distant antiquity to be connected to both Judeo-Christian and Greco-Roman myths of origin (Baudot, 1977; Dupeyron, 2002; Laird, 2016). The producers of the Mexican herbal thus took pains to embed signs of both Spanish and Nahua learning in their gift for the Spanish king. As befitted their European humanist education they wrote the *Libellus de medicinalibus indorum herbis* in Latin and it followed a Galenic structure. But at the same time, this work served to highlight the extent of indigenous knowledge of nature, while demonstrating its authors' ability to synthesize classical, Christian and Nahua representational codes.

References

Bakewell, L. and Hamann, B. E. (2011) 'Painting History, Reading Painted Histories: Ethnoliteracy in Prehispanic Oaxaca and Colonial Central Mexico' in W. H. Beezley (ed.) *A Companion to Mexican History and Culture*. Wiley Blackwell: Oxford, 163–192.

Baudot, G. (1977) *Utopie et histoire au Mexique. Les premiers chroniqueurs de la civilisation mexicaine (1520–1569)*. Privat: Toulouse.

Bierhorst, J. (1992) *History and Mythology of the Aztecs: The Codex Chimalpopoca*. University of Arizona Press: Tucson.

Cervantes de Salazar, F. (1971) *Crónica de la Nueva España* (2 vols.). Biblioteca de Autores Españoles, Editorial Atlas: Madrid.

Cruz, M. de la and Badiano, J. (1991) *Libellus de medicinalibus indorum herbis: Versión española con estudios y comentarios por diversos autores*. Fondo de Cultura Económica: Mexico City.

Dupeyron, G. R. (2002) *Indios imaginarios e indios reales en los relatos de la conquista de México*. Universidad Veracruzana: Xalapa.

Durán, D. (1995) *Historia de las Indias de Nueva España e islas de tierra firme* (ed. A. M. Garibay). 2 vols. Porrúa: Mexico City.

Emmart, E. W. (1940) *The Badianus Manuscript (Codex Barberini, Latin 241) Vatican Library: an Aztec Herbal of 1552*. Johns Hopkins University Press: Baltimore.

Fernández, J. (1991) 'Las miniaturas que ilustran el códice' in Cruz and Badiano (1991), 101–106.

Friedlander, W. J. (1992) *The Golden Wand of Medicine: A History of the Caduceus Symbol in Medicine*. Greenwood Press: Westport, CT.

Grieco, A. J. (1991) 'The Social Politics of Pre-Linnean Botanical Classification'. *I Tatti Studies: Essays in the Renaissance* 4: 131–149.

Hamann, B. E. (2013) 'Object, Image, Cleverness: the *Lienzo de Tlaxcala*'. *Art History* **36**(3): 518–545.

Hamann, B. E. (2004) 'In the Eyes of the Mixtecs/To View Several Pages Simultaneously'. *Visible Language* **38**(1): 68–123.

Hassig, D. (1989) 'Transplanted Medicine: Colonial Herbals of the Sixteenth Century'. *RES, Anthropology and Aesthetics* **17/18**: 30–53.

Heyden, D. (1983) *Mitología y simbolismo de la flora en el México prehispánico*. UNAM: Mexico City.

Hoffeld, J. (1967-1968) 'Adam's Two Wives'. *Bulletin of the Metropolitan Museum of Art* **26**: 430–440.

Houston, S. (2009) *Veiled Brightness: A History of Ancient Maya Color*. University of Texas Press: Austin.

Karttunen, F. (1992) *An Analytical Dictionary of Nahuatl*. University of Oklahoma: Norman.

Kobayashi, J. M. (1974) *La educación como conquista*. Empresa Franciscana en México: Mexico City.

Laird, A. (2015) 'The Teaching of Latin to the Native Nobility in Mexico in the mid-1500s. Contexts, Methods and Results' in E. Archibald, W. Brockliss and J. Gnoza (eds.) *Learning Latin and Greek from Antiquity to the Present*. Cambridge University Press: Cambridge, 118–135.

Laird, A. (2016) 'Aztec and Roman Gods in Sixteenth-Century Mexico: Strategic Uses of Classical Learning in Sahagún's *Historia General*' in J. M. D. Pohl and C. L. Lyons (eds.) *Altera Roma: Art and Empire from Mérida to México*. UCLA Cotsen Institute of Archaeology Press: Los Angeles, 147–167.

López Luján, L. (2006) *La Casa de las Águilas: un ejemplo de arquitectura religiosa de Tenochtitlan* (2 vols.). Instituto Nacional de Antropología e Historia: Mexico City.

López Luján, L. and López Austin, A. (2007) 'Los Mexicas en Tula y Tula en México-Tenochtitlan'. *Estudios de Cultura Nahuatl* **38**: 33–83.

Maldonado-Koerdel, M. (1964) 'Los minerales, rocas, suelos, y fósiles del manuscrito' in Cruz and Badiano (1991), 291–299.

Mathes, W. M. (1985) *The America's First Academic Library: Santa Cruz de Tlatelolco*. California State Library: Sacramento.

Mendieta, G. de (1993) *Historia Eclesiástica Indiana* (ed. J. García Icazabaleta) Porrúa: Mexico City.

Retief, F. P. and Cilliers, L. (2006) 'Snake and staff symbolism in healing'. *Acta Theologica* **26**(2): 189–199.

Romm, J. (1994) 'New World and "novos orbes": Seneca in the Renaissance Debate over Ancient Knowledge of the Americas' in W. Haase and R. Meyer (eds.) *The Classical Tradition and the Americas*. Walter de Gruyter: Berlin and New York, 77–116.

Romm, J. (2001) 'Biblical History and the Americas: The Legend of Solomon's Ophir' in P. Bernardini and N. Fiering (eds.) *The Jews and the Expansion of Europe to the West 1545–1800*. Berghahn Books: New York, 27–46.

Sahagún, B. de (1577) *Historia general de las cosas de Nueva España*. Manuscript: Ms. Med. Palat. 219, Biblioteca Laurenziana Medicea: Florence.

Sahagún, B. de (1982) *Florentine Codex: Introductory Volume* (A. J. O. Anderson and C. E. Dibble eds.). School of American Research and University of Utah: Santa Fe.

Sholem, G. (1971) 'Lilith' in *Encylopedia Judaica*, Vol. **2**. Macmillan: New York, 245–250.

Somolinos d'Ardois, G. (1991) 'Estudio histórico' in Cruz and Badiano (1991), 165–192.

Steck, F. B. and Barlow, R. H. (1944) *El primer colegio de América, Santa Cruz de Tlatelolco*. Centro de Estudios Franciscanos: Mexico City.

Stols, A. A. M. (1992) 'Descripción del códice' in J. Kumate et al. (eds.) *Estudios Actuales sobre el Libellus de Medicinalibus Indorum Herbis*. Secretaría de Salud: Mexico.

Waele, F. J. M. (1927) *The Magic Staff or Rod in Graeco-Italian Antiquity*. J. van der Doesstraat: The Hague.

Zetina, S. *et al.* (2008) 'Painting Syncretism: A Non-Destructive Analysis of the Badiano Codex' in 9th International Conference of NDT of Art, Jerusalem, Israel, 25–30 May 2008. [WWW document]. URL https://www.ndt.net/article/art2008/papers/121Ruvalcaba.pdf [accessed 8 July 2018].

4

Comparison and Seeing in the Mediterratlantic

BYRON ELLSWORTH HAMANN

This essay is about questions of comparison – specifically, comparisons of Mesoamerican and Mediterranean worlds in the sixteenth century. This is a familiar topic with regard to classical traditions in Latin America – and from both European and indigenous perspectives. On the European side, the works of Sahagún, las Casas, and Acosta all contain comparisons of indigenous cultural practices with those of the pagan Mediterranean (Pagden, 1982; Laird, 2016; Olivier, 2016). On the indigenous side, Serge Gruzinski (2002) has argued that the status of the classical pagan past for early modern Iberians enabled native American nobles and artists to reclaim their own pre-Christian past.

But irrespective of who made them, such Mediterratlantic comparisons were often misleading. The Aztec Tlazolteotl was not really the same as the Roman goddess of love. James Lockhart (1985) has used the phrase 'double mistaken identity' to refer to situations where cultural practices that on the surface seemed to be shared between Mesoamericans and Europeans actually concealed deeper differences. Or, in the words of Marshall Sahlins (1981: 81), these were 'working misunderstandings'. If comparison can reveal similarities, it can also reveal contrasts. In this essay, I consider a visual comparison in which the *differences* between indigenous American and European practices (specifically, material cultures of seeing) were dramatised, brought together in sharp relief. The project of Mediterratlantic comparison in sixteenth-century New Spain could sometimes break down, and reveal the mistaken similarities of 'double mistaken identities'.

Figure 1 shows facing pages from the *Codex Magliabechiano*, a spine-bound manuscript created in mid-sixteenth-century Central Mexico. This 92-folio work begins with paintings of indigenous textile designs, and then moves on to an overview of pre-Hispanic religion: the structure of the calendar, the names and insignia of principal deities, descriptions of key ceremonies. Folio 55 *recto* (which falls on the reader's right) depicts two humans wearing dance costumes. The man on the left personifies one of the *pulque* gods – *pulque* being an alcoholic beverage made from maguey cactus sap. The man on the right is dressed as a monkey. Each holds a black and white feathered staff in his right hand. We know that the two figures are dancing, and the beings they represent, because of the facing alphabetic text on folio 54 *verso*. It reads:

Figure 1.   *Codex Magliabechiano,* mid-1500s, fol. 54v–55r

Note: *Codex Magliabechiano XIII. Manuscrit mexicain post-columbien de la Bibliothèque nationale de Florence; reproduit en photochromagraphie aux frais du duc de Loubat* (1904).
Source: Photograph by author of image in public domain.

Este demonio se llamaua tlal tegauoa. En el qual arieto q[ue] a este se hazia y va delante vn yndio vestido vn pellejo de mona q[ue] dellos llaman en su lengua cuçumate.

This demon was called *Tlaltegauoa,* (shown) in the dance which was performed for him. And in front is an Indian wearing the skin of a monkey, which they call *cuçumate* in their language.

The style of both figures is strongly pre-Hispanic: bold black outlines; solid washes of colour. But one key feature reveals the painting's viceregal facture. The monkey-man holds a round shield before him. The shield's form is indigenous – it is a *chimalli* – yet its surface is decorated with a curiously fisted hand. This is a European gesture drawn in a European style. The black on white hand is a small detail, yet it opens up great vistas across space and time.

Specifically, the fist is clenched to make an *higa,* a gesture of deep antiquity that turned the hand into a vagina. In other words, it was the structural opposite of 'the finger', another legacy of the pagan Mediterranean. The *higa* was a sexualised gesture, to be sure, and prior commentaries on the *Magliabechiano* have focused on this detail's aggressive erotic content (Anders, 1970: 61–62; Boone, 1984: 26–27; Anders *et al.,* 1994: 190; Batalla Rosado, 1999: 472). Putting a forceful gesture like this on a shield underscores the *chimalli's* function: it wards off would-be attackers. I would also add that the placement of this vaginal device in the hands of a monkey-impersonator shows that the indigenous artist understood sexual iconographies from both sides of the Atlantic. In Mesoamerican thought, monkeys were lascivious beasts. Indeed, this monkey-dancer's hip cloth has been provocatively knotted to create a

Figure 2. Twenty-first century *higas*

Note: Left to right: Santiago de Compostela, Spain, 2013 (jet, collected at Praza San Miguel dos Agros); Vila Nova de Guia, Portugal, 2009 (wood, collected at the Vandoma market, Porto; carving by Florentino Santos); São Paulo, Brazil, 2012 (plastic, collected at Edifício Copan); Mexico City, Mexico, 2013 (painted wood, collected at Insurgentes 409).
Source: Photograph by the author.

projecting frontal phallus, a sort of Mesoamerican codpiece with an ancient history (Taube, 1996: 500–554; Persels, 1997).

The painter of this image may have known about the *higa* from enacted gestures. In 1545, the diary of a Dominican friar Tomás de la Torre – en route to the Chiapas of Bartolomé de las Casas – describes how a European 'gave two *higas* to an indigenous *cacique* in the Yucatan (1985: 141). But our painter was probably also familiar with the *higa*'s more permanent manifestations as well. *Higa* amulets were a common feature of early modern Iberian dress. At least two have been found in excavations of early viceregal contexts in Mexico City (Kelly, 1977: 24; Olvera, 1992: 37).

These objects were (and still are) mass produced in Galicia, in northwestern Iberia, and from shipping records we know that hundreds were imported to sixteenth-century New Spain (Kelly, 1977). They are even listed in sixteenth-century wills: the probate inventory of Amador Gutierrez Paez, written in Taxco and dated 19 June 1598, lists *una caxita de palo y en ella unas higas y coraçones de vidrio para gargantillas* (a wicker box containing some *higas* and glass hearts for necklaces) (Archivo General de la Nación, Mexico City, *Bienes Nacionales* vol. 414 exp. 9, unfoliated *verso*). But if the *higa* was – at least according to the commentaries on the *Magliabechiano* – such an offensive erotic gesture, why did people wear it as a piece of jewelry (Figure 2)? The answer has deep Mediterranean roots. From ancient Rome onward, *higa* amulets were used as protection against the evil eye. The first part of this essay will explore the history of these apotropaic jewels, and explain how such objects were understood to function.

But my explorations of visual-material culture will not end with this European *longue durée*. When *higa* amulets arrived in Mesoamerica, indigenous people interpreted them according to their own theories of vision, and in light of the artifacts they themselves had created to engage the projective powers of sight. Two of these artifacts are shown in the *Magliabechiano* scene – the feathered black and white staves – and they reveal that the artist not only understood the *higa*'s sexual force (since it is carried by a monkey), but also its close connection to the powers of sight. The feathered staves held in the right hands of the two dancers are the Central Mexican *tlachialoni*, literally a 'device for seeing'. Near the top of their long feather-decorated batons, both *tlachialoni* are ornamented with chequered black and white discs, pierced in the centre. These are representations of mirrors, made of obsidian or pyrite mosaic. The second part of this essay therefore shifts from Mediterranean to Mesoamerican theories of sight, and to the material culture produced by those New World ideas. I conclude by bringing these two deep Mesoamerican and Mediterranean histories together, considering how *higa* amulets – especially those made of jet – would have appeared to Mesoamerican eyes. This will bring us back to the monkey-dancer's round shield. We know that such dance paraphernalia were made from feather mosaics, a medium whose material substance was understood to have compelling optical-social effects. In sum, this essay reflects on material legacies of classical traditions in the early modern Mediterratlantic world – traditions which, in sixteenth-century Latin America, were brought into dialogue with analogous traditions from the pre-Hispanic Mesoamerican past.

In the background of all this is the work of Alfred Gell (1998) and his interest in 'tacky' objects – artifacts that had the power to attract people to their forms and, by extension, to their makers and owners. Gell argued that one globally common strategy for producing tackiness is the use of decorative patterns. The arts of ornamentation – of lime containers, Victorian furniture, canoe prows, tattooed bodies, dinosaur bed sheets – appear throughout Gell's work. The technologies of tackiness are also a concern in what follows. However, rather than exploring surface decoration, my approach to the arts of enchantment focuses on four *substances* that were understood by different early modern cultures to be visually attractive: jet, amber, obsidian and feathers. Objects made from these substances were seen to be socially compelling, not because of any surface ornamentation, but by the very fact of their physical being.

Mediterranean Histories

Fascination, in ancient, medieval and early modern Europe, was a form of enchantment cast by the eyes. To be fascinated was to suffer from the malevolent gaze of another: an evil eye (Salillas, 1905; Villena, 1994; Ciapparelli, 2005; Bartsch, 2006: 138–152). Ancient Greek and Roman theories of vision understood sight to be extromissive – that is, the eyes saw not by collecting and focusing external light, but by actively projecting their own lines of force onto the surrounding world. Since the eyes were closely linked to the soul, if one person looked on another with envy, or anger, those poisonous emotions could be visually projected across space and into the body of the observed victim. Sickness, weakness and wasting would result.

In order to protect against the evil eye, the ancient Romans created amulets called *fascina* (Bartsch, 2006: 142–144). Often made of bone or bronze, these took the form of a phallus or, in double-ended versions, of a phallus and a vaginal gesture: the *higa*. Since the eye, like the penis, was thought to be an organ of emission, images of the male member had the power both to attract the eye and to attack its malevolent gaze. In contrast, the fisted hand manifested an organ normally inaccessible to sight, an organ whose display had a complex mythic history, causing unexpected laughter (as in the Greek legend of Demeter and Baubo) or petrification (which was linked to the face of the Gorgon) (Olender, 1990: 90; Vernant, 1991: 113–114; Fornés Pallicer and Rodríguez-Escalona, 2005: 140–142).

Tracking the continuity of these ancient ideas forward to early modern Iberia is somewhat difficult, although the evil eye is discussed in a number of treatises by Muslim and Jewish authors from al-Andalus (Carr, 2000). In 1411, Enrique de Villena wrote a treatise on the evil eye, the *Tratado de la fascinación o de aojamiento*, which lists a number of ways to combat potentially harmful gazes, including the use of 'small hands of silver' – probably an *higa* reference – and 'broken pieces of mirror'.

Similar discussions of the evil eye appear in two early sixteenth-century treatises on superstitions and witchcraft: Martín de Castañega's 1529 *Tratado de las supersticiones y hechicería*, and Pedro Ciruelo's 1530 *Reprobación de las supersticiones y hechicerías*. Castañega describes how 'the most subtle impurities of the body come out through the eyes like rays, and the more subtle they are the more they penetrate and are most infectious' (Castañega, 1946: 71–72; Darst, 1979). Similar discussions were published shortly thereafter in Mexico City. In 1557 the Augustinian friar Alonso de la Vera Cruz included a chapter on the evil eye in his *Physica Speculatio* (Moreno Corral, 2004). A final example leads us from Mexico City to Madrid, where Sebastián de Covarrubias published a lengthy definition of '*higa*' as part of his 1611 *Tesoro de la Lengua Castellana*. It is worth quoting in full, for it brings us full circle back to ancient Rome:

> HIGA, es vna manera de menos precio que hazemos cerrando el puño, y mostrando el dedo pulgar por entre el dedo indice, y el medio, es disferaçada pulla. La *higa* antigua era tan solamente vna semejança del

miembro viril, este[n]dido el dedo medio, y encogiendo el indize, y el auricular: y assi se dezia *medium vnguem ostendere.* Iuvenal *satyra* 10.

> *Quum fortuna ipse minaci*
> *Mandaret laqueum, mediumque ostenderet vnguem.*

Dize vn prouerbio, Mee yo claro, y vna *higa* para el medico: dixolo Marcial, lib. 6, epig. 69 *Sexaginta & c. ibi:*

Ostendit digitum, sed impudicum
Alconti, Dasioque, Symmachoque.

Estos eran medicos famosos del tiempo de Marcial en Roma. Tambien es cosa vsada al que ha parecido bien darle vna *higa*, diziendo, Toma porque no os ajoen. Colgar a los niños del hombro vna *higa* de azabache es muy antiguo, y comunmente se ignora su principio. Pudo tener origen de la misma materia, porq[ue] el succino, o ambar, y el azabache escriuen tener propiedad contra el ojo: y tambien porque en quanto a la figura es supersticiosa deruiada de la Ge[n]tilidad que estaua persuadida tener fuerça contra la fascinacion la efigie priapeya, que como tenemos dicho era la *higa*, de todo esto no ay que hazer caso. (Covarrubias Orozco, 1611: 471r-v)

HIGA, is a manner of giving insult, which we form by closing the fist and showing the thumb between the index and middle fingers, this is a disguised obscenity. The ancient *higa* was just an imitation of the male member with the middle finger extended and the index and ring fingers hidden; and so it was called *medium vnguem ostendere*. Juvenal, *Satire* 10:

For he, when Fortune was in a threatening mood,
Would bid her go hang, and show the middle finger.

A proverb says, 'I pissed clear, and an *higa* for the doctor. So said Martial in Book 6, epigram 69, which starts '*Sexagesima* … ':

He shows his finger, and the insulting one at that,
To Alcon, to Damasius and to Symmachus.

These were famous doctors from the time of Martial in Rome. It is also the custom for the person who has decided to give the *higa* to say 'Take this, so they don't put the evil eye on you!' Hanging an *higa* of jet around the shoulders of children is long-established, and its origins are not generally known. It could have its origins in the raw material itself, because they say that succinite, or amber, and jet have powers against the eye: and also because the shape is superstitious, deriving from pagan times when it was believed that the priapic effigy had power against the evil eye, which, as we have said, was the *higa*. It isn't necessary to believe any of this.

Overall, the basic contours of fascination theory for early modern Iberians were those set out in antiquity. Vision was projective, and potentially harmful, but such dangerous visual disruptions could be deflected by specially designed amulets. But how exactly were early modern *higas* thought to function? What were the secrets of their cultural force? We can better understand the technologies of enchantment that made such items socially effective if we look first at their material substance, and then at their physical form. The first topic raises Alfred Gell's theme of tackiness; the second brings us to his ideas about apotropaics and extended personhood.

Early modern apotropaics were often shining things. Villena mentions 'tiny hands' (*manezillas*) made of reflective silver; both he and Castañega mention the use of mirror fragments. Such glinting ornaments were eye-catching objects in a very literal sense, as Castañega makes clear: 'they [who have dangerous sight] will look at the mirror before [looking at] the eyes of the child'. Jet and amber, the *higa*-making materials mentioned by Covarrubias, were also shining stones. But they had other virtues as well. Covarrubias claims that jet and amber 'have powers against the eye', and his phrasing suggests this idea is attested in written sources (*porque el succino, o ambar, y el azabache escriuen tener propiedad contra el ojo*). However, neither Pliny nor Dioscorides (authors Covarrubias cites in his earlier entries for 'AMBAR' and 'AZAVACHE') mentions any connection of jet or amber to the eyes, or to the treatment of optical ailments. Instead, Covarrubias is probably recalling Castañega (see below).

The use of jet and amber to make early modern *higas* can probably be explained by a curious property that both substances share. These black and golden stones were composed of originally organic materials: jet from fossilised wood, amber from fossilised sap. When rubbed against cloth, both build up a magnet-like static charge. In other words, like 'the glassy parts of the eyes' (to quote Castañega), both jet and amber could generate projective lines of force, irradiations that had the power to transform their surrounding world. Castañega actually discusses this shared property in his 1529 treatise: 'Amber and jet, when dry, clean and cold and shined against one's clothing, have the same property, attracting dry straw'. Covarrubias also mentions this property in his 1611 discussion of amber stones: 'They have the power to attract straws to themselves and light feathers'.

For Alfred Gell, jet and amber were a kind of early modern flypaper – and this brings us to his discussion of apotropaics. He understood apotropaic images to be weapons used by their creator-artists to combat the malign effects of other social beings, especially evil spirits. Gell also pointed out the frequency with which complex decorative designs – like knots or labyrinths – were used as 'demonic flypaper', with the power to intrigue, and thus distract, would-be evildoers (1998: 83). In contrast, the tackiness of *higas* made from silver or amber or jet did not involve any decorative patterning: no knots or labyrinths. Rather, the tackiness was understood to be built into their very substance: mirror-like silver could trap the onlooker's image; jet and amber had innate powers of attraction.

If the material substance of these early modern amulets was one factor in their perceived power against the evil eye, then that material potential was further enhanced by their physical form. Gell's own concept of extended personhood is a way of describing how art-objects can function as material amplifications of human bodies, expanding the social force of their owners or makers out into the world. Such extensions often take prosthetic form, such as cast-off body effluvia like skin, hair, fingernails, or photographs (Covarrubias 1998: 49–50, 102–115). As Covarrubias makes clear, the ancient sexual genealogy of the *higa* was still remembered in the early 1600s. In Gell's language, it was an apotropaic image that took the form of an extended – and thus distracting – human body part. Or more accurately, *higas* were effigy body parts two times over: they were hands, but hands fisted to create symbolic genitalia. *Higa* amulets were prosthetic extensions of their wearers, detachable members that served as durable decoys for potentially hostile onlookers. These items distracted the malevolent gaze of potential onlookers with a doubled decoy-organ, a false hand mimicking a false vagina. The full force of any dangerous look would thus be directed to an extended prosthetic of the would-be victim's body, providing an inanimate target impervious to attack.

The Mediterranean *higa* had the power to combat violent projective sight through materialities of tackiness combined with strategies of decoy and prosthesis. But when *higa* amulets arrived in sixteenth-century Central Mexico, what visual and material topographies did they encounter?

Mesoamerican Histories

We actually know a great deal about indigenous Mesoamerican understandings of vision. In part this is thanks to sixteenth-century alphabetic texts, but even more important are pre-Hispanic representations of the act of seeing itself. As in the ancient Mediterranean, Mesoamerican people thought of sight as extromissive, as a force that projected from the eyes. The pre-Hispanic Maya hieroglyph for the verb 'to see' shows an eyeball in profile, with two lines of vision emerging from its pupil: one curves up, the other curves down. Maya inscriptions also reveal how Maya elites organised social space through the projective power of their eyes (Houston and Taube, 2000: 286–289). Pre-Hispanic screenfold books from the Mixtec depict elites with 'feathered' or 'fiery' or 'smoking' sight. In contrast, it was generally forbidden for subordinates to gaze directly at their superiors, and certain sacred images were too powerful to look at (Gruzinski, 2000: 75; Hamann, 2004). Moving forward in time, a famous image from the *Codex Mendoza* (painted in 1540s Mexico City) shows an astrologer looking up at the stars with extromissive sight: a dotted line connects his face to a disembodied eyeball floating between him and the semicircular sky on which he gazes (Houston and Taube, 2000; Hamann, 2015: 102–107).

Mesoamerican ideas about vision are also fossilised in pre-Hispanic 'instruments of seeing', prosthetic devices that amplified sight (Headrick, 2003; Hamann, 2004: 94–95). These instruments took a variety of forms, but mirrors are perhaps the best known. Crucially, Mesoamerican mirrors did not provide perfect reflections, but warped and skewed their images: formative concave mirrors turn their images upside down; pyrite mosaic mirrors shatter their reflections into tiny shards; and obsidian mirrors trap their targets within translucent dark glass, creating an eerie hologram.

The longstanding Mesoamerican interest in optically disruptive mirrors was probably connected to their theories about the nature of the world and monistic philosophy. The apparent variety and plurality of the visible, physical world was understood to be a superficial façade, masking the deep interconnectedness of vital forces (Houston and Taube, 2000: 289–290). Because of this, as John Monaghan has argued, in Mesoamerica manifestations of the sacred often focused on the manipulation of surfaces, such as masks and clothing, or flayed skins (2000: 29–30). The idea that instruments of seeing, like mirrors, could pierce the apparent solidity of time and space explains the formal structure of the various *tlachialoni* shown in the *Magliabechiano*. A black and white chequerboard disc (probably indicating mosaic, but perhaps referring to light flashing off obsidian) has, at its centre, a round circle. On the one hand (and this is point to which we will return below) this made the whole apparatus look like a stylised eye, such as the round eye of the monkey dancer in Figure 1. However, the *tlachialoni* held by Tezcatlipoca on folio 33r of the *Magliabechiano* makes clear that the central circle is a *pierced* hole, through which we can see the brown wood of the *tlachialoni*'s central staff. Instruments of seeing were used to pierce the apparent spatio‑temporal boundaries of the present moment, and so it makes sense that they themselves would be pierced. As Annabeth Headrick argues, the hole functions 'as a window between realms' (2003: 33). Monism, optical disruptions, piercings: just as the substance and form of early modern *higas* explain why those amulets were effective against the evil eye, so too do the substance and form of Mesoamerican mirrors explain why those artifacts were thought to offer visions across New World space and time.

The mirrored *tlachialoni* staves from the *Codex Magliabechiano* raise another question. Why are instruments of seeing being carried by a *pulque* god and his monkey companion? The *tlachialoni* is more commonly carried by the god Tezcatlipoca ('Smoking Mirror'), as he does when he appears elsewhere in the same codex. But in addition to our two dancers, several other *pulque* deities in the codex also carry a *tlachialoni* (58r, 59r, 62v). One explanation for this connection of visual instruments to *pulque* has to do with the beverage's visual and cognitive effects.

I have never had more than one glass of *pulque* at a time, but the reports of recent bloggers describe mildly hallucinogenic results when the beverage is consumed in large quantities (Cogswell, 2012; see also: Taylor, 1979: 31; Corcuera de Mancera, 1991). A parallel, if hostile, account appears in a report on *pulque* and criminality given before Mexico's National Academy of Medicine in 1900 (Macouzet, 1901). Moving back in time, viceregal texts refer to potent alcoholic beverages that may involve *pulque* enhanced with other drugs, such as *nanacatl* mushrooms (Berdan and Anawalt, 1994: 232–233). Pre-Hispanic mirrors, as I mentioned, created reflections that were optically distorted in various ways: perhaps the altered visual effects created by *pulque* were understood to produce a similarly enhanced, if warped, view of the world.

Mediterratlantic Comparisons

We have moved from the evil eye and the *higa* in Mediterranean history to Mesoamerican theories of vision and 'instruments of seeing'. The image on folio 55r of the *Magliabechiano* brings these two traditions into dialogue. I now want to ask how indigenous people in Central Mexico – such as the creator of the *Magliabechiano* image – thought about the imported *higa* amulets they encountered.

Central Mexicans were no doubt struck by the fact that such amulets made of jet were optically associated devices made from a substance that looked a great deal like their own optically associated obsidian. This was certainly a connection made by the Europeans, such as Dominican friar Diego Durán (Heyden, 1988: 218). Jet, then, may have been interpreted as a kind of European obsidian which, like its Mesoamerican counterpart, had important optical properties.

The *higa*'s form as a disembodied human hand would have also intrigued indigenous viewers. Mesoamerican societies had a long history of creating talismans from, or shaped like, human body parts: trophy heads, ancestral bones, even – to take a particularly macabre Central Mexican example – the severed finger of a woman who died in childbirth (thought to give warriors strength on the battlefield). If jet was seen as a kind of European obsidian, and if the fisted *higa* amulet was understood to parallel Mesoamerican body-part artifacts, then similar kinds of material-conceptual translations may be signalled in the black-on-white *higa* shown at the centre of our monkey-dancer's shield.

Indigenous dances like the one shown here were spectacular events, and continued to be performed throughout the sixteenth century. Many of them involved lavish featherwork costumes, some inherited from pre-Hispanic times and others newly-made in Mexico City's thriving featherwork ateliers (Mundy, 2014). In the capital during the mid-1560s, the indigenous author of the *Annals of Juan Bautista* described preparations made for the dance ceremonies to honour the arrival of a new viceroy (Reyes García, 2001: 135). Special featherwork shields were made for indigenous participants, at least four examples of which survive today (Castelló Yturbide, 1993: 60, 66, 67, 69).

The *higa*-ornamented shield carried by the monkey-dancer on folio 55r was probably meant to represent a *featherwork* shield. If so, this adds yet another level of optical play to the painting. Feathers, with their often-iridescent, light-reflecting qualities, were understood in Mesoamerican aesthetics to be particularly visually arresting things. They were very 'tacky', in Alfred Gell's terms. Several of the scenes of viceregal featherworking included in the circa 1580 *Florentine Codex* mark plumed creations with a round disembodied eye-ball, indicating an irresistible optical attractiveness. Featherworks provided literally eye-catching surfaces (Peterson, 1988: 287; Leibsohn, 2007).

In other words, the *higa*-ornamented shield painted in the *Magliabechiano* points to an artifact that joined three levels of optical-conceptual play. The monkey's *chimalli* features a glittering representation in Mexican featherwork of a gesture often materialised in shining jet amulets, Mediterranean ornaments whose substance and forms were thought to attract, and thus deflect, dangerous optical emanations. This densely symbolic shield is, in turn, juxtaposed with images of two Mesoamerican 'devices for seeing'.

But what does this visual confrontation mean?

Double Mistaken Identity?

En estos bailes, cuando esta tierra se comenzó á conquistar, tractaban los indios la muerte y destruición de los españoles á que el demonio los persuadía. Son los indios tan aficionados á estos bailes, que, como otras veces he dicho, aunque estén todo el día en ellos, no se cansan [...] pero ellos son tan inclinados á su antigua idolatría que si no hay quien entienda muy bien la lengua, entre las sacras oraciones que cantan mesclan cantares de su gentilidad, y para cubrir mejor su dañada obra, comienzan y acaban con palabras de Dios, interponiendo las demás gentílicas, abaxando la voz para no ser entendidos y levantándola en los principios y fines, cuando dicen 'Dios'. (Cervantes de Salazar, 1914: 39)

In these dances, when this land began to be conquered, the Indians represented the death and destruction of the Spaniards, which the devil persuaded them to do. The Indians are so enamoured of these dances that, as I have said other times, even if they should be at it all day they do not become tired [...] but they are so inclined to their ancient idolatry that if there is no one present who understands their language well, then among the holy orations which they sing they mix songs from their pagan world, and in order to better conceal their damned work, they start and end with words of God, placing between them other pagan utterances, lowering their voices so as not to be understood, and raising them at the beginning and end, when they say 'God'.

These are the words of Francisco Cervantes de Salazar, a professor at the University of Mexico who actually owned a version of the *Codex Magliabechiano* manuscript in the middle of the sixteenth century (Boone, 1983: 5, 93–101). His claims about indigenous dances help place our own *pulque* performance in a wider context. The codex was one of a number of manuscripts about pre-Hispanic religion created in sixteenth-century New Spain. Many of these documents were produced as tools for extirpation. In order to eradicate problematic indigenous customs in the present, their past history needed to be studied, so that they could be recognised (Gruzinski, 2002: 191–198).

The *pulque*-dance painting on folio 55r makes subtle reference to such conflicts of viceregal conversion – European missionaries often commissioned these manuscripts, but their artists were usually indigenous people who had complex feelings about the pre-Christian past. And this brings us back to the questions of comparison and contrast with which I began. In this scene, pre-Hispanic artifacts for *enhancing sight* are juxtaposed with a viceregal artifact (made from Mesoamerican materials and decorated with a European gesture) for *warding off the evil eye*. In other words, the artist of this page is staging a confrontation between two types of visual-material culture, the *higa* and the *tlachialoni*. But despite their surface similarities, these artifacts engaged with sight in very different ways. One enhanced the user's gaze. The other warded off the dangerous gazes of others.

But did the artist realise how different these two artifacts were? Or is this juxtaposition just another example of double mistaken identity? One way to answer this question is to think about how the image of the *higa* nonetheless functions as an actual *higa* even though it is painted, and not carved in jet or gestured by a living hand. To an early modern European viewer, this fisted detail would have been the most recognisable part of the page. The painted *higa* would have literally drawn the European eye to it (just as an *higa* should). That European eye was potentially the source of a very hostile gaze, an evil eye which condemned the painted practices it looked down upon.

Indeed, the painted *higa* continues to dominate the iconography of this page, drawing the attention and commentary of present-day scholars, who always (as mentioned at the start of this essay) explain the symbol as a sexualised gesture of insult and attack. But because this painted *higa* is so successful in attracting eyes trained to look from the Western tradition, it manages to deflect attention from other aspects of the page: appropriately functioning as an apotropaic device. It is not accidental, then, that no previous commentaries on this page have pointed out that the *higa* is *also* connected to ancient ideas about the evil eye, and that its combination with two *tlachialoni* staves is probably not accidental. In other words, this painted *higa* functions in similar ways to the orations sung to God interspersed with pagan formulae that so annoyed Cervantes de Salazar: it provides a kind of camouflage for a complex indigenous discourse.

This painted meditation on two contrasting regimes of visuality is, at the same time, presented in the context of a dance honouring one of the *pulque* gods, patron of a beverage that viceregal church and government were eager to suppress (Corcuera de Mancera, 1991). Thas may explain why the *Magliabechiano* contains a special sub-section of *pulque* gods and goddesses, spanning folios 48v to 59v. These twelve folios provide a kind of alcoholic rogues' gallery. And near the end of the volume, on 85r, a *pulque*-centered fiesta is shown – the kind of event that would have accompanied the *pulque*-dedicated dance on 55r (Figure 3). In the centre, one of the *pulque* gods uses a straw to drink directly from a large ceramic *olla* filled with the foaming beverage. An overserved woman sits on the ground in front of him, vomiting. Visible seams are painted on her clothes, as well as on the clothes of two male participants. This is a curious detail, and does not appear anywhere else in the manuscript. Perhaps it was meant to indicate poverty, the patched-up garments of habitual drinkers. In the upper-right corner, a man and a woman drink facing each other. He holds a bouquet in his right hand, which she reaches out to stroke. Flowers were common symbols of sexuality in Mesoamerican art, often drawn in explicitly genital shapes (Klein, 1993: 23). Like the dancing monkey-man, this scene suggests the libido unleashed by drink. The main caption – labelling a woman in the lower centre holding a cup of *pulque* in front and a bouquet behind her back – reads: 'this was she who served the wine [*pulque*] to the others, until they got drunk'.

Figure 3.   *Pulque* festival, *Codex Magliabechiano*, mid-1500s, fol. 85r.

Source: Photograph by author of image in public domain.

Conclusion

The transfer of classical traditions to early modern Latin America was made possible, in part, by the transatlantic travels of missionaries and educated officials: men who carried knowledge of Latin grammar and ancient mythology in their heads. But this transfer of traditions was also made possible through the movement of material objects. Books for language instruction are perhaps the best documented. Thousands of copies of Antonio de Nebrija's Latin grammar crossed the Atlantic in the sixteenth and seventeenth centuries: a transmission well documented by ships' registers and library inventories (Leonard, 1949: 222, 268).

The travels of *higa* amulets reveal another medium through which classical traditions were brought to the Americas. In the first section of this essay, I mentioned that two such amulets have been recovered from excavations of sixteenth-century sites in Mexico City. The locations where these *higas* were excavated are significant, and underscore how ancient legacies both Mediterranean and Mesoamerican played a role in the visual culture of sixteenth-century New Spain.

One *higa* was found in excavations at Santiago Tlatelolco. As Alejandra Rojas' contribution to this volume makes clear, this was the site of an innovative Franciscan school where native Mexicans received a Renaissance humanist education which enabled them to become fluent in Latin and acquainted with Roman literature. The other *higa* was found in excavations above the House of the Eagles, home in pre-Hispanic times to an

Aztec warrior society. A stone bench within this building was carved in a self-consciously archaic style (modelled on a bench at the already archaeological site of Tula, a site abandoned centuries before the Aztecs came to power). The House of the Eagles was itself adjacent to the Aztec Great Temple, a massive pyramid whose fifteenth-century dedication rituals involved the burial of already ancient Mesoamerican objects: a Formative-period greenstone head, a stone mask from Classic-period Teotihuacan (Umberger, 1989). (The routine references made by archaeologists today to a 'Classic' period of pre-Hispanic Mesoamerican history reveal another connection to the ancient Mediterranean, but that is a story told elsewhere [Hamann forthcoming]).

One of these archaeological *higas*, then, was found in a place where imported centuries-old traditions from the ancient Mediterranean were taught to Native Americans. The other *higa* was found in a place already filled with centuries-old artifacts from ancient Mesoamerica.

References

Anders, F. (1970) *Codex Magliabechiano*. Akademische Druck- und Verlagstanstalt: Graz.

Anders, F., Jansen, M. and Reyes García, L. (1994) *Libro de la Vida*. Akademische Druck- und Verlagstanstalt and Fondo de Cultura Económica: Graz and Mexico City.

Bartsch, S. (2006) *The Mirror of the Self*. University of Chicago Press: Chicago.

Batalla Rosado, J. J. (1999) *El Códice Tudela o Códice del Museo de América y el Grupo Magliabechiano*. Unpublished doctoral dissertation, Universidad Complutense de Madrid, Madrid.

Berdan, F. F. and Anawalt, P. R. (eds.) (1992) *The Codex Mendoza*. Vol. 1. University of California Press: Berkeley.

Boone, E. H. (1983) *The Codex Magliabechiano and the Lost Prototype of the Magliabechiano Group*. University of California Press: Berkeley.

Carr, D. C. (2000) 'Arabic and Hebrew *auctoritates* in the Works of Enrique de Villena' in A. E. C. Canitz and G. R. Weiland (eds.) *From Arabye to Engelond*. University of Ottawa Press: Ottawa, 39–60.

Castañega, M. de (1946) *Tratado de las supersticiones y hechicerias*. Gráficas Ultra: Madrid.

Castelló Yturbide, T. (1993) *El arte plumaria en México*. Fomento Cultural Banamex: Mexico City.

Cervantes de Salazar, F. (1914) *Crónica de la Nueva España*. Hispanic Society of America: Madrid.

Ciapparelli, L. B. (2005) 'Medicina y Literatura en el Tratado de Fascinación de Enrique de Villena'. *Cuadernos de Historia de España* **71**(1): 31–56.

Ciruelo, P. (1977) *Pedro Ciruelo's A Treatise Reproving All Superstitions and Forms of Witchcraft Very Necessary and Useful for all Good Christians Zealous for their Salvation* (trans. E. A. Maio and D. W. Pearson). Fairleigh Dickinson University Press: Rutherford.

Cogswell, G. (2012) 'Pulque Power'. *Roads and Kingdoms*, 25 July. [WWW document]. URL   http://roadsandkingdoms.com/2012/pulque-power/ [accessed 5 July 2018]

Corcuera de Mancera, S. (1991) *El fraile, el indio y el pulque*. Fondo de Cultura Económica: Mexico City.

Covarrubias Orozco, S. (1611) *Tesoro de la lengva castellana, o española*. Luis Sanchez: Madrid.

Darst, D. H. (1979) 'Witchcraft in Spain'. *Proceedings of the American Philosophical Society* **123**(5): 298–322.

Fornés Pallicer, M. A. and Puig Rodríguez-Escalona, M. (2005) 'Insultar con los gestos en la Roma antigua y hoy'. *Minerva* **18**: 137–151.

Gell, A. (1998) *Art and Agency*. Clarendon Press: Oxford.

Gruzinski, S. (2002) *The Mestizo Mind* (trans. D. Dusinberre). Routledge: New York.

Hamann, B. E. (2004) 'In the Eyes of the Mixtecs/To View Several Pages Simultaneously'. *Visible Language* **38**(1): 68–123.

Hamann, B. E. (2015) *The Translations of Nebrija: Language, Culture, and Circulation in the Early Modern World*. University of Massachusetts Press: Amherst.

Hamann, B. E. (forthcoming) 'The Middle Ages, Middle America, and the Book' in B. Keene (ed.) *The World in a Book: Illuminated Manuscripts and the Global Middle Ages*. Getty Publications: Los Angeles.

Headrick, A. (2003) 'Seeing through Sahagún'. *Mesoamerican Voices* **1**: 23–40.

Heyden, D. (1988) 'Black Magic' in J. K. Josser and K. Dakin (eds.) *Smoke and Mist: Mesoamerican Studies in Memory of Thelma D. Sullivan*. (2 vols.). BAR: Oxford, **1**: 217–236.

Houston, S. and Taube, K. (2000) 'An Archaeology of the Senses'. *Cambridge Archaeological Journal* **10**(2): 261–294.

Kelly, I. (1977) 'Some Sixteenth-Century Jet Imports to the New World'. *Bead Journal* **3**(2): 24–28.

Klein, C. F. (1993) 'Teocuitlatl, "Divine Excrement"'. *Art Journal* **52**(3): 20–27.

Laird, A. (2016) 'Aztec and Roman Gods in Sixteenth-Century Mexico' in J. M. D. Pohl and C. L. Lyons (eds.) *Altera Roma: Art and Empire from Mérida to Mexico*. Costen Institute of Archaeology: Los Angeles, 167–188.

Leibsohn, D. (2007) 'Seeing In-Situ: Mapa de Cuauhtinchan No. 2' in D. Carrasco and S. Sessions (eds.) *Cave, City and Eagles' Nest*. University of New Mexico Press: Albuquerque, 389–426.

Leonard, I. (1949) *Books of the Brave: Being an Account of Books and of Men in the Spanish Conquest and Settlement of the Sixteenth-Century World*. Harvard University Press: Cambridge MA.

Lockhart, J. (1985) 'Some Nahua Concepts in Postconquest Guise'. *History of European Ideas* **6**(4): 465–482.

Macouzet, R. (1901) 'El pulque y la criminalidad'. *Revista de legislación y jurisprudencia* January–June: **(20)**: 27–34.

Moreno Corral, M. A. (2004) 'La *Physica speculatio*, primer libro de física escrito y publicado en el continente americano'. *Revista Mexicana de Física* **50**(1): 74–80.

Mundy, B. (2014) 'Indigenous Dances in Early Colonial Mexico City' in D. Pierce (ed.) *Festivals and Daily Life in the Arts of Colonial Latin America*. Denver Art Museum: Denver, 11–30.

Olender, M. (1990) 'Aspects of Baubo' in D. M. Halperin, J. J. Winkler and F. I. Zeitlin (eds.) *Before Sexuality*. Princeton University Press: Princeton, 83–113.

Olivier, G. (2016) 'The Mexica Pantheon in Light of Graeco-Roman Polytheism' in J. M. D. Pohl and C. L. Lyons (eds.) *Altera Roma: Art and Empire from Mérida to Mexico*. Costen Institute of Archaeology: Los Angeles, 189–214.

Olvera, H. J. (1992) 'Arqueología histórica poscortesiana' in *Encuentro de intelectuales Chiapas-Centroamérica, Volúmen 2: Patrimonio cultural*. Gobierno del Estado de Chiapas: Tuxtla Gutiérrez, 35–45.

Pagden, A. (1982) *The Fall of Natural Man*. Cambridge University Press: Cambridge.

Persels, J. C. (2007) 'Bragueta Humanística, or Humanism's Codpiece'. *Sixteenth Century Journal* **28**(1): 79–99.

Peterson, J. F. (1988) 'The Florentine Codex Imagery and the Colonial *Tlacuilo*' in J. J. Klor de Alva, H. B. Nicholson and E. Quiñones Keber (eds.) *The Work of Bernardino de Sahagún*. Institute for Mesoamerican Studies, The University at Albany, State University of New York: Albany, 273–293.

Reyes García, L. (2001) *¿Cómo te confundes? ¿Acaso no somos conquistados? Anales de Juan Bautista*. Centro de Investigaciones y Estudios Superiores en Antropología Social: Mexico.

Sahlins, M. (1981) *Historical Metaphors and Mythical Realities*. University of Michigan Press: Ann Arbor.

Salillas, R. (1905) *La fascinación en España*. Eduardo Arias: Madrid.

Taube, K. A. (1996) 'The Olmec Maize God'. *Res: Anthropology and Aesthetics* **29/30**: 39–81.

Taube, K. A. (2004) *Olmec Art at Dumbarton Oaks*. Dumbarton Oaks: Washington, DC.

Taylor, W. B. (1979) *Drinking, Homicide and Rebellion in Colonial Mexican Villages*. Stanford University Press: Stanford.

Torre, F. T. de la (1985) *Diario de Viaje de Salamanca a Ciudad Real de Chiapas*. Editorial OPE Caleruega: Burgos, 1544–1545.

Umberger, E. (1987) 'Antiques, Revivals, and References to the Past in Aztec Art'. *Res: Anthropology and Aesthetics* **13**: 62–105.

Vernant, J.-P. (1991) *Mortals and Immortals*. Princeton: Princeton University Press.

Villena, E. de (1994) 'Tratado de la fascinación' in *Obras completas, 1*. Fundación José Antonio de Castro: Madrid, 325–341.

5

The Inca Garcilaso in Dialogue with Neoplatonism

ERIKA VALDIVIESO

Un Antartico, nacido en el nuevo mundo, alla debaxo de nuestro hemisferio, y que en la leche mamo la lengua general de los Yndios del Perú, que tiene que ver con hazerse ynterprete entre Ytalianos, y Españoles? y ya que presumio serlo, porque no tomo libro qualquiera, y no el que los Ytalianos mas estimavan, y los Españoles menos conocian?
(Inca Garcilaso de la Vega, Prologue to *Historia General del Perú* 1617)[1]

An inhabitant of the southern continent, born in the new world, far below our own hemisphere, who imbibed in his mother's milk the *lingua franca* of the Indians of Peru – what business does he have acting as interpreter between Italians and Spaniards? And now that he has presumed to be one, why did he not choose some other book, not one which the Italians admired more and the Spaniards knew less?

Francisco Murillo, Cathedral Chancellor of Córdoba, put this question to the Inca Garcilaso de la Vega in the 1590s. Even today, readers of the *Diálogos de Amor* (Dialogues on Love), might well wonder why an author of Peruvian and Spanish parentage would begin his career in Castilian literature by translating a series of Italian philosophical dialogues. Readers today might also seek to comprehend the relationship between this obscure translation and the Inca's celebrated historical works, *La Florida* (History of Florida), and the *Comentarios Reales* (Royal Commentaries). The issues of identity and origin, raised in an apparently adversarial manner by the Cathedral Chancellor, continue to bear on interpretations of the Inca Garcilaso as an author.

The present discussion will begin with a brief overview of the Inca's life, surveying his trajectory from Cuzco in Peru to Córdoba in Andalusia. An introduction to the *Diálogos de Amor* will outline their structure and distinctive

---

1 Sáenz de Santa María (1960, 3:14). Original spelling is retained for all quotations from the Inca's works.

features, and consider the merits of the Inca's translation. The *Diálogos* will then be contextualised within the intellectual history of the Renaissance and Spanish America. Consideration of this text sheds light upon the construction of the Inca's *mestizo* or mixed race identity, as well as the role classical literature could play in the dialogue between antiquities of the New World and the Old.

From Cuzco to Córdoba

The Inca Garcilaso de la Vega was born Gómez Suárez de Figueroa in 1539 to a conquistador, Sebastián Garcilaso de la Vega y Vargas, and to a member of the Incan royal family, Isabel Chimpu Ocllo.[2] His first language was Quechua, but he received a Spanish-style education in the new viceroyalty of Peru. His schooling took place in a period of civil unrest, in which his father Sebastián often played an ambivalent role. Amidst 'the fire and tempest of the cruellest civil wars', the youth was, as he put it, 'more familiar with horse riding than Latin declensions'. After his father's death, at the age of twenty Gómez took his inheritance and travelled to Spain, where he eventually settled with his paternal uncle in Andalusia. His petitions to the Council of the Indies for the financial compensation owed to his father only renewed the rumours about Sebastián's role in the various rebellions in Peru. Gómez would spend the rest of his life attempting to vindicate his father's reputation, and he assumed his father's name in Spain for this reason (Porras Barrenechea, 1955; Fernández, 2004: 83–84).

Garcilaso turned to writing after a brief stint in the army. His first publication in 1590, *La Traduzion del Indio de los tres Diálogos de Amor* (The Indian's Translation of the three Dialogues on Love) rendered a popular Italian work into Spanish. The dedication to Philip II showed that this was only the start of Garcilaso's literary career: he wrote that he had already begun *La Florida*, an account of the exploits of the Spanish conquistador Hernando de Soto in North America, and he stated his intention to write a history of Peru. Garcilaso altered his name in this first publication: he now called himself 'Garcilaso Inga de la Vega'. The addition of 'Inga', in combination with 'Indio' in the title, called attention to his *mestizo* identity, a bold move in sixteenth-century Spain. Blood purity, a legacy of the *Reconquista*, the reconquest of Iberia from Muslim control, was prominent in contemporary discourses about miscegenation in the Americas. The name 'Garcilaso Inga de la Vega' thus confronted

---

2 Details about the Inca's life are drawn from the dedication to Felipe II (Sáenz de Santa María, 1960; Soria Olmedo, 1995).

Spanish readers with evidence of that miscegenation, cleverly promoting this unknown Peruvian author.

After a move to Córdoba in 1591, Garcilaso published *La Florida,* an often impertinent survey of the many failures of De Soto's expedition. With this second book, Garcilaso made a further change to his name. He now called himself '*The* Ynca Garcilaso de la Vega'. That addition of the definite article, along with the movement of 'Ynca' to the front of his name, transformed Garcilaso into a symbol of Peru, evoking the juxtaposition of two irreconcilable empires (Sommer, 1995). It was as 'the Inca' that he undertook his two-part history of the Peruvian conquest, in which Garcilaso sought to address lacunae that he, the offspring of Incas and Spaniards, was uniquely suited to fill.

The first volume, the *Comentarios Reales*, related the Incan history of Peru. The second volume, the *Historia General del Perú*, narrated the events of the conquest. In each of these books, the Inca reflected upon his identity. In the *Comentarios Reales* (1609) he called himself a *mestizo* with pride, because 'the phrase was coined by our fathers, and signified the union of two nations' (Sáenz de Santa María, 1960, 2: 373–374). The history of his Spanish heritage, the *Historia General*, was published posthumously in 1617. In his prologue, addressed to 'the Indians, *mestizos,* and *criollos* [American-born Spaniards]' of the empire of Peru, the Inca said it was his purpose, as a Peruvian, to show that the New World was far from barbarous. His history of the conquest was thus meant to facilitate communication between the two nations he represented. Though he was best known as the leading expert on the Incan Empire, Garcilaso's epitaph gave equal prominence to each of his books: 'he commented on the *Florida*, he translated León Hebreo, and composed the *Comentarios Reales*' (Sáenz de Santa María, 1960, 1: 66).

Love and Translation

It is easy to overlook a work of translation in an author's *oeuvre* simply because it is not seen as an original composition. For this reason, in the trilogy of the Inca's works, his translation of León Hebreo's dialogues on love is often forgotten. Yet the *Diálogos* were, for Garcilaso, of great importance because they marked the beginning of his career. Their structure and content can and should be seen in relation to the Inca's other works. The depth of his engagement with the original Italian text and the merits of his methods as a translator are very evident. Furthermore, the *Diálogos de Amor* throw light upon the Inca's self-fashioning.

Three dialogues on the nature of love are held between Filón (Love) and Sofía (Wisdom) – their names together constitute *filosofía*, philosophy. The desire for Sofía/Wisdom can never be satisfied, yet Filón/the Lover never ceases to press his suit. The *Diálogos* combine the language of courtship and philosophy to create a pleasing and erudite text. Without needing to understand each step of the argument, readers are drawn along by the fictional romance that frames the dialogue. The philosophical courtship falls into three parts. In the first dialogue, they discuss the difference between love and desire. The next time they meet, in the second dialogue, they discuss the universality of love. Filón begins with the particular, his love for Sofía, and then shows that love is all around them, even in the heavens. In the third and final dialogue, Filón tells Sofía about the origin of love, which leads to a discussion of the soul and the divine.

It was this mixture of seduction and the sublime that first led Garcilaso to articulate his theory of translation in the prologue to the *Diálogos*:

> De la mia [parte] puedo afirmar que me costaron mucho trabajo las erratas del molde, y mucho mas la pretension que tome, de interpretarle fielmente, por las mismas palabras, que su autor escrivio en el Italiano, sin añadirle otras superfluas, pues basta que le entiendan por las que el quiso decir, y no por mas (Garcilaso de la Vega, 1590: Dedication to Maximilian of Austria)

> For my part, I can confirm that the errors in the printed edition cost me a great deal of work, and what cost even more was my determination faithfully to interpret, using the very same words that the author wrote in Italian, not adding anything superfluous; it is enough for people to understand him through the words he wanted to say and no more.

As a translator, Garcilaso focused upon the author's intention and diction, so that readers could draw their own conclusions about the argument. Comparison of a passage in Hebreo's original Italian to Garcilaso's Spanish version shows that the Inca was able to give a word-for-word translation:

> Il sommo Dio con amore produce e governa il mondo e collegalo in una unione [...]. Ancora: gl'inferiori s'uniscono con li suoi superiori, il mondo corporale con il spirituale, e il corruttibile con l'eterno, e l'universo tutto col suo creatore mediante l'amore che gli ha e il suo Desiderio che ha d'unirsi con lui e di beatificarsi ne la sua divinità. (Hebreo, 2008: 159).

> El sumo Dios produze con amor, y govierna el mundo, y lo ayunta en una unión [...]. Assí mismo los inferiores se unen con sus superiores, el mundo corporal con el espiritual, y el corruptible con el eterno, y el universo todo con su Criador, mediante el amor que les tiene, y el desseo

suyo que les da de unirse con el, y de beatificarse en su divinidad. (Garcilaso de la Vega, 1590: 130r)

Through his love, the highest God creates and governs the world and binds it together in unity […]. In the same way, inferiors unite themselves with their superiors, the corporeal world with the spiritual, the corruptible with the eternal, and the universe with its Creator, by means of the love which holds sway over them and the desire it imparts to unite themselves with Him and be made holy in his divinity.

This translation is as close to the Italian text as it is polished.[3] The original *Dialoghi d'amore* were reprinted in Italian and translated 24 times between 1535 and 1607. There were two Spanish translations before the Inca's: one in 1568 by an Iberian Jew, Guedella Yahia, and one in 1584 by Carlos Montesa, a Spanish noble. Montesa's text was more elegant than Yahia's but it significantly altered the Italian, purging any content that could be construed as licentious, or worse, heretical (Bacich, 2007: 160). There is no way to know whether or not Garcilaso read Montesa's rendition, published six years before his own. Garcilaso's method of translation, however, demanded that the translator think of himself in partnership with Hebreo, the text's Jewish author – something Montesa would never have contemplated.

The true identity of León Hebreo adds further complexity to our understanding of the Inca's translation. Hebreo was born Judah ben Isaac Abravanel, to a prominent Jewish family from Portugal.[4] Before 1492, Abravanel's father had served as minister to the thrones of Portugal and Castile, while Abravanel himself had been Ferdinand and Isabella's physician. Like the Inca, Hebreo also gradually transformed his name to reflect changes in his circumstances. In Spain, Judah changed his name to León, alluding to the association of lions with the tribe of Judah. After the expulsion of the Jews, the family settled in Naples, where Leone, as he was now called, forsook his distinguished surname, Abravanel, for the generic 'Hebreo', 'the Hebrew'. His *Dialoghi d'amore* dramatise an exchange of ideas between Renaissance and Jewish philosophy, and the Jewish nature of the *Dialoghi* was evident from the title page of each edition, where the author's surname, Hebreo, appeared.

---

3   The renowned nineteenth-century critic Marcelino Menéndez y Pelayo praised the quality of Garcilaso's prose, comparing the Inca's work favourably with previous translations of the *Diálogos* (Menéndez y Pelayo, 1894: CLXII).

4   Hughes (2007), Veltri (2008: 60–72), Idel (2011) and Panizza (2011) discuss the Abravanels, contextualising their works within broader philosophical and literary trends.

The title of *La Traduzion* thus linked the Inca to a fellow mediator between two traditions: '*The Indian's* translation of the three dialogues of love by León *the Hebrew*'.

Dialogues of Love

How Garcilaso came to read León Hebreo, and indeed how León Hebreo came to write the *Dialoghi* in the first place, is best understood in the context of a broader Renaissance intellectual history. A good place to begin is the inventory of the Inca's library, taken shortly after his death (Durand, 1948). It may seem surprising that he owned relatively few texts in Castilian, but possessed many more copies of books by Italian authors – but this was far from unusual for educated Spaniards of his time (Gómez Moreno, 1994). In addition to works by Dante, Petrarch, Boccaccio, Bembo and Castiglione, the Inca possessed at least five different editions of Hebreo's work, as well as a volume of Marsilio Ficino. Careful review of the inventory shows a surprising pattern: Bembo, Castiglione, Hebreo and Ficino were all Neoplatonists who wrote extensively on the philosophy of love. The Inca's translation thus appears to be part of a Neoplatonic tradition. Ancient and Renaissance Neoplatonists alike shared an interest in Plato and the Platonic school, but Renaissance thinkers engaged more with the Platonic theory of love. The *Diálogos de Amor* are in fact based upon Plato's own treatment of love in his *Symposium*, yet Hebreo and the Inca's reading of this text were mediated by both ancient and Renaissance Neoplatonism.

For example, in the second dialogue, Filón describes love as the mediator between the lover and the beloved (Garcilaso de la Vega, 1590: 130r). This was first expressed in Plato's *Symposium*, where Socrates maintained that Love was the child of *Poros*, 'resourcefulness', and *Penia*, 'poverty'. As a result, Love was neither immortal nor mortal, but a *daimon*, who mediated between gods and men:

> καὶ γὰρ πᾶν τὸ δαιμόνιον μεταξύ ἐστι θεοῦ τε καὶ θνητοῦ […] ἐν μέσῳ δὲ ὂν ἀμφοτέρων συμπληροῖ, ὥστε τὸ πᾶν αὐτὸ αὑτῷ συνδεδέσθαι [...] θεὸς δὲ ἀνθρώπῳ οὐ μίγνυται, ἀλλὰ διὰ τούτου πᾶσά ἐστιν ἡ ὁμιλία καὶ ἡ διάλεκτος θεοῖς πρὸς ἀνθρώπους […] εἷς δὲ τούτων ἐστὶ καὶ ὁ Ἔρως.
>
> (Plato, *Symposium*, 202e-203a [ed. Burnet, 1922])

> The spiritual is between the divine and the mortal […] for since it is in the middle it causes each to supplement the other, so that everything is bound together in it […] for god does not associate with man, but all communion and communication between the gods and men takes place through the spiritual […] and one of these [spirits] is Love.

The gulf between gods and men, between the transcendent and the physical world, is thus mediated by Love. Yet love between individuals was but a step on the ladder to higher forms of love, culminating in contemplation of the good and beautiful. Romantic love was not unimportant for Plato, but it cannot be said to have been his sole focus either.

Plotinus initiated Neoplatonism in the third century AD by developing Plato's metaphysics.[5] He elaborated the division Plato had made between the physical and the transcendent world. Plotinus further divided the transcendent world into three levels: the One, the Intellect, and the Soul, which Plotinus regarded as distinct 'hypostases', or beings. The One was the source of all things, and from it emanated the Intellect. From Intellect came the Soul, and from the Soul came the physical world. Each level of his universe reflected and imitated the one above it, so that his hierarchical vision had a fundamental unity: all things were a reflection of the One.

As their universe was hierarchical, Neoplatonic philosophers were drawn to the idea of Love, the *daimon*, as a mediator between each level of the world. For Plotinus, love created unity, but its action was directed toward the One or the All:

> Ἐχέτω δὴ ἡ μὲν ὅλη ὅλον, αἱ δ᾽ ἐν μέρει τὸν αὐτῆς ἑκάστη [...]. συνεῖναι δ᾽ αὖ καὶ τὸν ἐν μέρει τῇ ἐν μέρει καὶ τῇ ὅλῃ τὸν μέγαν ἐκεῖνον καὶ τὸν ἐν τῷ παντὶ τῷ παντὶ πανταχοῦ αὐτοῦ· καὶ πολλοὺς αὖ τὸν ἕνα τοῦτον γίνεσθαι καὶ εἶναι, φαινόμενον πανταχοῦ τοῦ παντὸς οὗ ἂν θέλῃ.
>
> (Plotinus, *Enneads* 3.5.4 [ed. Henry and Schwyzer, 1964: 297])

> Let us grant that the universal Soul has a universal Love, and that each of the particular souls has its own love [...]. Now particular love attends the particular soul and that great Love attends the universal Soul and the Love that is in the All attends the All and is everywhere. Furthermore the same Love becomes and is many loves, appearing wherever he wishes in the All.

He posited that each individual soul participates in the universal Soul, and so each individual love participated in the universal Love. All of these kinds of loves were then subsumed in the One, the source from which Soul and the souls derive. Plotinus' reading of the *Symposium* was abstract; his cosmic scope eclipsed the individual almost entirely. Plato's *daimon* had shuttled between gods and men, as well as between humans, but Plotinus made more

---

5   Smith (2004) provides an introduction to Neoplatonism. See further Gerson (2010).

of love's vertical mediation than the horizontal mediation of human experience.

Neoplatonic philosophy had enjoyed a strong following in late antiquity until the rise of Aristotelianism: the lack of knowledge of Greek relegated Plato's work to obscurity in the West. Greek returned in the fifteenth century with the Italian humanists, whose renewed interest in the languages of the Bible also led to a demand for Hebrew (Kraye, 2004; Hankins, 2007). This demand coincided with the forced migration of many Hebrew scholars from Spain into Renaissance Italy, which in turn fostered an exchange of ideas between Jews and Christians there. Biblical humanists perceived many similarities between the Jewish, Christian and pagan traditions, which they explained by positing the existence of the *prisca theologia* (ancient theology), that manifested itself in various religious and philosophical doctrines. To recover this tradition, the Florentine Marsilio Ficino turned to Plato and Neoplatonic writers of late antiquity.

Ficino came to be the epitome of Renaissance Neoplatonism (Hankins, 1990). He provided eloquent Latin translations and commentaries on Plato's works and produced widely influential studies of his own. Ficino assumed that Platonic philosophy was part of the *prisca theologia*, and it was this assumption that made his work on Platonic love appealing to León Hebreo in the early sixteenth century. Hebreo's father, Isaac Abravanel, had written about the connections between the Kabbalah and hermetic texts, arguing that the *prisca theologia* was in fact Mosaic revelation, which Plato had learned from the prophet Isaiah in Egypt (Idel, 2011: 166–168). León Hebreo's *Dialoghi* built upon his father's work, uniting the *prisca theologia* of Neoplatonism with contemporary Jewish philosophy. Its format, moreover, was inspired by the Renaissance vogue for *trattati d'amore* (treaties on love), which drew upon Ficino's modification of the Platonic philosophy of love. The single greatest difference between the *Dialoghi* and the *trattati d'amore*, however, was their treatment of human sexuality (Kraye, 1994; Panizza, 2011). While Bembo and Castiglione had written dialogues of love between male interlocutors, Hebreo's *Dialoghi* were staged as the courtship of a man and a woman. Furthermore, as the passage on love as a cosmic principle has shown, the corporeal world is as important as the spiritual world, with which it is in union ('el mundo corporal [se une] con el espiritual', Garcilaso de la Vega, 1590: 122v-130r, page 69 above). Bodies are not things to be overcome but rather conduits of the love that draws us back to the divine.

It remains to consider the place of the Inca in this Neoplatonic tradition at the end of the sixteenth century. A study of the *Traduzion* shows that Garcilaso did not receive this tradition passively, but interpreted the arguments made by Hebreo in the *Dialoghi*. That is clear from the notes printed in the margin of the Inca's translation. Such notes had already been a feature of Sauvage's

French translation (1551), Sarraceno's Latin translation (1564) and Yahia's Spanish translation (1568).[6] For Filón's discussion of cosmic love, the number of notes given by Sauvage and Sarraceno are almost equivalent: 21 in French and 24 in Latin. Yahia, on the other hand, gives only five notes, because he limited his interventions to highlighting Jewish thought in the text. Furthermore, while Sauvage gave short summaries, Sarraceno recapitulated almost every detail he deemed necessary.

Garcilaso provided 24 notes on this section, the same number as the Latin edition. While the Latin and Spanish editions comment upon many shared passages, the Inca rarely reduplicated information, and if he did so, his comments were succinct. Compare, for example, the annotations offered by Sauvage, Sarraceno and Garcilaso to the section on cosmic love, excerpted above, discussing the union of the corporeal with the spiritual:

> Conclusion par une generale diffinition d'amour.
> (Sauvage, *Philosophie d'Amour* ([1551] 1595: 349))

> Conclusion with a general definition of love.

> Amor non secus ac vinculum quoddam commune superiora cum inferioribus, infernaque cum supernis; spiritalia cum corporeis, corporaque cum spiritibus; aeterna cum mortalibus, necnon caduca cum perpetuis; creatorem cum rebus ipsis procreatis, resque ab eo conditas cum ipso tandem conditore copulat atque coniungit.
> (Sarraceno, *De Amore Dialogi Tres,* 1564: 161)

> Love, like a universal chain, couples and yokes together superiors with inferiors, and earthly things with heavenly things, the spiritual with the corporeal, and bodies with spirits, the eternal with the mortal, and also the perishable with what is everlasting, the creator with his own creations, and finally created beings with the author of their being.

> Quantas cosas i quan grandes une el amor.
> (Inca Garcilaso de la Vega, *La Traduzion,* 1590: 130r)

> The quantity and magnitude of the things love unites.

The register of the Inca's comment lay in between the extremes of the terse French and the pleonastic Latin. In general, he preferred to use his annotations

---

6   Bacich and Pescatori (2009) list all editions of the *Dialoghi* and discuss the Spanish translations of Hebreo.

to provide a brief resumé rather than detailed declarations of the argument, encouraging readers to interpret the text for themselves. Furthermore, his word choice was elegant. Where Sarraceno opted for the erotic innuendo of 'copulat et coniungit' – 'to couple and yoke together' – in his Latin gloss, the Inca simply wrote 'unir', 'to unite' – the same verb used in his translation. His notes show the fruit of his study of previous editions of the *Dialoghi* and of Neoplatonic sources. As a result, he could highlight passages that required special attention and guide readers through the argument.

Antiquities, New and Old

The Inca went beyond merely participating in the development of an exchange of ideas which had hitherto been confined to a European elite. In his own translation, he demonstrated mastery of the text, improved upon previous translations and clarified the argument presented by Hebreo. The *Dialoghi* blended ancient and contemporary philosophy, as well as Christian and Jewish beliefs. In the face of conflict between these different traditions, Hebreo had chosen to create a dialogue between them. A similar strategy can be found in the Inca's *Comentarios Reales*. Renaissance ideas like the *prisca theologia* took on a new significance in Spanish America, where new cultures challenged existing schemas of human knowledge. For example, Garcilaso would claim that the Incas had a conception of God as the Platonic prime mover (Garcilaso de la Vega, 1609 2.2: 25r-27v). The sun, he argued, was the visible deity worshipped by the Incas, but Pachacamac, the creator, 'does to the universe what the soul does to the body'. This distinction between the visible god and the unknowable divine showed a debt to Hebreo and his *Dialoghi*, for it reflects the teachings of the Kabbalah about the *séfirot*, the visible manifestation of a God who surpasses human understanding (Mazzotti, 2006; Bernand, 2006, 2010). Faced with conflict between Christian monotheism and Incan practice, Garcilaso offered a metaphysical, Neoplatonic interpretation that transcended the issue altogether.

Neoplatonism, therefore, could reconcile the New World with the Old, while Neoplatonic love could unify the two sides of the Atlantic. The vision of the world presented in the *Diálogos* is hierarchical, but it is a hierarchy in which every member of society is linked by love. When, in the *Comentarios Reales*, Garcilaso described the expansion of Incan territory, he said that the people of the Andes were only able to love each other because they now spoke Quechua, the official language of the empire (*Comentarios Reales*, 7.1: 165r-166v). For the Inca, language was the key to true understanding and acceptance of another culture. He would in fact argue that poor translation had led to armed conflict between Spaniards and Incas and perpetuated misconceptions about Incan culture (Zamora, 1988). Mediation and love were exactly what was needed in the viceroyalty of Peru, plagued as it was by cycles of conflict. Language, love and empire thus coalesced in the Inca's first publication.

At the same time, in the context of the Counter-Reformation, the *prisca theologia* seemed as unorthodox as Hebreo's learning appeared dangerous. The interpretation of classical antiquity was thus a double-edged sword. Garcilaso's *Historia General* was published posthumously, in part due to Inquisitorial concerns about the content, which exposed deep-seated division in the viceroyalty. The *Diálogos* themselves, because they accommodated Jewish and pagan thought along with Christian principles, were placed on the *Index Librorum Prohibitorum* by 1612. The Inca's Neoplatonism, therefore, could as easily spark controversy as it could inspire reconciliation.[7]

References

Bacich, D. (2007) 'Translation and Coded Dialogue in the Spanish Empire'. *Pacific Coast Philology* **42**(2): 156–168.

Bacich, D. and Pescatori, R. trans. (2009) *Dialogues of Love: Leone Ebreo*. University of Toronto Press: Toronto.

Bernand, C. (2006) *Un Inca platonicien: Garcilaso de la Vega, 1539–1616*. Faynard: Paris.

Bernand, C. (2010) 'Soles. Platón, Heliodoro, León Hebreo y el Inca Garcilaso' in C. Mora, G. Serés and M. Serna (eds.) *Humanismo, mestizaje, y escritura en los Comentarios Reales*. Madrid: Iberoamericana, 31–50.

Burnet, J. (ed.) (1922) *Platonis Opera Vol. II*. Clarendon Press: Oxford.

Durand, J. (1948) 'La biblioteca del Inca'. *Nueva Revista de Filologia Hispanica* **2**(3): 239–264.

Fernández, C. (2004) *Inca Garcilaso: imaginación, memoria e identidad*. Fondo Editorial, Universidad Nacional Mayor de San Marcos: Lima.

Garcilaso de la Vega, Inca (1590) *La Traduzion del Indio de los Tres Diálogos de Amor de Leon Hebreo*. Pedro Madrigal: Madrid.

Garcilaso de la Vega, Inca (1609) *Primera Parte de los Comentarios Reales de los Incas*. Pedro Crasbeeck: Lisbon.

Gerson, L. (ed.) (2010) *The Cambridge History of Philosophy in Late Antiquity*. Cambridge University Press: Cambridge.

Gómez Moreno, A. (1994) *España y la Italia de los humanistas. Primeros ecos*. Gredos: Madrid.

Hankins, J. (1990) *Plato in the Italian Renaissance* (2 vols.). Brill: Leiden.

Hankins, J. (ed.) (2007) *The Cambridge Companion to Renaissance Philosophy*. Cambridge University Press: Cambridge.

---

7   This paper benefited from several questions raised by Jorge Cañizares-Esguerra at the Warburg Institute in May 2016. I would like to thank Andrew Laird for helpful suggestions on an earlier draft.

Hebreo, L. (2008) in D. Giovannozzi (ed.) *Dialoghi d'amore*. Edizione Laterza: Bari.

Henry, P. and Schwyzer, H.-R. (eds.) *Plotini Opera. Tomus I*. Clarendon Press: Oxford.

Hughes, A. (2007-2008) 'Epigone, Innovator, or Apologist? Judah Abravanel and his *Dialoghi d'Amore*'. *Studia Rosenthaliana* **40**: 109–125.

Idel, M. (2011) *Kabbalah in Italy, 1280–1510: A Survey*. Yale University Press: New Haven.

Kraye, J. (1994) 'The Transformation of Platonic Love in the Italian Renaissance' in A. Baldwin and S. Hutton (eds.) *Platonism and the English Imagination*. Cambridge University Press: Cambridge, 76–85.

Kraye, J. (ed.) (2004) *The Cambridge Companion to Renaissance Humanism*. Cambridge University Press: Cambridge.

Mazzotti, J. (2006) 'Otros motivos para la *Traduzion*: el Inca Garcilaso, los *Diálogos de amor* y la tradición cabalística' in R. Chang-Rodríguez (ed.) *Franqueando Fronteras: Garcilaso de la Vega y La Florida del Inca*. Pontifica Universidad Católica del Perú, Fondo Editorial: Lima, 131–148.

Menéndez y Pelayo, M. (1894) *Antología de Los Poetas Hispano-Americano*. Vol. 3. Sucesores de Rivadeneyra: Madrid.

Panizza, L. (2011) 'Platonic Love on the Rocks: Castiglione Counter-Currents in Renaissance Italy' in F. Clucas P. J. Forshaw and V. Rees (eds.) *Laus Platonici Philosophi: Marsilio Ficino and his Influence*. Brill: Leiden, 199–226.

Porras Barrenechea, R. (1955) *El Inca Garcilaso en Montilla, 1561–1614*. Editorial San Marcos: Lima.

Sáenz de Santa María, C. (ed.) (1960) *Obras completas del Inca Garcilaso de la Vega*. (4 vols.). Ediciones Atlas: Madrid.

Sarraceno, J. (1564) *De amore dialogi tres*.Venice.

Sauvage, D. [1551] (1595) *La sainte philosophie de l'amour*. Chez Rouille: Lyon. [orig. *Philosophie d'amour de M. Leon Hebreu*].

Smith, A. (2004) *Philosophy in Late Antiquity*. Routledge: London.

Sommer, D. (1995) 'Mosaic and Mestizo: Bilingual Love from Hebreo to El Inca'. *Jewish Studies Quarterly* **2**(3): 253–291.

Soria Olmedo, A. (1995) *Traducción de los Diálogos de Amor de León Hebreo*. Biblioteca Castro: Madrid.

Veltri, G. (2008) *Renaissance Philosophy in Jewish Garb: Foundations and Challenges in Judaism on the Eve of Modernity*. Brill: Leiden.

Zamora, M. (1988) *Language, Authority and Indigenous History in the Comentarios Reales de los Incas*. Cambridge University Press: Cambridge.

6

Universal History and New Spain's Indian Past: Classical Knowledge in Nahua Chronicles

ANDREW LAIRD

By the early seventeenth century, a number of native authors in the Valley of Mexico had written histories of the region from its mythical beginnings to the time of the Spanish incursion. These chronicles contain valuable information about the various Mexican polities, their ruling families, and the alliances and conflicts between them. In some of these works there are also occasional references to Greco-Roman antiquity and to early Christian literature, which provide clear evidence of the humanist learning the Amerindian writers had acquired. But the aim of the discussion to follow is to examine the specific ways in which those writers made use of classical sources, in order to reveal more about the rhetorics and agenda which shaped their narratives. The following survey of three major chroniclers – Tezozomoc, Alva Ixtlilxochitl and Chimalpahin – will show that each one accommodated European antiquarian learning as part of a strategic design to assert the significance of the Mexican past and its relevance to world history.[1]

Tezozomoc

Hernando de Alvarado Tezozomoc was born in Mexico-Tenochtitlan in the 1520s. His *Corónica mexicana* (1598) began with the legendary migration of the Aztecs from Aztlan to Mexico City, and culminated in the early events of the Spanish conquest. Though this history may have been rooted in oral tradition, it is written in Castilian and adopts a Christian perspective. More remarkably, it contains at least two illustrative analogies drawn from Greco-Roman

---

1 Earlier native chronicles include Pomar [1582] (1986); Múñoz Camargo [1591] (2013), recalling Plato, Isidore and other classics (2013: 41), and Múñoz Camargo [1584–1585] (Richter, 2015: 129), which mentions Artaxerxes. References to primary sources below provide original book, chapter or folio numbers, citing modern editions where possible. English translations are my own unless otherwise indicated.

literature. The first occurs in a description of the trusted counsellors of Montezuma II, ruler of the 'Aztecs' or Mexica:

> estauan muy secretos, que nenguno de la çiudad sabían dellos, porque el senado mexicano guardauan mucho secreto, como los r[r]omanos lo guardauan en el Capitol[l]io. (Alvarado Tezozomoc, 1598: chapter 97)

> They were very secretive, so that no one in the city knew of them because the Mexican Senate kept much secret, just as the Romans did in the Capitol.

Accounts of Roman senatorial practice were widely available: Alvarado Tezozomoc repeatedly referred to the Mexican council as a 'senate' to convey to Spanish readers the seriousness of the Aztec officials' role and the importance of their procedures.[2]

Secondly, the *Corónica mexicana* connected some creatures in a prophecy made to Montezuma with figures from the European imagination:

> algunos antiguos les dexaron profetizado que los que abían de benir a rreynar y pobrar estas tierras que abían de ser llamados tzoçuilycxique y por otro nombre çenteycxiques, que son aquellos que están los desiertos de Arabia que el alto sol ençiende, son, que tienen un pie solo, de una pata muy grande, con que se hazen sombra, y las orejas les sirben de fraçadas, tienen la cabeça en el pecho. (Alvarado Tezozomoc, 1598: chapter 110)

> Some people of old predicted that there would come and populate these lands ones who were to be called *tzoçuilycxique* [Goldfinch-foot] or else named *çenteycxique* [One-foot]: they are those that are found in the deserts of Arabia burned by the high sun, and they have just one foot on a very large leg that they use as their shade, they use their ears as coverings, and have heads in their chests.

This passage conflates three fantastical humanoid species described in the *Etymologies*, the popular Latin encyclopaedia compiled by Isidore of Seville in the seventh century:

> Blemmyas in Libya credunt truncos sine capite nasci, et os et oculos habere in pectore. […] Panotios apud Scythiam esse ferunt, tam diffusa

---

2   Compare Cicero, *Letters to Atticus*, 4.17.3; and the Roman *Historia Augusta,* 12: 'senatus consultum tacitum fieret […] ne quid forte proderetur': 'a secret decree of the Senate was passed […] so that nothing could end up being disclosed'. That text circulated in several editions which succeeded Bonus Accursius' 1475 *editio princeps.*

Figure 1.   Monstruous figures including a Sciopod and a Blemmyan depicted in Sebastian
Münster, *Cosmographia* (Basel: Henricus Petrus 1544)

magnitudine aurium ut omne corpus ex eis contegant [...]. Sciopo-
dum gens fertur in Aethiopia singulis cruribus et celeritate mirabili:
quos inde σκιόποδας Graeci vocant, eo quod per aestum in terra
resupini iacentes pedum suorum magnitudine adumbrentur. (Isidore,
Etymologies, 11.3.19–23 ed. Lindsay, 1985)

People believe that the Blemmyans in Libya are born as trunks without heads, with mouths and eyes in their chests. [...] They tell of the
Pannotians of Scythia, whose ears are so large that they cover all the
body. [...] The race of Sciopods is said to live in Ethiopia; they have only
one leg, and are amazingly fast-moving. The Greeks call them *skiopodes*
('shade-footed ones') because when it is hot they lie back on the ground
and are shaded by the great size of their feet.

Pliny (*Natural History*, 7.2), the source for Isidore's account, was also highly
influential and recalled by Augustine (*City of God*, 16.8) so that the Blemmyans, Pannotians and Sciopods had all been represented in medieval and
Renaissance iconography [Figure 1]. It is significant that the creatures in the
Mexican prophecy recounted by Tezozomoc are not merely compared to these
figures from classical myth, but actually identified with them – presumably
in order to demonstrate their existence as well as to make them recognisable to
European readers. The equivalences drawn between Aztec and Roman gods
in Fray Bernardino de Sahagún's *Historia general*, book 1 had a similar purpose
(Laird, 2016: 152–155).

Another work in Nahuatl, long credited to Hernando de Alvarado Tezozomoc, is now attributed to Chimalpahin.[3] The *Chronica mexicayotl* (Chronicle of what is Mexico), glorified Tenochtitlan and its rulers. The text began with a teleological narrative about the Aztecs' foundation of the *altepetl* or city state, which was attributed alternately to two divine agencies: the demonic Huitzilopochtli 'conversed with the *azteca* and lived among them as their friend' during their migration to Mexico, but the Christian God also inclined them to move southwards to their destined home in Mexico for another reason:

> so that the Spaniards would go to them and change their way of life, and so that their spirits and souls would be saved, in the way that in times past the people of Rome brought it about, as well as the people of Spain, *the Spaniards who then expanded over all the world [yn españolesme yn huel ixquich yc omocenmanque in ipā cemanahuatl]*. (Chimalpahin, 1997 1: 67)

The italicised phrase echoes the language Alvarado Tezozomoc used, only a few lines before, to describe the divine plan for the *Aztecs* to 'spread, expand everywhere over various lands' (*omotecaco omoçecenmanaco y nepapan nohuiampa tlallipan*). The early history of the Mexica is thus set in parallel to that of the Romans and Spaniards, to indicate its stature and importance.

Alva Ixtlilxochitl

Fernando Alva Ixtlilxochitl was born in the 1570s, not in Tenochtitlan, but in the neighbouring principality of Texcoco (Alva Ixtlilxochitl, 1997; Brian, 2016). He produced several lengthy historical works in Spanish, but his 1608 *Compendio histórico del reino de Texcoco* (Historical Compendium of the Kingdom of Texcoco), and the *Relación sucinta*, a history of New Spain in just a few pages, gave particular prominence to Nezahualcoyotl (Figure 2), a renowned ruler of pre-Hispanic Texcoco, from whom Alva Ixtlilxochitl could claim descent (Alva Ixtlilxochitl, 1997 1: 415–521; 395–413).

The sixteenth-century Franciscan chroniclers Gerónimo de Mendieta and Juan de Torquemada, drawing from Fray Andrés de Olmos, had already presented Nezahualcoyotl as an opponent of polytheism and a scrupulous legislator (Baudot, 1995: 75–81). Juan Bautista Pomar, a *mestizo* writer from Texcoco who was their contemporary, also affirmed the king's interest in 'the

---

3　The transmission of the *Chronica mexicayotl* is complex (Schroeder, 2011). Alvarado Tezozomoc wrote a 1609 preface affirming he was the grandson of Montezuma II (Chimalpahin, 1997 1: 60–65).

Figure 2.   *Codex Ixtlilxochitl*, fol. 106r, Bibliothèque Nationale, Paris. Early 1600s

Note: Depiction of Nezahualcoyotl with caption *'neçahualcoyotzin Rey de Texcoco'*.

true God and creator of all things' (Pomar, 1986: 69; Brian, 2016: 101). The missionary Fray Toribio de Benavente or 'Motolinía' had first compared the ruler to the biblical King David – and it was long believed that he had been the composer of some of the Nahuatl lyrics collected in the *Cantares mexicanos* and in the *Romances* appended to Pomar's chronicle (Motolinía, 1971: 321–322, 322–359; Lee, 2008: 44). According to Alva Ixtlilxochitl's *Compendio histórico*, the ancient Mexican historians who 'painted' the life of Nezahualcoyotl accomplished what the classical Athenian historian Xenophon had achieved in his life of Cyrus, king of the Persians, by presenting their subject as a paradigm for other kings. 'Nezahualcoyotl', Alva continues, 'was a model to good and outstanding princes' (Alva Ixtlilxochitl, 1997 1: 439 [*Relación* 11]).[4]

---

4   Brian (2016: 96–107) considers the bearing of Renaissance historiography and princely education on Alva Ixtlilxochitl's project.

Alva Ixtlilxochitl has done most to inspire modern popularisations of Nezahualcoyotl as a philosopher king (León-Portilla, 1959, 1972). The *Relación sucinta* laid stress on Nezahualcoyotl's qualities as a sage:

> Fue hombre sabio, y por su mucho saber declaró estas palabras que siguen que el divino Platón y otros grandes filósofos no declararon más, que fue decir: *Y pan yn Chahconauhtla manpan meztica intloque nahuaque ypal nenohuani teyocoyani ic el téotl oquiyócox yníxquex quéxquix mita ynamota*, que quiere decir: 'Después de nueve andanas está el criador del cielo y de la tierra, por quien viven las criaturas, y un solo dios que crió las cosas visibles y invisibles'. Asimismo llamó al cielo Ylhuicac, lugar de gloria inacabable, y al infierno Mictlan, que quiere decir lugar de muerte sin fin. Todas estas cosas declaró y alcanzó, y anduvo muchos años especulando divinos secretos, y como le faltó la ley evangélico siguió la idolatría, aunque él, como se ve en los cantos que tienen hoy día los naturales y en las historias y pinturas, muchas veces dijo que Huitzilopuchtli, dios de los mexicanos, y los ídolos eran demonios que les traían engañados, y que aunque ellos les hiciesen sacrificio no era sino porque no los hiciesen daño en sus personas y bienes temporales, porque siempre les amenazaban. (Alva Ixtlilxochitl, 1997 1: 404–405).

He was a wise man, and in his great knowledge he pronounced the following words to which divine Plato and other great philosophers added nothing: *Y pan yn Chahconauhtla manpan meztica intloque nahuaque ypal nenohuani teyocoyani ic el teótl oquiyócox yníxquex quéxquix mita ynamota*, which means 'Beyond the nine levels [of heaven] is the creator of heaven through whom all creatures live, and one sole god who created all things visible and invisible'.[5] Accordingly he called Heaven *Ilhuicac*, a place of endless glory, and Hell he called *Mictlan*, which means place of death without end. He attained and declared all these things, and he spent many years reflecting on the secrets of divinity, and as he did not have the law of the gospel, he kept to idolatry, although, as can be gleaned from the songs the natives sing to this day and from their histories and paintings, he often said that Huitzilopochtli, god of the Mexicans, and their idols were demons who kept them deceived, and that although they sacrificed to them, it was for no other reason than that they should not suffer harm to their persons and worldly goods, since they were always threatened by them.

---

5   Alva Ixtlilxochitl's Nahuatl is garbled. Whittaker (2016: 48) has reconstructed this passage from the manuscript.

In his edition of Alva Ixtlilxochitl's text, Edmundo O'Gorman suggested that the Nahuatl words attributed to Nezahualcoyotl could have come from a traditional song. As it happens, they do resemble part of a composition in the *Cantares Mexicanos* 68 (59v), entitled *Atecuilizcuicatl,* (Water-Pouring Song), which recalls the Aztecs' war against the Spaniards and their leaders' colourful voyage to another world. There the expressions *chiucnāuhtlāmanpan*, 'the nine levels', and *ycelteotl*, 'one God alone', are also conjoined in a description of the Christian heaven:

> Can chiucnautlamantlini yc onnemio in mopillohuā in Agelosme mitzhuelamachtia on ycelteotl huiya Alcagel, Biltotesme, Potestates, Pilincipatos. (Bierhorst, 1985: 338).

> For in nine levels dwell Thy princes, Angels, and they give Thee pleasure, God alone: Archangels, Virtues, Powers, Principates.

The fusion of Platonic and Christian thinking found both in this lyric and in the quotation ascribed to Nezahualcoyotl looks as if it originated in the thought of the Italian Neoplatonist Marsilio Ficino. Ficino had been a luminary of the Renaissance in Florence and his Latin works circulated all over Spanish America (see Valdivieso and Arbo in this volume).

In the eighteenth and final book of his *Theologia Platonica* (Platonic Theology), Ficino also described the nine levels of heaven under the Empyreum (Figure 3). The same passage of the work set out a celestial region inhabited by angels, to which souls akin to them were carried up, and the contrasting nine levels of the false demons, to which souls akin to them sank down (Ficino, 2001 6: 13 [1482, Book 18, chapter 8]).[6] These realms have correspondences in Nezahualcoyotl's glorious heaven of Ilhuicac and deathly hell of Mictlan – and Alva Ixtlilxocitl seems to have aligned Huitzilopochtli and the other Aztec idols which Nezahualcoyotl called *demonios* with Ficino's *reprobi daemones* or false demons. It is no coincidence that missionaries in New Spain who were well versed in early Christian literature had regarded Aztec divinities as deceiving demons (Laird, 2016: 150–156).

---

6   The Latin text of the passage summarised above reads: *His novem felicium gradibus apud Platonicos octo caelorum plagae ac nona super caelum excogitata regio congrue accommodari videntur; apud Orphicos autem octo caeli atque sub luna aethereus ignis; apud Christianos circuli sub empyreo novem. Quilibet enim ad illam potissimum regionem habitu quodam simili, quasi naturali levitate, feruntur, cuius habitatoribus angelis sese in vita praecipue similes reddiderunt. Similiter quoque Christiani reprobos animos in novem reproborum daemonum gradus quibus se vivendo fecere similes ipsa similitudine quasi pondere naturali, putant praecipitari.*

Figure 3. Diagram showing arrangement of the celestial spheres in Peter Apian, *Cosmographia* (Antwerp: Arnold Berckman 1539)

The account of Nezahualcoyotl's wisdom in the *Relación sucinta* closes with an unusual detail:

> y en memoria de las nueve andanas que hallaba, según él lo entendía, mandó hacer una torre en Tezcuco de nueve sobrados que hoy día se ve en sus ruinas, que se llamaba Chililitli. (Alva Ixtlilxochitl, 1997 1: 405)

> In memory of those nine levels of heaven as he understood it, he ordered a tower of nine storeys to be constructed in Tezcoco, the ruins of which can be seen to this day, which was called *Chililitli*.

There is also a construction representing the cosmos in another passage from Ficino's *Platonic Theology*:

> Archimedes Siracusanus aeneum caelum fecit in quo omnes septem planetarum motus verissime conficiebantur ut in caelo et ipsum

> volvebatur ut caelum. Mitto Aegyptiorum pyramides, Romanorum Graecorumque aedificia, metallorum officinas et vitri. (Ficino, 2004 4: 170 [1482, Book 13, chapter 3])

> Archimedes of Syracuse made a bronze model of heaven in which all the movements of the seven planets were very accurately worked just as they are in the heavens, and the device itself revolved like heaven. I leave aside the pyramids of Egypt, the buildings of the Romans and Greeks and their work in metal and glass.

Archimedes' technical feat, the Egyptian pyramids and Greek and Roman monuments were described in the part of Book 13 of Ficino's work which was devoted to 'diligence in the arts and in governance' (artium et gubernationis industria) (Toussaint, 2002). This association might therefore have appealed to Ixlilxochitl as he sought to portray the princely virtues of his royal ancestor. But the *Relación sucinta* offered no explanation for Nezahualcoyotl supposedly calling the tower 'Chililitli', or of what the name meant. The Nahuatl word *chililitli* appears to have been used for a copper cymbal struck by a pine mallet (Sahagún, 1951: 77 [*Historia general*, Book 2, chapter 25]; Stevenson, 1968: 39–40).

Chapter 45 of Alva Ixtlilxochitl's *History of the Chichimeca* (1608–1616) reveals more about the tower and its name. This architectural representation of the nine heavens was topped by a spire to honour the unknown and unseen creator of all things:

> era por la parte de afuera matizado de negro y estrella, y por la parte interior estaba todo engastado en oro, pedrería y plumas preciosas, colocándolo al dios […] sin ninguna estatua ni formar su figura. (Alva Ixtlilxochitl, 1997 2: 126)

> the exterior was adorned with stars on a black background, and inside it was inlaid with gold, gems and precious feathers set out for the god […] without any statue or attempt to represent his image.

We are also told that the ninth storey of the tower contained various musical instruments including a dome-shaped bell called a *tetzilacatl*, a very large drum, and most importantly a *chililitli*, after which both the tower and temple were named.

The musical instruments in this longer description and the naming of such a building after a copper cymbal might suggest that the intimations of Nezahualcoyotl's Christian Platonism were being blended with an authentic Mexican tradition. But this was not the case. The description of the universe at the end of Plato's *Republic* – the main source for Ficino's account of the heavenly regions – had also presented the cosmos as a musical harmony of the spheres. According to Plato, a Siren was positioned on each of the eight rotating concentric circles of the cosmos, seven of them planetary and one with fixed stars constituting the outermost revolving orbit: 'Each Siren [...] sounded a single note, and all eight notes together made a single harmonious sound [*harmonia*]'. There is also a detailed visualisation of the whole arrangement in this passage of the *Republic* (10: 616c-617c): 'one is bound to picture it as a hollow wheel with the others fitting snugly inside it like those jars which fit into one another [...] and their circular rims looked at from above form a solid surface'.

Plato had further argued in the *Laws* (7: 810–822) that music had a direct bearing on statecraft because it could exert a strong influence on the character of individuals and of society as a whole. Ficino placed even more emphasis on the importance of music for the soul than Plato did (Kristeller, 1943: 289–323; Walker, 2000: 3–29; Vanhaelen, 2017). He enlarged on its utility in government and explained in a 1472 letter (3. 29–30) to the Count of Gazzoldo that music should be part of a prince's moral education, developing his judgement and his ability to instill true laws and values (Rees, 2002: 355). Associations like these led Alva Ixtlilxochitl to portray Nezahualcoyotl as having an interest in musical instruments. The *chililitli*, in particular, had a special iconological significance: the disc, suspended vertically, approximates to Plato's image of the circular rims of the rotating planets which looked like a solid surface when viewed from above. If it was made of copper or of a copper alloy, it could also recall Archimedes' revolving bronze model of the celestial bodies. The round gong or cymbal symbolised the cosmos – and that is why the tower was named after it.

In the end, Alva Ixtlilxochitl used Renaissance Neoplatonism as the source for all the thought he attributed to Nezahualcoyotl in order to aggrandise the king in the eyes of Spanish readers. The writer had explicitly compared the king to *divino Platón* at the outset, but in so doing he gave away his own literary debt to Marsilio Ficino, who routinely used the same epithet in Latin: *divinus Plato*.

Chimalpahin

Domingo de San Antón Muñón Chimalpahin, born in 1579, was a prolific author, best known for two annalistic works: the eight cycles of the *Relaciones* and the *Diario*. The *Diario* covers the years 1589 to 1615, containing long entries about events in Mexico City and New Spain, some of which the author observed himself. At the end of the entry for 1608 (fol. 72), Chimalpahin counts back to the very creation of the world:

Yn iquac yn itzinpeuhyoc. yn ochihualoc yn yocoyalloc cemanahuatl.
ye caxtoltzonxihuitl ypan caxtolpohualxihuitl. Ypan yepohualli ypã ce
xihuitl. Ynic axcan ypan in yn itlamian yxiuhtzī tt° Dios. de 1608 años.
(Chimalpahin, 2006: 116)

When the universe was made and created at the very beginning, it was
6,361 years before now at the end of the year of our Lord God 1608.

The Flood and the foundation of the city of Rome provide further points of
chronological reference to situate the first settlement of Mexico 1,524 years
earlier, in AD 84: 'it was then the ancient Chichimeca who had come to Aztlan
Teocolhuacan gradually began to come in this direction, to […] disperse here
in the land called New Spain'.

Yet the next entry for the year 1609 returns to the time in which Chima-
pahin was writing: the focus moves abruptly from indigenous history to the
election of officials for the Audience of New Spain and other contemporaneous concerns. The Roman Emperor Vespasian's sack of Jerusalem in AD 70 is
then cited as well as the Creation, the Flood, the foundation of Rome and the
crucifixion of Christ. The destruction of Jerusalem was a prominent theme in
writing from post-conquest New Spain, not least for dramatic productions in
Nahuatl as well as in Spanish (Sell and Burkhart, 2009: 243–280). The subject's
appeal lay in its similarities to the fall of the Aztec capital of Mexico Tenochtitlan – similarities which Franciscan authors had interpreted in a variety of
different ways.

Chimalpahin's *Relaciones* are his *magnum opus*, covering the years (including those in which no events are recorded) from the Creation and the story of
Adam and Eve up to 1612. Both the Mexican year count and Christian system
of dating are used to head each annual entry: this is clearly visible in the original manuscript (Chimalpahin, 1949–1952). Along with records of the Mexican
past, the *Relaciones* accommodate further data from classical Greco-Roman
and Judaeo-Christian history. This is especially true of the second *Relación,*
where the year count begins with the year 1 Rabbit, or 3 BC.

Scholars dealing with Chimalpahin refer to his 'typical annalistic style',
and his adherence to 'the ancient tradition of indigenous record-keeping –
annals' (Schroeder, 2010: 102). But this needs to be probed further: of what
ancient tradition was this discourse really 'typical'? Chimalpahin's format is
directly modelled on the *Chronicon* of Isidore of Seville. This was the archetype
of all post-classical European chronicles, including even the *Annals of Tiger-
nach* in Scotland or the Welsh *Annales Cambrienses,* and it was in turn based on
St Jerome's adaptation of Eusebius' chronicle. Isidore incorporated a shorter
version of his *Chronicon* in the *Etymologies* – a work which was printed more
than ten times between 1470 and 1530 and widely read in New Spain. Isidore

counted from the creation of the world, 5,210 years before Christ was born, dividing the world into six ages. Chimalpahin's count has a different starting point, but Isidore provided the source for much of his material as well as the manner in which his own work is set out. Even some of the expressions Isidore uses are echoed in Nahuatl, such as 'God alone knows' for information which is not available to mortals.

There is another important indication of a debt to Isidore. Chimalpahin's second *Relación* (11r) followed the Proclamation of the Birth of Christ from the Roman rite in using three classical points of reference to date the nativity in *Año 4 calli* or AD 1: the Olympiad of 194 BC, the 753 BC foundation of Rome, and the 42 years of the principate of Octavian or Caesar Augustus:

> in nechipahualiztli yn motenehua la olimpiada ye iuh chiuhcnapo-
> hualxihuitl ypan matlactli onnahui xihuitl; auh ye iuh centzonxihuitl
> ypan caxtolpohualxiuitl ypan onpohualli onmatlactli ypan ome xiuitl
> yn iquac yn motlalli ynic tlatalili altepetl Roma. yhuan ye iuh onpohualli
> ypan ome xihuitl ynic tlahtocati ynic Emperadorti yn itoca Octaviano,
> yn iquac on in çan ye inmah yn tlacemicnopilhuilizcahuipan yn ipan
> yn omotlacatilitzino yn totecuiyo Dios omochiuh [...]. (Chimalpahin,
> 2003, 1: 60).

> From the cleaning that is called the Olympiad it was 194 years. And it was 752 years from the establishing and founding of the city of Rome. And it was also 42 years that the Emperor named Octavian was ruler. It was then at that time of blessed fortune it came about that our Lord God deigned to take human form [...].

Of special interest here is the implicit etymology for *olimpiada* as a 'cleaning', *nechipahualiztli*. 'Olympiads' of course really took their name from the Olympic Games which were held every four years, but modern editors assume Chimalpahin was thinking of *limpiar*, the Spanish for cleaning. He was, however, better informed than is at first apparent.

Before Isidore set out his *Chronicle* in Book 5 of the *Etymologies*, he had defined the units of time in days, weeks, months, seasons and years. He explained the origin of olympiads and he also explained that a *lustrum* was a five-year period, said to have been set every fifth year by the Romans, following the example of the olympiads and that 'it was called *lustrum* because the city of Rome was *purified* (*lustrabatur*) every five years' (*Etymologies* 5.37.2). That explains Chimalpahin's association of the olympiad with purification or cleaning. It remains to note that the Aztecs used four signs to name their years – Rabbit, Reed, Flint and House – and that as early as the 1530s the Franciscan Motolinía had referred to those Mexican cycles as *olympiades* in chapter 16 of his *Memoriales* (Motolinía, 1903 1: 48).

So far scholars are aware only of the classical, medieval and contemporary sources for the *Relaciones* which are actually named in the text. As Isidore was never mentioned by Chimalpahin, his foundational influence on the Mexican chronicler has not yet been recognised. There are many other latent European influences on Chimalpahin. For instance, his comment in connection with the fall of the Aztec empire – made in Spanish – that 'everything in the world waxes and wanes' (todas las cosas deste mundo cresen y menguan, Chimalpahin, 1997 2: 54) is not Nahua wisdom. It is, rather, a commonplace derived from Scripture and several school texts in standard use (Ecclesiastes 1; Wisdom 5: 9; 1 Corinthians 7: 31; Seneca, *Epistles*, 107.8; Herodotus, 1.86–87; Xenophon, *Cyropaedia*, 7.2; Plutarch, *In Solon*, 8.24; Justinus, 1.7; Boethius, *Consolatio*, 2.2). This adage had already been applied to the changing fortunes of Montezuma and the Aztecs by the mid-1500s (Cervantes de Salazar, 1971 [*Crónica de la Nueva España* Book 4, chapter 113]; Sahagún, 1982, 1: 47 [*Historia general*, Book 1, Prologue]).

Chasing down the authorities whom Chimalpahin does name reveals much about the way he worked. His acknowledgment of the *Antiquae lectiones*, an anthology of ancient texts by the classical commentator Caelius Rhodiginus, indicates he may have consulted other Renaissance encyclopaedias and commonplace books like Reisch's *Margarita Philosophica* and Johannes Ravisius Textor's *Officina*. Nonetheless it is surprising to find Nahuatl renderings of quotations from the classical Greek authors Sophocles and Diogenes Laertius – authors who were little known even in Europe. The Sophocles citation is as follows:

> Auh ca no yhuan ytla yn cenca acotlacpacca yn itlatzontequilliz yn itenanamiquilliz, yn mitohua motenehua ypa yn *isentencias* in iyamauh yn itoca *Sophocles poeta tragico* quitohuaya: "Ca ça niman amotle oncatqui qualli yectli ytzonquizca y nepepeuhcayotl yn iquac totecuiyo Dios yn achtopa ytlacamo huallehua yehuatzin ytechpatzinco yn tlachihualliztli". Auh oncan in ic peohuac hualla y yn ohuican quimo[no]chillia yn totecuiyo Dios yn ipa yn itzitzinpeuhcapa yn ixquich yn quexquix. (Chimalpahin, 2003 1: 32)

> And indeed something exalted is the verdict which is stated and pronounced in the text of the *Sententiae* of one named *Sophocles the tragic poet*: "For there was nothing, only then was there a good holy source and beginning when the Lord God was the first lord and master of creation." And so from the beginning, from its coming, in all parts of the world we call on our Lord God at the beginning of the making of all things that are made.

There never was a collection of *sententiae* or 'sayings' by Sophocles. The quotation is based on a spurious fragment (1126) attested by a number of early Christian authors (Pearson, 1917 3: 172–173), notably Eusebius, in his *Preparation for the Gospel* (13: 680d), a text well known to missionaries in New Spain (Laird, 2016: 157–159). Eusebius, though, was not the source for Chimalpahin's knowledge that Sophocles was a 'tragic poet'. Just as classical scholars today search other ancient sources for independent testimonia on their primary texts, the Nahua chronicler adduced a remark on Sophocles which he found in Isidore's *Chronicon*:

> Xerxes ann. XX. Sophocles et Euripides tragoedi celebrantur IVMDC-CXXXIII. (Isidore, *Etymologies* 5.39.19 ed. Lindsay).

> 4733: Xerxes 20 years. Sophocles and Euripides are honoured tragedians.

Diogenes Laertius, who lived in the 200 s AD, did not, as Chimalpahin maintained, 'show the people how the wisdom of divinity, our Lord God, generated the initial discourse, in his papers' (Chimalpahin, 2003 1: 32). Diogenes was not in fact a Christian. The Nahua annalist purloined this extravagant interpretation of Diogenes' *Lives of the Philosophers* from Ambrogio Traversari's 1433 dedication of the *Vitae Philosophorum* to Cosimo de Medici, printed in Rome in 1472. Traversari had claimed that Diogenes' doctrines were 'largely in agreement with Christian truth' (Stinger, 1977; Kraye, 2007: 98). It is significant that Chimalpahin embedded this remark into the opening of his own work: the first chapter of his first *Relación*, where the importance of God as the first creator is repeatedly affirmed as part of a similar apologetic strategy:

> Auh i yehuantin yn aquique tlacuilloque yn cenca ye huecauh mochipa pehuaya ytechpatzinco ycatzinco yn Dios ynic yehuatzin Dios. Auh i yehuatl ytoca Diogenes Laercio yn ipa ynnemilliz yn tlamatinime, yn mitohua motenehua philosophos, i ye quitoz quitenehuaz yn itzinpeuhcapa yn tlamachilliztli philosophia, niman ic compehualtia yn quiteytitia quitenextillia yn queni teoixtlamachilliztzintli yn totecuiyo Dios yn quichiuh tlatolpeuhcatenonotzalliztli yn ipan iamauh oncan quihto. Auh i yehuantin achto yn tlamanitique yn iuh quichihuaya, ca teopixque catca gentiles yn tlapallehuiaya yn ixquich tlamantli ca teoyotl […]. (Chimalpahin, 2003 1: 32)

> And those who wrote a long time ago always began in, and with, God since he is God. And the one called Diogenes Laertius in his *Lives of the Sages*, those that are said to be and are called *philosophers*, at the point

of talking about or referring to the principle of knowledge, of *philosophy*, in making his beginning, he causes the people to see, he shows the people how the wisdom of divinity, our Lord God, generated the initial discourse, in his papers where he said it. And those who first set out things in this form, who were doing this, were *gentile* priests who were well disposed to all that was divine [...].

Conclusions

The works of the three chroniclers briefly surveyed here, though doubtless aimed at different audiences or readers, appear to have a common agenda. In their particular ways these writers were affirming a global value for their histories by establishing an enduring Nahua 'archive' and epistemology – more than a century before Eguiara y Eguren attempted to construct a monument to creole learning in the *Bibliotheca Mexicana* (see Introduction, page 15 above). While Alvarado Tezozomoc had made only incidental references to Roman antiquity in his *Corónica mexicana*, the Nahuatl *Chronica mexicayotl* dignified the Indians of New Spain, implicitly aligning them with the Romans and the Spaniards. To refine and consolidate Texcoco's distinctive legacy, Alva Ixtlilxochitl glorified his ancestor by adopting the kind of strategy early Christian apologists had used to ennoble classical authors. Much as pagans like Virgil or Seneca had been shown to anticipate church teaching in their writings, Nezahualcoyotl was characterised as a Platonic philosopher ahead of his time. Chimalpahin should not be romanticised as a custodian or spokesman for the pre-Hispanic past simply because he wrote in Nahuatl. He was writing for posterity and the innovative employment of the Mexican language in the Spanish genre of the *Relación* is therefore not so innocent. The old-fashioned Christian chronicle format served Chimalpahin's modernising endeavour to elevate Nahuatl and canonise it as a literary medium.

Classical texts, Greco-Roman history and ancient thought thus provided instruments as well as inspiring analogies for all three authors. In this regard, the opening of Fernando Alva Ixtlilxochitl's dedication to his *Sumaria Relación* is telling:

> Desde mi adolescencia tuve siempre gran deseo de saber las cosas acaecidas en este Nuevo Mundo que no fueron menos que las de los romanos, griegos, medos y otras repúblicas gentílicas que tuvieron fama en el universo; aunque con la mudanza de los tiempos y caída de los señoríos y estados de mis pasados, quedaron sepultadas sus historias [...]. (Alva Ixtlilxochitl, 1997 1: 526)

From my youth, I always had a great desire to know about events which took place in this New World which were no less than those of the Romans, Greeks, Medes and other pagan republics of universal renown; though, after the changing of the times and the collapse of my ancestors' dominions and estates, their histories remained in obscurity.

The symbolic value of European antiquity was very evident to Fernando Alva Ixtlilxochitl and his peers, as they endeavoured to confer prestige on Mexico's indigenous history and to place it on the world stage.

References

Allen, M. J. B., Rees, V. and Davies, M. (eds.) (2002) *Marsilio Ficino: His Theology, His Philosophy, His Legacy*. Brill: Leiden, Boston, Cologne.

Alva Ixtlilxochitl, F. de (1997) *Obras históricas* ed. E. O'Gorman. (2 vols.). Universidad Autónoma de México: Mexico City.

Alvarado Tezozomoc, H. de [1598] (2001) *Crónica mexicana* ed. G. Díaz Migoyo and G. Vasquez. Dastin: Madrid.

Bierhorst, J. (ed.) (1985) *Cantares Mexicanos. Songs of the Aztecs*. Stanford University Press: Stanford.

Brian, A. (2016) *Alva Ixtlilxochitl's Native Archive and the Circulation of Knowledge in Colonial Mexico*. Vanderbilt University Press: Nashville.

Cervantes de Salazar, F. [1560] (1971) *Crónica de la Nueva España* ed. M. Magellon. (2 vols.) Atlas: Madrid.

Chimalpahin Cuauhtlenahuanitzin, D. (1949-1952) *Eight Relations*. Facsimile reproduction by E. Mengin (3 vols.). Corpus Codicum Americanorum Medii Aevi: Copenhagen.

Chimalpahin Cuauhtlenahuanitzin, D. (1997) *Codex Chimalpahin* ed. and trans. A. J. O. Anderson and S. Schroeder. (2 vols.). University of Oklahoma Press: Norman.

Chimalpahin, D. (2003) *Las ocho relaciones y el memorial de Colhuacan*. Ed. and trans. R. Tena. (2 vols.). Cien de México: Mexico City.

Chimalpahin Cuauhtlenahuanitzin, D. (2006) *Annals of his Time* ed. and trans. J. Lockhart, S. Schroeder and D. Namala. Stanford University Press: Stanford.

Ficino, M. (1482) *Theologia Platonica*. Florence.

Ficino, M. (1975-2015) *The Letters of Marsilio Ficino*. Translated by members of the School of Economic Science (10 out of 12 vols. to date). Shepheard-Walwyn: London.

Ficino, M. (2001-2006) *Platonic Theology* ed. J. Hankins. (6 vols.). Harvard I Tatti Renaissance Library: Cambridge.

Kraye, J. (2007) 'The revival of Hellenistic philosophies' in J. Hankins (ed.) *The Cambridge Companion to Renaissance Philosophy*. Cambridge University Press: Cambridge, 97–112.

Kristeller, P. O. (1943) *The Philosophy of Marsilio Ficino*. University of Columbia Press: New York.

Laird, A. (2016) 'Aztec and Roman Gods in Sixteenth-Century Mexico: Strategic Uses of the Classical Learning in Sahagún's *Historia General*' in J. M. D. Pohl and C. L. Lyons (eds.) *Art and Empire from Merida to Mexico*. Cotsen Institute of Archaeology: Los Angeles, 147–167.

Lee, J. (2008) *The Allure of Nezahualcoyotl. Pre-Hispanic History, Religion and Nahua Poetics.* University of New Mexico Press: Albuquerque.

León-Portilla, M. (1959) *La filosofía náhuatl estudiada en sus fuentes.* UNAM: Mexico.

León-Portilla, M. (1972) *Nezahualcoyotl: su vida y pensamiento.* Gobierno del Estado de México: Texcoco.

Lindsay, W. M. (ed.) (1985) *Isidori Hispalensis Episcopi Etymologiarum sive Originum Libri XX.* (2 vols.). Clarendon Press: Oxford.

Motolinía [Fray Toribio de Benavente] (1903) *Memoriales* eds. F. Paso y Troncoso, V. de P. Andrade and J. M. de Agreda y Sánchez. Mexico: Casa del Editor; UNAM: Mexico.

Motolinía (1903) *Memoriales o libro de las cosas de la Nueva España* ed. E. O'Gorman. UNAM: Mexico City.

Múnoz Camargo, D. [1591] (2013) in L. Reyes García (ed.) *Historia de Tlaxcala (Ms. 210 de la Biblioteca Nacional de París)*. Universidad Autónoma de Tlaxcala: Tlaxcala.

Pearson, A. C. (1917) *The Fragments of Sophocles.* (3 vols.). Cambridge University Press: Cambridge.

Pomar, J. B. [1582] (1986) 'Relación de la ciudad y provincia de Texcoco' in R. Acuña (ed.) *Relaciones geográficas del siglo XVI* (vol. 3). UNAM: Mexico City.

Rees, V. (2002) 'Ficino's Advice to Princes' in Allen, Rees and Davies (eds.), 339–358.

Richter, A. (2015) *Geschichte und Translation im kolonialen Mexiko: Eine Untersuchung ausgewählter historischer Schriften von Fernando de Alva Ixtlilxochitl, Diego Muñoz Camargo und Hernando Alvarado Tezozomoc.* Georg Olms: Hildesheim, Zurich and New York.

Sahagún, B. de (1951) in A. J. O. Anderson and C. Dibble (eds.) *Florentine Codex. Book 2: The Ceremonies.* School of American Research and University of Utah: Santa Fe.

Sahagún, B. de (1982) in A. J. O. Anderson and C. Dibble (eds.) *Florentine Codex. Introductions and Indices.* School of American Research and University of Utah: Santa Fe.

Schroeder, S. (2010) 'Chimalpahin Rewrites the Conquest' in S. Schroeder (ed.) *The Conquest All Over Again: Nahuas and Zapotecs thinking, writing and painting Spanish colonialism.* Sussex Academic Press: Brighton, Portland, Toronto, 101–123.

Schroeder, S. (2011) 'The Truth about the *Crónica Mexicayotl*'. *Colonial Latin American Review* **20**(2): 233–247.

Sell, B. D. and Burkhart, L. M. (eds.) (2009) *Nahuatl Theater. Vol. 4: Nahua Christianity in Performance.* University of Oklahoma Press: Norman.

Stevenson, R. M. (1968) *Music in Aztec and Inca Territory.* University of California Press: Berkeley and Los Angeles.

Stinger, C. L. (1977) *Humanism and the Church Fathers: Ambrogio Traversari (1386–1439) and Christian Antiquity in the Italian Renaissance.* State of New York University Press: Albany.

Toussaint, S. (2002) 'Ficino, Archimedes, and the Celestial Arts' in Allen, Rees and Davies (eds.), 307–326.

Vanhaelen, M. (2017) 'Cosmic Harmony, Demons, and the Mnemonic Power of Music in Renaissance Florence: The Case of Marsilio Ficino' in J. Prins and M. Vanhaelen (eds.) *Sing Aloud Harmonious Spheres: Renaissance Conceptions of Cosmic Harmony*. Routledge: Abingdon, 101–122.

Walker, D. P. [1958] (2000) *Spiritual and Demonic Magic, from Ficino to Campanella*. Pennsylvania State University Press: University Park.

Whittaker, G. (2016) 'The Identities of Fernando de Alva Ixtlilxochitl' in G. Brokaw and J. Lee (eds.) *Fernando de Alva Ixtlilxochitl and his Legacy*. University of Arizona Press: Tucson, 29–76.

7

The Exemplary Power of Antiquity: Humanist Rhetoric and Ceremony in Seventeenth-Century New Spain

STUART M. McMANUS

On 30 November 1680, Tomás Antonio de la Cerda y Aragón made his first entry into Mexico City as the viceroy of New Spain. In the course of an elaborate celebration he processed through a triumphal arch, which the creole poet and polymath Carlos de Sigüenza y Góngora had designed and adorned with portraits of Mexican gods and rulers, accompanied by compositions in verse (Brading, 1992: 362–364). Another arch devised by the Jeronymite poet Sor Juana Inés de la Cruz ([1680] 2009) graced the cathedral of Mexico City for the same occasion (Paz, 1988: 150–151; Méndez Bañuelos, 2000; Andrews, 2007). Both structures were temporary, but secured a more enduring historical significance through the authors' explanatory descriptions, which have become well known in their own right: Sor Juana's *Neptuno alegórico*, 'Allegorical Neptune', laid claim to a classical and biblical genealogy for the incoming viceroy, and the *Theatro de virtudes políticas*, 'Theatre of Political Virtues', composed by Sigüenza y Góngora extolled the ancient Mexican rulers as models of conduct for the king's representative (Lorente Medina, 1994; Montiel Bonilla, 1999; Cañeque, 2007).[1]

The programme of these arches, involving both texts and images, was actually part of a larger tradition of exemplary rhetoric, perpetuated in the European Renaissance as a 'social technology' to improve a wide range of qualities and skills, from statesmanship to scholarship (Hankins, 2004). The same technology manifested itself in various civic rituals in Spanish America and Brazil, from triumphal processions to funeral commemorations of *exequias* or exequies. The discussion to follow will begin by providing a brief account of how European rhetorical culture was transmitted to New Spain. It then focuses on the oratory and iconography of the *exequias* performed for Philip IV in Mexico City in 1666 and the specific role of exemplarity in such performances – evident in visible monuments as well as in the speeches.

---

1 Sigüenza's pioneering research, drawn from indigenous codices and other testimonies, set a precedent for creole investigations of pre-Hispanic Mexico (More, 2012; Adorno, 2015).

The final section returns to the *Theatro de virtudes políticas*: the ceremonies orchestrated by Sigüenza y Góngora in 1680 show the extent to which humanist theories and practices of exemplarity – ultimately of Greco-Roman origin – pervaded the colonial elites, and held an important place in their intellectual history.

Humanist Rhetorical Culture in New Spain

Rhetoric – the codification of effective speaking and writing – was prominent in education, just as the practice of oratory loomed large in colonial civic life. The classical rhetorical tradition, first revived and placed at the centre of educational reforms by humanists of the Italian Renaissance and later throughout Europe, had encouraged emulation of ancient achievements in political and literary discourse. This new humanist current also influenced sacred oratory: the Council of Trent endorsed classical rhetoric as an efficacious means of reviving piety among the Church's erring flock, and educated clerics began to model their sermons on the discourses of the Church Fathers (O'Malley, 1979).

In the wake of the conquest, Renaissance rhetoric came to prominence in both sacred and secular oratory in New Spain. The discipline was a prerequisite for college and university, and the Jesuit curriculum of the *Ratio studiorum* demanded that students devote a full year to rhetoric. Their training focused on expression in Latin, but this also provided the basis for speaking in the vernacular, whether in the assembly hall or in the pulpit. Cipriano Soáres' *De arte rhetorica* (1568), frequently reprinted in Mexico City, served as a common introduction, along with collections of model classical texts including Cicero's letters and speeches, which were memorised and recited with attention to their style and subject matter. Students learned the classical canons of invention, arrangement, style, memory and delivery, from humanist handbooks or in class. They examined individual parts of an oration which contained appropriate examples of *exordia* (introductions) and *confirmationes* (substantiation) and kept commonplace books of passages from the authors they read. All this prepared them for their own efforts in composing and delivering declamations, which were required every month and on special occasions throughout the year (Osorio Romero, 1979: 44).

Thus, from the Jesuits' arrival in the Americas in the 1500s until the mid-eighteenth century, generations of clerics, administrators and merchants spent their formative years emulating the finest examples of classical eloquence. Knowledge and appreciation of rhetoric went beyond the Royal Audience and the Ecclesiastical Council of Mexico City to be shared by some members of New Spain's native elites (Lukács, 1995). Philip IV and Charles II each confirmed the rights of indigenous nobles to receive degrees on the same terms as the Spanish gentry in a succession of *cédulas* or royal seals promulgated between 1680 and 1697. In Mexico City, the San Gregorio Seminary College for Indians was entirely focused on training indigenous nobles, and the Council Seminary of Mexico City also provided *caciques* with an education very similar to that provided by the Jesuit colleges.[2] New Spain's caste system meant that students of native or *mestizo* extraction were generally unable to reach the most prestigious levels of the ecclesiastical and civil hierarchies, but some did receive degrees at the Royal and Pontifical University and a certain number would take up positions in local administration or join the secular clergy.[3] Nicolás del Puerto, for instance, a doctor in canon law who later became a professor of rhetoric and eventually bishop of his home diocese of Oaxaca in 1678, had distant indigenous ancestors, a fact he very likely obscured in his lifetime (Pérez Puente, 2005: 88; Villella, 2016: 235–241). This same Nicolás del Puerto delivered the Latin oration for the exequies of Philip IV in 1566 which is described below.

Classicising Eloquence in the Funeral Orations for Philip IV

Only a few years before the triumphal entry of New Spain's viceroy into Mexico City in 1680 orchestrated by Sigüenza de Góngora, the municipal authorities and ecclesiastical institutions in New Spain had been faced with a far greater challenge: planning the exequies in 1666 for Philip IV who had died the previous year. The commemorations involved the construction of a symbolic *túmulo* or funeral pyre. The structure, though ephemeral, was of an impressive height and richly decorated. No less civic pride would have been taken in the oratory prepared for the occasion which was in Latin and in Spanish: many would be able to judge its quality, whether they were hearing the speeches being delivered or reading them in the elaborate festival books which carefully documented and explained the ceremony. One such volume is an invaluable source for what occurred on this occasion: *Llanto del occidente en el ocaso del más claro sol de las Españas: fúnebres demonstraciones que hizo pyra real, que erigió en las exequias del Rey N. Señor D. Felipe IIII el grande*, 'The

---

2   The Jesuit Vicente López, whose Ciceronian dialogue prefaced the *Bibliotheca Mexicana* (1755), taught at the Colegio de San Gregorio in the second quarter of the eighteenth century, providing members of indigenous elites with a humanist formation (Menegus Bornemann and Aguirre Salvador, 2006: 103–105, 117–139, 93; Vargas Alquicira, 1987: XVIII-XX).

3   It would not be until 1772 that an Indian officially received a doctorate, although that predated by more than a century any such development in the former British colonies of North America.

Lament in the West on the setting of the brightest Sun of the Spains: the Funerary Display rendered by the Royal Pyre, erected for the Exequies of the King, Our Lord Don Philip IV, the Great'. The volume published in 1666 was compiled by Isidro Sariñana y Cuenca.

The exequies in the cathedral in Mexico City were organised by the Royal Audience. Two churchmen famed for their literary learning and authority were chosen to deliver the Latin funeral oration and a Castilian sermon. The responsibility for giving the speech in Latin fell to the aforementioned Nicolás del Puerto, a former student of the Jesuit College of San Ildefonso, who had been made a rector of the Royal University more than a decade earlier, in 1655 (Villella, 2016: 235). To achieve this level of distinction, he would have had to best the other candidates in a formal and rigorous *oposición* (competitive public examination), displaying his powers of eloquence and scholarly learning in a Latin lecture on a passage from a text by Cicero, chosen for him at random (Osorio Romero, 1976: 55–60).

The oration Nicolás del Puerto delivered from the pulpit of the cathedral in Mexico City was carefully designed to praise the particular qualities of Philip IV in his youth, in his adulthood and at the time of his death. Renaissance epideictic style for such occasions often demanded commendation of the deceased according to his or her virtues within a biographical narrative. A speech for a Habsburg monarch who had frequently been presented in the mode of a Roman emperor required illustrations from antiquity as well as later history and Scripture: in the Counter-Reformation biblical and classical antiquities served almost equivalently as guides to conduct for the present age (Tanner, 1993; Beaver, 2008).

Puerto thus affirmed that Philip was more clement than Constantine, more munificent than Alexander, more temperate than Leo the Great, more moderate than the five kings named Ferdinand, more humane than the twelve kings named Alphonso, milder than Charles V and more pious than the three Philips before him (Sariñana y Cuenca, 1666: fol. 131r-v). Commonplaces from Latin poetry enhanced the classicisation of the monarch: a comet supposedly presaging the death of Philip IV recalls a description in the Roman poet Lucan (*Pharsalia*, 1: 526–529) of the portent in the sky before the death of Julius Caesar (Sariñana y Cuenca, 1666: fol. 115r). Pliny's panegyric of Trajan and the Church Fathers' orations on the death of the Christian emperors, such as St Ambrose's eulogies of Theodosius and Valentinian II, provided textual models for this celebration of Philip's qualities (Sariñana y Cuenca, 1666: fols. 131v-132r).

The king's civic virtues, such as piety, clemency and liberality, were praised as well as his qualities of prudence, justice and fortitude. In this respect the speech conformed to the prescriptions in Nicholas Caussin's 1619 compendium of classical rhetorical theory and practice,

Eloquentiae sacrae et humanae parallela: copies of this sixteen-book work could be found in college libraries across the Americas (Caussin, 1619: 468–471, 478; Sariñana y Cuenca 1666, fols. 119r-132r). The structure of Del Puerto's oration also followed humanist convention. Opening with an *exordium* suited to the circumstances – '*ab adiunctis*' – the speaker's self-deprecating *captatio benevolentiae*, 'winning of the good will' of the audience, was in line with the advice in Cicero (*De oratore* 2.19.80) to make listeners 'favourable, attentive and receptive' which was a mainstay of humanist oratory (Caussin, 1619: 243, 384; Sariñana y Cuenca, 1666: fols. 113r-114v). It is significant that Puerto's *exordium* appears to be largely of his own invention – in contrast to that of a funeral oration delivered at the exequies also organised for Philip IV in the same year of 1666 by the Inquisition of Mexico City. On the latter occasion, the *captatio* was directly lifted from a Latin translation of a Greek oration which Gregory of Nyssa had made in AD 381 for the funeral of Meletius, Patriarch of Antioch (Monroy, 1666: fol. A1r).

The use of classical analogies and illustrations was not restricted to Latin oratory for a Latinate audience: a rhetorical education in seventeenth-century Spanish America also equipped students to perform in Spanish. The terminology used to describe vernacular funeral sermons – *oración fúnebre*, *oración panegírica* and *sermón panegírico* – shows that they belonged to the enduring tradition of the Latin *oratio funebris* and Greek eulogy often referred to as panegyric.[4] While Latin funeral oratory (as in the case of the oration for the death of Philip IV) more closely adhered to the purer classical conventions of humanist rhetoric, vernacular sermons represented a distinctive tradition, accommodating some models of medieval origin.[5] Inevitably there was a wide range of trends in practice: the classicising features of vernacular oratory varied according to the background of the speaker and the nature of his interests and education. But as a rule, ceremonial orations inaugurated by more prestigious cities or institutions made a more intensive display of classical learning.

Funeral Oratory and the Exemplary Tradition

As well as the precepts of epideictic rhetoric, Greco-Roman moral philosophy, mediated by Renaissance humanism, had a pervasive influence on baroque

---

4   An edition of Rafael Landívar's *Funebris declamatio* (Laird, 2006: 97–113) delivered in Guatemala in 1766 for Archbishop Figueroa, a century after the death of Philip IV, is evidence of this endurance: the practice continued in Mexico well after the baroque period.

5   Urrejola (2012) illustrates the confusion that can arise from scholars' attempts to unify these successive traditions.

funeral oratory in Spanish America (Hankins, 2007). That partly accounts for the considerable emphasis on the importance of virtue as the main, perhaps even the sole, criterion by which the achievements of emperors, kings, leading churchmen and statesmen were to be reckoned. Epideictic always contained an element of exhortation, and funeral orations put forward ideals of public and private behaviour as an example for emulation by local elites (McManamon, 1989: 2–3). The purpose of these ritualistic events was in the end to remind audiences of the values inculcated in them by their Christian humanist education (Muir, 2005: 4–5).

Thus, epideictic rhetoric, along with the classical exemplary tradition as a whole, was not about moving listeners to abandon previous beliefs and accept new dogmas: that was more the province of judicial or 'deliberative' oratory. Rather, epideictic served to repeat and reinforce commonly held ideas in an aesthetically pleasing form with the aim of improving local governance for the benefit of all (Caussin, 1619: 451–452). Funeral orations were certainly not concerned with advocating monarchy in preference to other constitutional models or with justifying the rule of the Habsburg monarchy, whether in the 'kingdom' of New Spain, the viceroyalty of Peru, or the Philippines. The focus was simply on virtue as the essence of good kingship, as vice was the essence of tyranny.

This ideal of the state ruled by a virtuous king had a long pedigree which stretched back from the early modern period through the Middle Ages to Greco-Roman antiquity, most notably in the genre of *principum specula* or 'mirrors for princes'. Such an ideal sat well with Christian ethical traditions that were themselves founded on, and continually informed and revitalised by, the successive introduction of further classical precedents as they emerged: Stoic ideas also circulated in Spanish America (Schmidt, 1997). The *specula* or mirrors were so called because monarchs were offered an idealised image of themselves in the way that the Roman philosopher Seneca had presented Nero with a vision of himself as a merciful ruler which could serve as a model for the young emperor (Stacey, 2007). Thus the business of funeral orations for monarchs, viceroys and the like was not just to praise the deceased, but also to incline listeners to follow in their footsteps. By carefully constructing a virtue-driven model of kingship illustrated by numerous examples taken from the past, whether in Greece, Rome, medieval Spain or more recent times, orators hoped to excel in what the Roman Quintilian (*Institutio oratoria*, 3.5.2) had identified as their first duty: to delight, move and teach those who heard them.

Although Philip IV's right to rule was presented as deriving from his virtuous actions, he was a hereditary monarch and his illustrious lineage was important too. In his oration, Nicolás del Puerto drew attention to the fact that Philip IV was the son, grandson and great-grandson of Philip III, Philip II and

Charles I respectively. But following the precepts of humanist rhetoric and moral philosophy, the importance of this lineage lay not in the royal and imperial authority that it transmitted, but in the continuity in virtue accorded by having such illustrious forebears (Caussin, 1619: 463; Sariñana y Cuenca, 1666: fols. 125v-127r). A noble lineage was necessary but not sufficient for kingship. It was how Philip measured up to his ancestors that really mattered, as an oration delivered in the cathedral of Puebla by Gregorio López de Mendizábal, a former chair of rhetoric at the university in Mexico City, made very clear:

> O! quales hinc, quantaeque volitant virtutum celsarum imagines, in vnum que coalent Philippi Magni simulacrum! cana imprimis Fides, prisca que Religio, bellica Fortitudo; oculata Prudentia, placidissima Pietas, aliae que innumerae virtutum Formae ex maiorum suorum cineribus certatim convolant ad Philippi effigiem, & praestantiorem, longè illà, quam Plato ideam Principis finxit, optimi Regis imaginem mihi sic sapientius concinnant […]. (Mendizábal, 1666: fol. 4r)

> Oh how many different images of lofty virtues fly about, to coalesce into one likeness of Philip the Great! Hoary Trust above all, ancient Religion, martial Fortitude, visible Prudence, most placid Piety and countless other forms of virtues vie with each other, as they fly from the ashes of his forebears to the representation of Philip. Far more outstanding than the 'idea' of the prince thought up by Plato is the image of the best King that they, very wisely as I see it, set in place.

In this and the other funeral orations, Philip did not rule his American kingdoms by virtue of his inherited power. Power itself was rarely the object of panegyric. Rather it was his excellence in the exemplary virtues of his predecessors which justified his right to his many crowns and served as a model to his representatives and subjects across the Americas.

Iconography in the Obsequies for Philip IV

As indicated at the outset, funeral commemorations involved visual elements which complemented the oratory. In the *exequias* performed for Philip IV in 1666, Nicolás del Puerto's presentation of the monarch as heir to the virtues of Constantine, Alexander and others was complemented by images of exemplary figures which decorated a vast but temporary *túmulo* or funeral pyre in the cathedral of Mexico City. Sigüenza y Góngora himself remarked that such constructions had ancient precedents, and were conceived as a reinvention of the funeral pyres on which Roman emperors were cremated (Sigüenza y Góngora, 1984: 169–171).

Figure 1. Sestertius of Faustina, AD 141–142

Harvard Art Museums/ Arthur M. Sacker Museum. © President and Fellows of Harvard College.

The *túmulo* erected for Philip IV in Mexico City resembles the structures depicted on Roman coins (such as the reverse of the AD 141–1142 Sestertius of Faustina I (Figure 1). It consisted of a number of storeys of decreasing size with a statue and the insignia to represent the body of the deceased monarch (Figure 2). Yet, unlike ancient funeral pyres, each storey also featured iconography, which made the same exemplary argument as the orator who would have stood in front of it during the ceremony.

The first storey of Philip's *túmulo* featured the famous military banner emblazoned with the christogram (combining the Greek letters *chi*, X, and *rho*, P) under which the first Christian emperor Constantine had marched into battle. It was surrounded by statues of classical figures, each of which represented a particular quality: piety was symbolised by Constantine himself; dedication to the cult of the Virgin Mary by Leo the Great; patronage of letters by Charlemagne; benevolence by Alexander of Macedon; victory over tyranny by King Theseus of Athens; constancy by Jason; public-spiritedness by Prometheus, and farsightedness by Janus. These figures in turn were flanked by statues of four women representing four names of Spain: Cetubalia, Iberia, Hesperia and Hispania: their role was to communicate the position ordained for Spain in world history – at least from a Judeo-Christian perspective. Each statue was inscribed with a legend to amplify this: for instance, Cetubalia's inscription stated that she had received laws from Tubal, the grandson of Noah (Sariñana y Cuenca, 1666, fol.: 85r). As the observers' gaze was drawn upwards to the tapering tiers of the funeral pyre, a statue of Philip IV, surrounded by four statues of Solomon, was visible

Figure 2.   Isidro Sariñana y Cuenca, Llanto de sol, Mexico City, 1666, fol. 40r

Digital image courtesy of the Getty's Open Content Program.

on the second level (Sariñana y Cuenca, 1666: fol. 89v). At the very top of the *túmulo* was the figure of Faith, the most exalted Christian humanist virtue.

Images and texts were combined in the emblems painted around the base of the pyre. The popular Renaissance genre of the emblem, which combined a moralising dictum with a relevant illustration, was common in civic displays in New Spain; although examples were often purloined from pre-existing compilations, new ones were produced for important occasions. The emblem of a lion with the face of Philip IV adorning the *túmulo* in his honour would have left observers in no doubt about whose virtues were being commended (Figure 3). Sariñana y Cuenca's festival book explained that the lion had

Figure 3.   Isidro Sariñana y Cuenca, Llanto de sol, Mexico City, 1666, following fol. 54v

Digital image courtesy of the Getty's Open Content Program.

been a symbol of physical prowess and generosity of spirit since antiquity, characteristics worthy of imitation that Philip had possessed. The actual text of the emblem, taken from Ovid's *Tristia*, 3.5.31 underlined this:

Quo quisque est maior, magis est placabilis ira

The greater one is, the more can his wrath be appeased.

For onlookers unfamiliar with Latin, clarification was provided by a lengthier Castilian poem.

Figure 4.   Isidro Sariñana y Cuenca, Llanto de sol, Mexico City, 1666, following fol. 63v

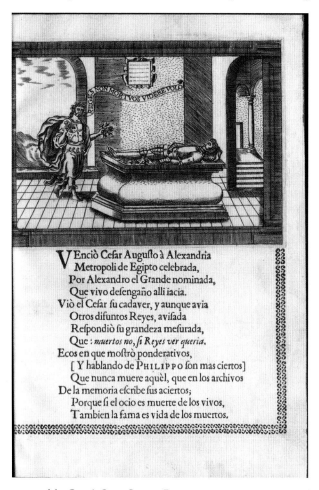

Digital image courtesy of the Getty's Open Content Program.

The emblems also incorporated imagery from Greco-Roman history: one emblem showed Caesar Augustus visiting the sepulchre of Alexander the Great in Alexandria after the battle of Actium (Figure 4). The text *Reges non mortuos videre volo*, 'I have no wish to see kings die', reflected Augustus's conviction that great monarchs should enjoy eternal fame as he ordered the tomb to be opened so that he could place a crown on Alexander's head and spread flowers around the body (Sariñana y Cuenca, 1666: fol. 64r-v). In the context of the *exequias*, not only was Philip a new Alexander, who was ruler of a vast empire by dint of his virtues, but like the Macedonian conqueror his virtues were to be recalled by the inhabitants of New Spain. They were thus induced to contemplate the exemplary conduct of both Alexander and Augustus Caesar as well as of Philip IV himself.

Sigüenza y Góngora's Arch in the Exemplary Tradition

The celebrations and the triumphal arch for the entry of the Viceroy into Mexico City in 1680 were evidently rooted in the rhetorical exemplary tradition. The erection of the *túmulo* with exequies for Philip IV, which had been enacted in the capital fourteen years before, provided a significant precedent for the ceremonies and the construction of the triumphal arch directed by Carlos de Sigüenza y Góngora. Sigüenza's *Theatro de virtúdes políticas* followed the same general conventions as Sariñana y Cuenca's volume recording the earlier occasion and it also made clear the function of such triumphal arches:

> a los príncipes sirvan de espejo, donde atiendan a las virtudes con que han de adornarse los arcos triunfales que en sus entradas se erigen para que de allí sus manos tomen ejemplo, o su autoridad y poder aspire a la emulación de lo que en ellos se simboliza en los disfraces de triunfos […]. (Sigüenza y Góngora, 1984: 171)

> they serve as a mirror for princes where they are concerned with the virtues, with which triumphal arches should be adorned and that are built for their entrances so that they may take it as an example for their own conduct, or so that their authority and power can aspire to the emulation of those who are represented in the guise of triumphs.

The message was the same: virtue was the highest accomplishment of any ruler and the ancients provided the most persuasive examples of this. But Sigüenza's vast arch – 90 feet high and 50 feet wide – included paintings of the god Huitzilopochtli along with twelve Mexica rulers. The particular qualities of the pre-Hispanic figures Sigüenza had selected were also spelled out in accompanying verses. For instance, the painting representing Huitzilopochtli, the god who had guided the Aztecs from the mythical place of their origin to the Valley of Mexico, featured the hummingbird (*huitzilin*) from which the god derived his name, alongside a left hand holding a lighted torch, explained by a text from Virgil:

> descendo ac ducente deo flammam inter et hostis
> expedior: dant tela locum flammaeque recedunt.[6]
> (Virgil, *Aeneid,* 2. 632-633)

---

6 Sigüenza y Góngora (1984: 197) did cite *Aeneid* book 2, but gave only the words: *'Ducente Deo'*, 'as God is in charge'.

I descend, and as God is in charge, I am freed from flames and enemies: the spears give way, and the flames recede.

In this way, Huitzilopochtli exemplified the need for princes 'to begin their actions with God in mind so that they are revealed and venerated as heroic' (*de principiar con Dios sus acciones para que descuellan y se veneran heroicas*) – thus conforming to both classical and Christian virtues. Similarly, the verses that accompanied the image of Huitzilopochtli also underlined the particular virtue that the god represented, offering a parallel exemplary argument:

> Acciones de fe constante
> que obra el príncipe, jamás
> se pueden quedar atrás
> en teniendo a Dios delante.
> los efectos los confiesan
> con justas demonstraciones
> pues no tuercen las acciones
> que solo a Dios enderezan.
> (Sigüenza y Góngora, 1984: 197)

> The actions a prince performs in constant faith never fall behind, if God lies ahead. Their effects reveal themselves with sure proofs because actions that steer straight to God do not go astray.

Citing a dictum which Livy (*Ab urbe condita*, 5.51) had attributed to the triumphant Roman general Marcus Furius Camillus – *omnia prospere evenisse sequentibus deos*, 'everything goes well for those who follow the will of the gods' – Huitzilopochtli was rendered a model of piety and obedience to God (Sigüenza y Góngora, 1984: 195). The Aztec monarchs on Sigüenza's triumphal arch included Axayacatl, Montezuma II and Cuauhtemoc, who respectively represented princely virtues of fortitude, liberality and constancy. Their role was completely analogous to the preceptive function of Alexander, Caesar and other rulers from European classical antiquity on the monument for Philip IV. Sigüenza's deployment of Mexican models in this context was a bold innovation, but his use of exemplarity could not have been more conventional.

References

Adorno, R. (2015) 'El México antiguo en el Barroco de Indias: don Carlos de Sigüenza y Góngora'. *Anales de Estudios Latinoamericanos* (Asociación Japonesa de Estudios Latinoamericanos, Tokyo) **35**: 1–42.

Andrews, J. (2007) 'The Negotiation of Mexican Identity in 1680: Sor Juana Ines de la Cruz's *Neptuno alegórico* and Carlos de Sigüenza y Góngora's *Theatro de virtudes políticas*' in J. Andrews and A. Coroleu (eds.) *Mexico 1680: Cultural and Intellectual Life in the Barroco de Indias*. HiPLAM: Bristol, 23–44.

Beaver, A. G. (2008) *A Holy Land for the Catholic Monarchy: Palestine in the Making of Modern Spain, 1469–1598*, Unpublished doctoral dissertation, Harvard University, Cambridge.

Brading, D. A. (1992) *The First America: The Spanish Monarch, Creole Patriots and the Liberal State 1492–1867*. Cambridge University Press: Cambridge.

Cañeque, A. (2007) 'El arco triunfal en el México del siglo XVII como manual efímero del buen gobernante' in J. P. Buxó (ed.) *Reflexión y espectáculo en la América virreinal*. Universidad Nacional Autónoma de México: Mexico, 199–218.

Caussin, N. (1619) *Eloquentiae sacrae et humanae parallela libri XVI*. S. Chappelet: Paris.

Hankins, J. (2004) 'Machiavelli, Civic Humanism, and the Humanist Politics of Virtue'. *Italian Culture* 32(2): 98–109.

Hankins, J. (2007) *Cambridge Companion to Renaissance Philosophy*. Cambridge University Press: Cambridge.

Inés de la Cruz, Sor Juana [1680] (2009) *Neptuno alegórico ed.* V. Marin. Cátedra: Madrid.

Laird, A. (2006) *The Epic of America: An Introduction to Rafael Landívar and the Rusticatio Mexicana*. Duckworth: London.

Lorente Medina, A. (1994) 'Don Carlos De Sigüenza y Góngora, educador de príncipes: el *Theatro de virtúdes políticas*'. *Literatura Mexicana* 5(2): 335–371.

Lukács, L. (1995) *Ratio atque institutio studiorum Societatis Iesu* [1599] in Lukács (ed.) *Monumenta paedagogica Societatis Iesu* (5 vols.). Monumenta Historica Soc. Iesu: Rome, V, 355–454.

McManamon, J. M. (1989) *Funeral Oratory and the Cultural Ideals of Italian Humanism*. University of North Carolina Press: Chapel Hill.

Méndez Bañuelos, S. J. (2000) 'Ingenio y construcción alegórica en dos arcos triunfales novohispanos' in A. Mayer (ed.) *Carlos de Sigüenza y Góngora. Homenaje 1700–2000*. Universidad Nacional Autónoma de Mexico: Mexico City, 35–65.

Mendizábal, G. L. de (1666) *Oratoria parentatio ... B.* Calderón: Mexico.

Menegus Bornemann, M. and Agirre Salvador, R. (2006) *Los Indios, el sacerdocio y la universidad en Nueva España, siglos XVI-XVIII*. Universidad Nacional Autónoma de México: Mexico.

Monroy, Antonio de (1666) 'Laudatio funebris ad regias Augustissimi Philippi IV...' in *Honorario túmulo, pompa exequial y imperial mausoleo*. Mexico City.

Montiel Bonilla, A. (1999) *El teatro de virtudes de Sigüenza y Góngora. ¿Pilar del nacionalismo o texto cortesano del siglo XVII?* Secretaría de Cultura: Puebla.

More, A. (2012) *Baroque Sovereignty: Carlos de Sigüenza y Góngora and the Creole Archive of Colonial Mexico*. University of Pennsylvania Press: Philadelphia.

Muir, E. (2005) *Ritual in Early Modern Europe*, (2nd ed.) Cambridge University Press: Cambridge.

O'Malley, J. W. (1979) *Praise and Blame in Renaissance Rome: Rhetoric, Doctrine, and Reform in the Sacred Orators of the Papal Court, c. 1450–1521*. Duke University Press: Durham.

Osorio Romero, I. (1976) *Tópicos sobre Cicerón*. Universidad Nacional Autónoma de México: Mexico.

Osorio Romero, I. (1979) *Colegios y profesores jesuitas que enseñaron latín en Nueva España*. Universidad Nacional Autónoma de México: Mexico City.

Paz, O. (1988) *Sor Juana Inés de la Cruz*. Belknap Press of Harvard University: Cambridge.

Pérez Puente, L. (2005) *Tiempos de crisis, tiempos de consolidación. La catedral metropolitana de la ciudad de México, 1653–1680*. Universidad Nacional Autónoma de México: Mexico.

Sariñana y Cuenca, I. (1666) *Llanto del occidente en el ocaso del más claro sol de las Españas: fúnebres demonstraciones que hizo pyra real, que erigió en las exequias del Rey N. Señor D. Felipe IIII el grande*. Por la viuda de Bernardo Calderón: Mexico.

Schmidt, P. (1997) 'Neoestoicismo y disciplinamiento social en Iberoamérica colonial' in K. Kohut and S. V. Rose (eds.) *Pensamiento europeo y cultura colonial*. Vervuert-Iberoamerica: Madrid, 181–204.

Sigüenza y Góngora, C. de [1680] (1984) 'Theatro de virtudes políticas que constituyen a un príncipe' in W. G. Bryant (ed.) *Seis obras*. Biblioteca Ayacucho: Caracas, 167–240.

Stacey, P. (2007) *Roman Monarchy and the Renaissance Prince*. Cambridge University Press: Cambridge.

Tanner, M. (1993) *The Last Descendant of Aeneas: The Hapsburgs and the Mythic Image of the Emperor*. Yale University Press: New Haven.

Urrejola, B. (2012) 'El panegírico y el problema de los géneros en la retórica sacra del mundo hispánico. Acercamiento metodológico'. *Revista Chilena de Literatura* (82): 220–247.

Vargas Alquicira, S. (1987) *Diálogo de abril: acerca de la Bibliotheca del señor doctor Juan José de Eguiara y del ingenio de los mexicanos*. Universidad Nacional Autónoma de México: Mexico.

Villella, P. B. (2016) *Indigenous Elites and Creole Identity in Colonial Mexico, 1500–1800*. Cambridge University Press: Cambridge.

8

Plato and the Guarani Indians

DESIREE ARBO

The Jesuits were already renowned as educators and missionaries in Europe and Asia when they first arrived in the southernmost regions of America in 1586. Although colleges were founded early on in Córdoba, Asunción and elsewhere, the success of early missionary expeditions in the region proved short lived and some were disastrous. In order to provide a more stable basis for evangelisation, in 1606 the Superior General of the Society of Jesus, Claudio Acquaviva, ordered efforts to be concentrated in the newly established Province of Paraguay. The 30 missions to the Guarani, located between the Paraná, Paraguay and Uruguay rivers, would become one of the most famous endeavours of the Jesuits in the New World, earning both praise and criticism from Europeans and neighbouring Spanish Americans alike (Imbruglia, 1983).

All this came to an end when Charles III of Spain decreed the immediate expulsion of all Jesuits from Spain's territories in 1767.[1] The decree was enforced in Córdoba on 12 July of that year. Abruptly woken by soldiers, the Jesuits were taken to Buenos Aires, from where they were transported to Europe. Among them was a Catalan, José Manuel Peramás, who had worked in the mission of San Ignacio Miní and taught in the College of Montserrat in Córdoba (Furlong, 1952: 7–24; Batllori, 1966: 345–354). Peramás was to end up living in exile in the Italian city of Faenza, where he produced several Latin works which were prompted by his knowledge and experience of the Americas, including an account of his expulsion, the *Annus Patiens*, 'Year of Suffering' (Suárez, 2010). His epic poem about Columbus, *De invento novo orbe*, 'On the Discovery of the New World', was published in Faenza (Peramás, 1777; Arbo and Laird, 2015; Feile Tomes, 2015a, 2015b).

Peramás also provided the last and most systematic elaboration of an analogy that earlier authors had drawn between the Jesuit missions in Paraguay and the projections of an ideal society in Plato's *Republic*. In a treatise entitled *De administratione guaranica comparata ad Rempublicam Platonis commentarius*, 'A Commentary on the Administration of the Guarani compared to Plato's *Republic*', Peramás adroitly used his classical learning

---

1   The exiled creole Jesuits' presence in Italy had various ramifications (Batllori, 1966; Guasti, 2006; Laird, 2006: 23–34, 2012).

to hint at his own ideas of identity and nation. This chapter will introduce Peramás' text in the context of the author's broader agenda, consider its place in a tradition of comparing Paraguayan missions to Plato's society, and analyse a sample passage from the *De administratione guaranica* to illustrate the idiosyncratic way in which Peramás appropriated the authority and works of Plato.

Peramás' Treatise on the Guarani

The *De administratione guaranica* is actually the introduction to a larger work, *De vita et moribus tredecim virorum Paraguaycorum,* 'The Lives and Habits of Thirteen Men of Paraguay', a set of biographies of Jesuit priests and coadjutor brothers who worked in the province. That introduction, however, which constituted roughly 35 per cent of the original 462-page octavo volume, has long been regarded as a self-contained work in its own right. The treatise sought to demonstrate that 'something similar to what was invented by Plato has existed among the Guarani Indians': 'quiddam simile exstitisse Platonis inventis inter Guaranios Indos' (Peramás, [1793: ii] 2004: 27).

Peramás made it clear he was highlighting that similarity by showing how Christian doctrine could promote the common good, which he considered to be the best argument to refute the anti-religious positions propounded by thinkers and philosophers of the eighteenth-century Enlightenment.

The 30 chapters of the *De administratione guaranica* are arranged as follows:

1-7: Description of the layout of the missions
8-15: Ethnographic accounts of marriage, educational practices, music, dance, work, feasts, and the arts
16-17: 'Digression' on the development of the arts and the origin of nations
18-23: Commerce, visitors, dress, authorities, laws and discipline, defending the labours of the Jesuits against slanders
24-25: Sustained refutation of Raynal and other *philosophes*
26-27: Punishments and funerals
28-30: Epilogue: 'Apostrophe against the liberal philosophers'
Conclusion: closing responses to irreligious philosophers and the French Revolution.

The text has attracted more attention than any of Peramás' other works – from philosophers and anthropologists as well as historians and Latinists. There were debates in the early twentieth century about the extent to which this account of the Paraguayan missions amounted to advocating communism

(Furlong, 1952: 78–79), but more recently there have been other related approaches. The treatise has been examined as a forthright retort to theories of American degeneracy propounded by De Pauw, Raynal and other Enlightenment authors (Gerbi, 1973; Batllori, 1966), as a response to the French Revolution (Morales, 2010; Melai, 2011), as well as part of a broad tradition of utopian literature from the myth of the Noble Savage to the mythologisations of the Jesuit missions (Cro, 1992, 1994a, 1994b, 2005). Yet to date there is no study of Peramás' openly acknowledged debt to Plato.

The Jesuits, Paraguay and Plato

Reports from members of the laity in Paraguay criticising the Jesuits provided ammunition for their opponents in Europe. Voltaire, for instance, was able to affirm that although the Jesuits were subject to a monarchy, in their missions they ruled as kings themselves, 'possibly the best obeyed on earth': 'peut-être les rois mieux obéis de la terre' (Voltaire, 1859 8: 112). Similarly, an article on Paraguay in volume 11 of Diderot's influential *Encyclopédie* held that 'in every parish there is a Jesuit whom everyone obeys, and who governs as a sovereign' (Diderot and D'Alembert, 1765: 900–902). And Bernardo Ibáñez de Echevarri, Peramás' former companion who had been expelled from the Society of Jesus, accused its members in Paraguay of dissolute behaviour and heresy, averring that they behaved as if they possessed an independent sovereign state, by enslaving Indians, avoiding taxes, and indiscriminately allowing foreigners into Spanish territory (Ibáñez de Echavarri, 1770; Bacigalupo, 1979: 475–494).

Peramás would answer these accusations in the *De administratione guaranica* by presenting the indigenous communities in the missions as ordered societies that were committed to the Spanish imperial project and composed of active and intelligent citizens – and he used the model of Plato's ideal republic to lend support to this case. But Peramás was by no means the first to mention Plato in such a context. As early as the 1500s, the French essayist Michel de Montaigne had done so as he characterised the native inhabitants of Brazil in his famous discourse, *Des cannibales*:

> C'est une nation, dirais-je à Platon, en laquelle il n'y a aucune espèce de trafic; nulle connaissance de lettres; nulle science de nombres; nul nom de magistrat […] nulle agriculture; nul métal […]. Il me déplâit que Lycurge et Platon ne l'aient eue; car il me semble que ce que nous voyons par expérience en ces nations-là, surpasse non seulement toutes les peintures de quoi la poésie a embelli l'âge doré […] mais encore la conception et le désir même de la philosophie. (Montaigne, 1998: 130)

This is a nation, as I would tell Plato, in which there is no form of trade, no knowledge of letters, no knowledge of numbers, no title of magistrate […] no agriculture, no metals […]. It is a pity that Plato and Lycurgus had not [been able to observe these indigenous peoples] because it seems to me that what we have seen through experience in the nations there surpasses not only all the depictions of the Golden Age beautified in poetry […] but also the conception and very aim of philosophy.

Peramás made no mention of Montaigne. Instead, his introduction to the *De administratione guaranica* credited Jacques Vanière, Lodovico Antonio Muratori and Pierre François de Charlevoix as his most important sources, all of whom were Jesuits or had received a Jesuit education. Vanière had praised the Indians of Paraguay in his influential didactic poem, *Praedium Rusticum* (1730); the antiquarian Muratori compared the missions they inhabited to early Christian communities; and Charlevoix decried the attempts of some members of Paraguay's secular population to discredit what the Jesuits had accomplished in the missions.[2] Though Peramás drew mostly from Muratori, it is significant that Charlevoix had made a specific reference to Plato and other utopian writers in his *Histoire du Paraguay* (1756):

> Je parle de ces Républiques chrétiennes, dont le Monde n'avoit point encore vu de modèles, et qui ont été fondées dans le centre de la plus féroce barbarie, sur un plan plus parfait que ceux de Platon, du Chancelier Bacon et de l'illustre Auteur du Télémaque. (Charlevoix, 1756, 1: 5)[3]

> I refer to those Christian republics, of which the world had yet no precedent, and that were founded in midst of ferocious barbarism with a plan more perfect than those of Plato, the chancellor Bacon or the illustrious author of the *Télémaque* [Fénelon].

---

2   Muratori's *Il cristianesimo felice nel Paraguay*, 'The Good Fortune of Christianity in Paraguay', (1743) had been cited by Voltaire and praised in the *Encyclopédie* (Imbruglia, 1983: 166–169). Venturi (1972) analysed Muratori's views in the context of the Italian Enlightenment, but without considering his work in relation to the New World.

3   Peramás would also have been familiar with Charlevoix's history in its expanded Latin version by the last provincial of Paraguay, Domingo Muriel (1718–1795). Peramás often referred to another of Muriel's works, *Rudimenta iuris naturae et gentium* (2 vols.) (Venice, 1791).

But another important Jesuit source which made mention of Plato was cited rather more discreetly (though at some length) by Peramás in his concluding chapters ([1793: cccv-cccvi] 2004: 199–200).

Giovanni Battista Noghera's *Riflessioni su la filosofia del bello spirito* (1775) commented on the introduction of the Christian religion to the people of Paraguay:

> un popolo convertito a Cristo [...] di maniera che d'innumerabili cov-
> ili di fiere insociabili e antropofaghe se ne compone oggimai una rep-
> publica sola migliori assai di costumi e più felice di stato che non è
> l'immaginata Repubblica di Platone. Ognuno intende ch'io qui parlo
> della Cristianità fioritissima del Paraguay. (Noghera, 1775: 121)

> a people converted to Christ [...] in such a way that out of the countless
> dens of unsocialised and man-eating savages has emerged one sole
> republic of better customs and in a happier state than the imagined
> Republic of Plato. Everyone understands that I am speaking here of the
> Christian faith flourishing in Paraguay.

Although Noghera's defences of religion and the infallibility of the Pope had been suppressed, his complete works were published in 1790, so Peramás would have been able to quote from them (O'Neill and Domínguez, 2001: 2829).

Jesuit defences of the missions had thus drawn glancing parallels or analogies with the society of Plato's *Republic* which were rhetorical in nature, but Peramás developed them in a far more systematic and comprehensive way. He may have felt a certain urgency to lay claim to Plato in the wake of the recent French Revolution: he noted that Montesquieu had commended Guarani society for its successful implementation of Plato's commonwealth, but passed over the French philosopher's view that the Guarani won happiness only at the expense of their freedom: 'Montesquieus autem suo illo in opere de natura, & ratione legum, Guaraniorum vivendi modum magnifice commendat': 'Montesquieu also, in his work on the nature and spirit of the laws, brilliantly commended the Guarani way of life' (Peramás, [1793: cclxxviii] 2004: 184).[4] More importantly, while Montesquieu saw the native communities as a potential social model for a republican society in which utopian idealism could shape political reality, Peramás presented his

---

4 Contrast Montesquieu (1979: 162 [cap. VI]): 'Le Paraguay peut nous fournir un autre exemple. On a voulu en faire un crime à la societé qui regarde le plaisir de commander comme le seul bien de la vie: mais il sera toujours beau de gouverner les hommes, en les rendant plus heureux': 'Paraguay can provide us with another

Guarani system as contingent on the historical conditions that gave rise to it (Imbruglia, 1983: 31–45). The *Republic* and to some extent the *Laws* (Plato's second dialogue on statecraft) served Peramás' defence of the Jesuits' missionary objectives – the actualisation of their principles and prescriptions in Paraguay was never meant to provide a paradigm to be universally applied.

Plato in the *De Administratione Guaranica*

The incorporation and interpretation of Plato in Peramás' text helps to illuminate its agenda. In this respect the word *commentarius* in the full title of the work – 'A *Commentary* on the Administration of the Guarani compared to Plato's *Republic*' – appears significant. In literary and philological scholarship, a commentary is a systematic elucidation of a text, provided by a lemma (an excerpt from that primary text) followed by comments explaining its content and meaning. That format inherited from antiquity continued to facilitate the study of Scripture and scholastic texts in Spanish American colleges and seminaries and it had also long served European humanists as the principal method of exegesis of classical authors (Kraus and Stray, 2015). The Latin translation and commentary on Plato's complete works produced by the Florentine Marsilio Ficino, for instance, was known to Peramás: it had first reached Spanish America in the early 1500s and was still highly regarded by Jesuits even in the eighteenth century (Byrne, 2015: 1–49, 210–213; Laird, Valdivieso in this volume).[5]

But Peramás was not concerned with explaining Plato's text and did not produce that kind of commentary. In classical Latin, *commentarius* had broader connotations and could denote nothing more complex than a linear succession of topics: Caesar's firsthand reports on the Gallic Wars and the notes appended to Cicero's speeches were alike called *commentarii* (Riggsby, 2006: 133–145). The cognate term in Spanish, *comentario*, was defined in the first dictionary of the *Real Academia Española* in 1729 (vol. 2) as 'Historia o cosa escrita con brevedad; lo mismo que Epitome', 'a history or thing written with brevity; the same as an epitome'. That sense of 'history' had been exemplified in Spanish America by the *Comentarios reales* (1609), the Inca

---

example. One could make it a crime for the Society that regards the pleasure of command as the only good in life, but it will always be a fine thing to govern people, making them happier by doing so'.

5   Peramás engaged with Ficino in his chapter on marriage customs among the Guarani, expressing his disagreement with Ficino's admiration of Plato even in instances where the Jesuit deemed Plato to be wrong, as in the advocating of wives held in common in *Republic* book 6.

Garcilaso de la Vega's original title for his account of Andean history and society. The use of the term *commentarius* in Peramás' title really signalled that the *De administratione guaranica* was a concise, historical report on the missions as well as a collection of notes to introduce the ensuing biographies of the Jesuits.

Peramás himself describes the way in which his text was conceived and set out:

> Is autem nobis scribendi erit modus: ponam compendio quid quaque in re voluerit Plato; dein dicam quid inter Guaranios fieret, ac tuum denique, collatis capitibus, pronunciare convenirent ne invicem utraque instituta, an contra discreparent. (Peramás, 1793: iv)

> This will be my manner of writing: I will summarise for each question what Plato had intended; next I will say what was done among the Guarani. Then it will be for you to determine, by comparing the major points, whether the two systems converge, or whether there is discrepancy between them.

This was a very selective reading of Plato: Peramás' summaries entailed inclusions and exclusions which amounted to pronounced interpretations of his chosen Platonic texts – mainly the *Republic* and the *Laws*. Moreover, Peramás also acknowledged that he was 'following the senses of both works here and there, not the words or the order' – in a loose application of the humanist practice of translating *ad sensum* rather than *ad verba*. A translation *ad sensum* aimed to convey the meaning of the source text, but often in a less precise manner, sometimes omitting or altering passages in favour of greater elegance and fluency (Botley, 2004: 164–177). Marsilio Ficino's adoption of this technique in translating all of Plato was part of a grand design to christianise the philosopher. Peramás seems to share Ficino's conviction that Plato had intimations of Christian thought and, like Ficino, he used the flexibility of the commentary to further his own agenda.

Peramás discerned an evolution in Plato's work and considered the *Laws* to be more prudent and moderate than the *Republic* as the work of a mature author, and he referred to it more often. The *Laws* was a dialogue in which three speakers – an unnamed Athenian, Cleinias the Cretan and Megillos the Spartan – discuss the ideal legislation for a new colony to be founded in Crete. Peramás seems to identify the wisdom dispensed by the old Athenian as Plato's own: his precepts are presented in the *De administratione guaranica* without any indication that they were ever a part of a dialogue. The kind of transposition and manipulation of the original text this afforded can be illustrated by quoting chapter 4 in its entirety. Here Peramás rehearses Plato's specifications for the kind of people that should be brought together in a city, before describing the Guarani inhabiting the missions:

De gente coalitura in urbem

PLATO

XIV. Gens sit una, & lingua; eaedem leges sint, eadem sacra, his enim mirifice coalescit civium amicitia. Qui e variis confluunt populis linguae variae, ii prae desiderio morum & legum, quibus antea assueverunt, non probant urbis, in quam adsciscuntur, leges, & mores, qui tamen mutandi temere non sunt, receptis usibus peregrinis. (Lib IV. de Legg.)

GUARANII

XV. In triginta Guaraniorum priscis oppidis (his bina adjecta fuerunt aetate nostra) gens una omnino erat, atque una lingua, quae viguit, atque etiam num viget, in maxima Americae meridialis parte ab Oceano Brasilico ad amnim usque Maranonium, atque hunc etiam ultra, usui enim est in Cayena. Qui terrarum tractus multo est amplior, quam quanto obtinuit olim lingua vel Graeca vel Latina, quibus Guaranica nihil cedit artificio & elegantia, de qua re dicemus in vita Ignatii Chomae. Amicitia autem inter Guaranios post suscepta christiana sacra tam erat solida & constans, ut solidior & constantior esse nusquam possit: nam *societate gentis, & linguae* (adde religionis) *quam maxime homines conjunguntur*, ait praeclare Tullius. (*De officiis* lib. I. c. XVI) (Peramás, 1793: chapters 14–15)

The people to come together in a city

PLATO

14. Let it be one people and language, with the same laws and sacred rites: by these, the bonds of friendship among citizens grow wonderfully. When people come together from several populations with several languages, because of the desire for customs and laws to which they had been accustomed before, they are not satisfied in their adopted city. Laws and customs however must not be changed rashly with the acceptance of foreign practices. ([Plato] *Laws* Book 4).

GUARANI

15. In the thirty former towns of the Guarani (of which two were founded in our time), there was one people, and one language which flourished, and still now flourishes, in a very great part of South America, from the Brazilian Ocean to the Marañon River [in Peru], and even beyond, for it is spoken in Cayenne. Thus its extension is over an area larger than Greek or Latin ever attained, and to these the Guarani language is in no way inferior in artifice and elegance. Of this we will speak further in the life of Ignatius Chomé. For now, friendship among

the Guarani after they received the Christian religion was so firm and constant, that it could not be firmer or more constant: for *in a society [a common] people and language* (to which is added religion) *bind men the most*, as Cicero eminently put it. (*De officiis*, 1.16).

The passage from *Laws* book 4 distilled here was transformed, as well as removed from its original context. In Plato, the Athenian had inquired whether the projected new colony in Crete would be founded with colonists from one city of origin or from several. Cleinias' reply – that they would probably be drawn from different cities – prompted a long meditation from the Athenian on the advantages and disadvantages of each option. Colonisation, he said, would be easier when one entire city moved. In Ficino's translation this is expressed as follows:

> Nam quod genus unum est unius linguae earumdemq[ue]; legum, cum sacrorum & huiusmodi omnium com[m]unione[m] habeat, amicitia quide[m] inter se aliqua copulatur, sed leges alias, gubernationisq[ue]; modum a pristino discrepantem non facile suscipit. (Plato, *Laws*, 4: 708b-d; Ficino, 1567: 533).

> For this one people has one language and has the same laws, since it has commonality in sacred things and all such matters, is bound to itself by a certain bond of fellow-feeling, but it does not so easily sustain others' laws and a method of government diverging from the one it had before.

The Athenian went on to observe that people gathered together from different locations, on the other hand, would probably be more willing to obey new and unfamiliar laws, though it would take them longer 'to breathe together and grow to be united as one and the same, like horses under a single yoke' (ut conspirare, & tamquam sub uno iugo equi, unum idemq[ue], ut dicitur, coalescere possint) (Plato, *Laws*, 4:708d; Ficino, 1567: 533).

But Peramás' summary has Plato state something rather different: it is the people coming from different locations that would pine after their old laws, and a city should not introduce foreign customs lightly. Peramás' Plato would approve not only of the Guarani missions being composed of people from the same ethnic and linguistic group, but also of their isolation from the rest of the Spanish American world. Unity of people, language, laws and religion is the key to a happy society.

It is also conveyed that the sense of community among the Guarani was enhanced and consolidated after the arrival of the Jesuits and their conversion. Although he does refer in this chapter to Ignacio Chomé, whose biography appears later in the volume, Peramás does not spell out that a unified Guarani language was precisely the result of Jesuit missionary activity: Antonio Ruiz de Montoya's influential grammar and lexicon, *Arte y vocabulario de la lengua guaraní* (1640), for instance, standardised the Guarani language from a multiplicity of dialects (Nickson, 2009: 5). Overall, this chapter, in the manner of the entire treatise of which it forms a part, marshals the authority of Plato (and indeed Cicero) to defend the importance of the Christian religion as a fundamental component of civilised society.

Conclusion

In his final chapters, Peramás made explicit his criticism of the French Revolution and his concern that liberal philosophers would use Plato and other utopian writers to propagate their doctrines in Europe. Like Muratori before him, Peramás insisted that the *administratio* or system he set out could function only in primitive societies – those of the Guarani, the Germans in Tacitus' *Germania* or the first Christian communities – and not in modern societies. European nations had reached a point where it was impossible to revert from being complex societies that recognised inequality of power, possessions and talents, and rewarded or punished accordingly. José Manuel Peramás' alignment of the Guarani missions with the Platonic republic, once taken as a blueprint for communism, was effectively made to support the *ancien régime*. This author's evident devotion to the Jesuit principles of hierarchy and order and his lament for the tranquillity lost after the French Revolution, along with his Christian vision of the conquest (which would now be deemed eurocentric), all suggest a conservative agenda.

The interest of Peramás' *De administratione guaranica* lies in the extent to which debates about the Jesuit missions played some part in shaping European thought about the nature of the state, from the early modern period through to the Enlightenment. The prominence of Plato in Peramás' text, as well as in the web of sources that influenced it, highlights the significance of both the common references and the different interpretations that characterised intellectual debates in Europe and the New World. In both regions, Greco-Roman authors had long been symbolic elements as well as sources in debates on states and nations. The intellectual histories of Europe and colonial Spanish America with their respective classical traditions were inextricably linked, but the Latin and vernacular literature about the New World produced on each continent also shows that the traffic of ideas moved across the Atlantic in two directions.

References

Arbo, D. and Laird, A. (2015) 'Columbus, the Lily of Quito and the Black Legend: The Context of José Manuel Peramás' Epic on the Discovery of the New World, *De invento novo orbe inductoque illuc Christi Sacrificio* (1777)'. *Dieciocho* 38(1): 7–32.

Bacigalupo, M. (1979) 'Bernardo Ibáñez de Echevarri and the Image of the Jesuit Missions of Paraguay'. *The Americas* 33(4): 475–494.

Batllori, M. (1966) *La cultura hispano-italiana de los jesuitas expulsos*. Editorial Gredos: Madrid.

Botley, P. (2004) *Latin Translation in the Renaissance: The Theory and Practice of Leonardo Bruni, Giannozzo Manetti, and Desiderius Erasmus*. Cambridge University Press: Cambridge.

Byrne, S. (2015) *Ficino in Spain*. University of Toronto Press: Toronto.

Caturelli, A. (1992) 'Ciudad platónica y ciudad cristiana en el Nuevo Mundo: el pensamiento de José Manuel Peramás'. *Verbo* 301–302: 17–32.

Charlevoix, P.-F. (1756) *Histoire du Paraguay*, Vol. 3. Chez Ganeau, Bauche [et] D'Houry: Paris.

Charlevoix, P.-F. [1756] (1779) (trans. D. Muriel). *Historia Paraguajensis Petri Francisci-Xavierii de Charlevoix, ex Gallico Latina cum animadversionibus et supplemento*. F. Sansoni: Venice.

Cro, S. (1992) 'Empirical and Practical Utopia in Paraguay'. *Dieciocho* 15: 171–184.

Cro, S. (1994a) 'Guaranica: De administratione guaranica comparata ad rempublicam Platonis commentarius'. *Canadian Journal of Italian Studies* 17: 48–49. Symposium Press: Hamilton.

Cro, S. (1994b) 'Classical Antiquity, America and the Myth of the Noble Savage' in W. Haase and M. Reinhold (eds.) *The Classical Tradition and the Americas*. W. De Gruyter: Berlin and New York, 379–418.

Cro, S. (2005) 'La utopia de las dos orillas (1553-1793)'. *Cuadernos para investigación de la literatura hispánica* 30: 15–268.

De Pauw, C. (1768) *Recherches philosophiques sur les américains, ou Mémoires intéressants pour servir à l'histoire de l'espèce humaine*. G.J. Decker: Berlin.

Diderot, D. and D'Alembert, M. (1765) *Encyclopédie ou Dictionnaire Raisonné des Sciences, des Arts et des Métiers*. Samuel Faulche: Neufchastel. [WWW document]. URL htpps://encyclopedie.uchicago.edu [Accessed 4 May 2016]

Feile Tomes, M. (2015a) 'News of a Hitherto Unknown Neo-Latin Columbus Epic, Part I. José Manuel Peramás's *De Invento Novo Orbe Inductoque Illuc Christi Sacrificio* (1777)'. *International Journal of the Classical Tradition* 22(1): 1–28.

Feile Tomes, M. (2015b) 'News of a Hitherto Unknown Neo-Latin Columbus Epic, Part II. José Manuel Peramás's *De Invento Novo Orbe Inductoque Illuc Christi Sacrificio* (1777)'. *International Journal of the Classical Tradition* 22(2): 223–257.

Ficino, M. (1567) *Divinis Platonis Opera Omnia Marsilio Ficino Interprete*. Antoine Vincent: Lyon.

Furlong, G. (1952) *José Manuel Peramás y su diario del destierro (1768)*. Librería del Plata: Buenos Aires.

Gerbi, A. [1955] (1973) (trans. J. Moyle). *The Dispute of the New World: The History of a Polemic, 1750–1900* Media Directions Inc.: Pittsburgh, London.

Guasti, N. (2006) *L'esilio italiano dei gesuiti spagnoli: identità, controllo sociale e pratiche culturali (1767–1798)*. Edizioni di Storia e Letteratura: Rome.

Ibáñez de Echavarri, B. (1770) *Regno Gesuitico del Paraguay dimostrato co'documenti piu classici de'medesimi Padri della Compagnia, i quali confessano, e mostrano ad evidenza la regia sovranità del R. P. Generale, con independenza e con odio verso la Spagna. Anno 1760.* Impressão Regia: Lisbon.

Imbruglia, G. (1983) 'Introduction' in *Ludovico Antonio Muratori, Relation des missions du Paraguay* (trans. F. E. de Lourmel). La Découverte-Maspero: Paris.

Imbruglia, G. (1987) *L'invenzione del Paraguay.* Bibliopolis: Naples.

Kraus, C. and Stray, C. (eds.) (2015) *Classical Commentaries: Explorations in a Scholarly Genre.* Oxford University Press: Oxford.

Laird, A. (2006) *The Epic of America, an Introduction to Rafael Landívar and the Rusticatio Mexicana.* Duckworth: London.

Laird, A. (2012) 'Patriotism and the Rise of Latin in New Spain. Disputes of the New World and the Jesuit Construction of a Mexican Legacy'. *Renaessanceforum* **8**: 231–261.

Melai, F. (2011) 'Sul significato del "platonismo" di Peramás nel suo *Commentarius* (1793)'. *Società e Storia* **134**: 673–688.

Montaigne, M. [1580] (1998) *Essais* (Ed. M. Fragonard). Pocket: Paris.

Montesquieu, M. [1748] (1979) *De l'esprit des lois* (ed. V. Goldschmidt). Garnier-Flammarion: Paris.

Morales, M. (2010) '¿Guaraníes? No, aqueos. Una lectura de la obra de José Manuel Peramás De Administratione Guaranica comparate ad Rempublicam Platonis commentarius (1793)' in P. Chinchilla (ed.) *Los jesuitas formadores de ciudadanos. La educación dentro y fuera de sus colegios. Siglos XVI-XVI.* Universidad Iberoamericana: Mexico City, 209–243.

Muratori, L. [1743] (1964) 'Il cristianesimo felice nelle missione de' padri della Compagnia di Gesù nel Paraguai descritto da Lodovico Antonio Muratori' in G. Falco and F. Forti (eds.) *Opere di Lodovico Antonio Muratori* (vol. 1). Riccardo Ricciardi: Milan, 964–1013.

Nickson, R. A. (2009) 'Governance and the Revitalization of the Guarani Language in Paraguay'. *Latin American Research Review* **44**(2): 3–26.

Noghera, G. (1775) *Riflessioni sulla filosofia del bello spirito.* Remondini: Bassano.

O'Neill, C. and Domínguez, J. M. (2001) *Diccionario Histórico de la Compañía de Jesús Biográfico-Temático.* Institutum Historicum/Universidad Pontificia Comillas: Rome and Madrid.

Peramás, J. M. [Josephus Emmanuelis Peramasius] (1777) *De invento novo orbe inductoque illuc Christi sacrificio libris tres.* Ex Chalcographia Josephi Antonii: Faventiae (Faenza).

Peramás, J. M. (1793) *De vita et moribus tredecim virorum paraguaycorum.* Ex Typographia Archii: Faventiae (Faenza).

Peramás, J. M. [1793] (1946) *La República de Platón y los guaraníes* (trans. J. Cortés del Pino, with prologue by G. Furlong). Emecé Editores: Buenos Aires.

Peramás, J. M. [1793] (2004) *Platón y los Guaraníes* (trans. F. Fernandez Pertíñez, with prologue by B. Melià). Centro de Estudios Paraguayos 'Antonio Guasch': Asunción.

Peramás, J. M. [1766] (2005) *José Manuel Peramás Laudationes Quinque: Cinco alabanzas al ilustre Sr. Dr. Ignacio Duarte Quirós* (trans. M. Suárez). Biblioteca de la Nación Argentina: Buenos Aires.

Raynal, G. (1770) *L'histoire philosophique et politique des établissements et du commerce des Européens dans les deux Indes.* Amsterdam.

Real Academia Española (1726-1739) *Diccionario de la lengua castellana en que se explica el verdadero sentido de las voces, su naturaleza y calidad, con las phrases o modos de hablar, los proverbios o refranes.* Imprenta de Francisco Del Hierro: Madrid.

Riggsby, A. (2006) *Caesar in Gaul and Rome: War in Words.* University of Texas Press: Austin.

Suárez, M. (2010) 'Peramás y la doble redacción sobre el exilio jesuítico' in A. Schniebs (ed.) *Debates en Lenguas Clásicas.* Colección Libros de Filo, Universidad de Buenos Aires: Buenos Aires, 151–175.

Venturi, F. (1972) *Italy and the Enlightenment: Studies in a Cosmopolitan Century* (trans. S. Corsi). New York University Press: New York.

Voltaire (1859) *Oeuvres complètes.* Vol. 8. Ch. Lahure Hachette: Paris.

9

Classicism in Modern Latin America from Simón Bolívar to Roberto Bolaño

ROBERT T. CONN

Classical traditions proved to be just as instrumental in the culture and history of nineteenth- and twentieth-century Latin America as they were for the post-independence United States (Winterer, 2004; Richard, 2009). This chapter surveys the turn to 'classicism' – the uses or invocations of texts or models from the Greco-Roman world – in modern Latin America. It illustrates the variety of ideological and political purposes for which classical references were invoked. It deliberately ranges over nearly two centuries in order to convey the extent to which writers and political figures turned to the literature of European antiquity in search of universals to authorise their varied projects of nation-making. My argument is that certain cultural practices forged in a series of specific historical moments gave rise to classicism, leading to the conception and identification of new subjectivities, while others were rendered marginal or subordinate, or displaced altogether.

Formation of States, Nations and Identities, from the Nineteenth to the Twentieth Century

Simón Bolívar (1783–1830) looked to classical antiquity in order to find the models with which to defend the process of independence and build the governmental structures of the new nations he imagined. Bolívar made many references to the classical world in his writings, but his comparison of the imminent collapse of Spain's empire to that of Rome in his 1815 *Letter from Jamaica* – a comparison repeated in his *Angostura Address* of 1819 – is without doubt the best known (Lynch, 2006; Bartosik-Vélez, 2016). Yet in 1815 at least, developments on the ground meant that Spain's decline was anything but a foregone conclusion: New Granada and Venezuela had fallen back into the hands of the royalists and Bolívar himself was on the run, with no clear path back to the mainland. Yet his goal in evoking the decline of Rome's imperial power was to signal independence as inevitable.

Over the course of the nineteenth century, several influential statesmen made a show of their classical learning, including Andrés Bello (1781-1865) in Chile, Juan Montalvo (1832-1899) in Ecuador, and some members of the Argentine intellectual movement known as the 'Generation of 1837' who were opposed to the dictator Juan Manuel de Rosas. One of them, Juan Cruz Varela, penned plays on ancient themes, including a *Dido*, and *Argia*, a drama based on the *Antigone*. The most famous writer in the group, Domingo Faustino Sarmiento, who eventually became president of Argentina, contrasted Varela's preference for classical authors to his own liking for James Fenimore Cooper. Sarmiento saw the North American author as a model for the new literature he believed himself to be creating in *Facundo* (Sarmiento, [1845] 1981: 39). Nonetheless his autobiographical recollections provided evidence of his reading of classical works (Sarmiento, 1850). In Venezuela, Felipe Larrazábal (1816-1873) produced an epistolary biography of Bolívar in 1865 which dressed the leader up as a Cincinnatus, a Roman leader renowned for his selfless public service (Livy, *Ab urbe condita*, 3.26; Larrazábal, 1866). This portrayal, which transformed the military hero into a model statesman embodying the requisite republican virtues, became a seminal text in Venezuela's Bolivarian tradition.

Classicism took on new importance for writers and intellectuals as it spread across the Spanish-speaking countries of the Americas under the impetus of *modernismo*. Conceived both within and against the Latin American state of the late nineteenth century, the literary movement not only launched a critique of the bourgeois, capitalist forces at play at this time but also directed its attention to an industrialising United States that was moving 'south' in its economic and political ventures, taking Cuba and Puerto Rico in 1898, and well on its way to building an expansive political and economic network to manage the hemisphere in the decades ahead.

The cultural capital of Greece and Rome was not lost on the *modernistas*. The Nicaraguan poet Rubén Darío was a central figure who drew from the classical world and Asia, as well as German, French and Spanish literatures, each of which took the form of a citation of sorts in his construction of a cosmopolitan poetic universe. In his 1905 poem *Los cisnes*, 'The Swans', which warns of a future in which English will be the dominant language of Latin America, the poet renders the full name of Ovid in Spanish as 'Publio Ovidio Nasón', to appropriate ownership of a tradition that has been incorporated and celebrated by writers elsewhere in time but now formed clearly part of the Spanish-language literary tradition (Darío, 1931).

The Cuban writer and political leader José Martí had already seen the writing on the wall with regard to future United States dominance when he settled in New York City in 1880. His *Nuestra América* (1891) expressed the need for Latin America to defend its sovereignty by organising itself culturally, constructing its own Greece to legitimise and celebrate its unique and hard-fought place in history. Similarly, the Uruguayan José Enrique Rodó, in his momentous essay of 1900, *Ariel*, aligned Latin America with the values of the classical world, pitching them against capitalism and pragmatism as represented by the power to the north (Rodó, 1967; Martí, 1985).

Latin American intellectuals in the early twentieth century were ever more conscious of their standing, not only in relation to general populations but also to the rest of the world, and they used classicism to promote their interests. In Argentina, the novelist and poet Leopoldo Lugones found inspiration in ancient Greece as well as in his engagement with *gauchesca* poety. But in Mexico, in the aftermath of the 1910 revolution, classicism became politically significant in quite different ways as it was applied by Alfonso Reyes and José Vasconcelos to various state-building projects, ranging from refined scholarly inquiry to the education of the masses and to the packaging of local Mexican traditions for urban and international consumption.

For Alfonso Reyes (1889-1959), classicism went beyond serving as a framework for acquiring and disseminating knowledge to become a virtual end in itself. He sought to align genres of modern Mexican literature with their analogues in classical drama, poetry and prose. Reyes rewrote Mexico's complex linguistic and cultural past, purging it of the spontaneous vernacular quality that had enlivened it, turning a highly politicised tradition into a new form of *belle-lettrisme*. The Spanish language and Spain's literary tradition, combined with knowledge of the classics, assumed a normative role, uniting the hitherto distinct conceptions of the state and of culture. Reyes set aside the critiques of modernity represented by Nietzsche (whose writings and categories circulated among the *modernistas* of the nineteenth century) as he reorganised the Mexican literary sphere in order to change the values underlying it, subordinating, in Matei Calanescu's terms, aesthetic to bourgeois modernity (Calinescu, 1987).

In the wake of the Mexican Revolution, much of Reyes' prose writing took the form of far-reaching histories which found their beginnings in ancient Greece – though in the midst of the Revolution he had posited the past existence of an autochthonous state in the Aztec period in which Mexicans could see their distinguished origin. Reyes also incorporated critical categories used by authors whose ideological positions he did not share, strategically placing them in the new totalising schemes of his own and creating through a kind of textual performance the consensus he desired for the intellectual community. Thus, during the later years of Porfirio Díaz' dictatorship in Mexico at the turn of the century, Reyes' views were in conflict with those of Rubén Darío; he clashed with the renowned thinker Miguel de Unamuno and the novelist Pío Baroja in the Spain of the 1910s and 1920s; with the *americanista* models of José Vasconcelos and the US writer Waldo Frank in 1930s Argentina and Brazil; and with the new archaeology and anthropology of Alfonso Caso and Fernando Ortiz in the 1940s. Through all those phases, Reyes repeatedly harnessed classicism as an interpretive framework to keep the enterprise of

'Culture', as he understood it, in alignment with the liberal state he envisaged and hoped one day to see come to fruition (Conn, 2002).

José Vasconcelos (1882-1959), together with Alfonso Reyes, Pedro Henríquez Ureña and Antonio Caso, had founded Mexico's Greek-inspired *Ateneo de la Juventud* or 'Young People's Athenaeum'. Classicism provided the cultural content of the projects he conceived to improve conditions for the Mexican masses. As secretary of education in the early 1920s, Vasconcelos acted as patron of the Mexican muralist painters and urged that they follow classical themes rather than simply portray Mexican realities (Rochfort, 1998: 33-44). The muralists in the end did not abide by Vasconcelos' aesthetic principles, but their influence can nonetheless be seen in Rivera's *La Creación* (The Creation), a work depicting the nine Greek muses in a largely indigenous setting which occupies centre stage at the *Anfiteatro Simón Bolívar* in Mexico City. Like Reyes, Vasconcelos was responding to European conceptions of Latin America, turning on their heads the primitivising visions of such European thinkers and writers as Chateaubriand and Hegel (Gerbi, 1973).

If Reyes saw himself as re-instrumentalising European models, Vasconcelos, in contrast, imagined a new Latin American culture that would transcend that of Europe and the United States. The important role that the dyad of Rome and Greece played in that vision is evident in his famous 1925 essay, *La raza cósmica* (The Cosmic Race). There Vasconcelos used Rome to characterise Latin America's past, as the Spanish colonial regime had fallen into decline on account of its imitation of Roman imperial models. Greece, on the other hand, conveyed the region's future ascendance, as Pythagoras was set forth as a model for the new Latin American race and Plato's mythical Atlantis was transplanted to the prehistory of the South American continent.

Vasconcelos would later propose a pedagogical function for cinema to counter that of Hollywood, bringing classical music and ballet to the Mexican masses (Conn, 2009). In a prologue to his 1939 screenplay about Simón Bolívar which was never put into production, he envisaged a sound track with German music. But through all the changes in his ideological positions, even during his final alignment with Germany and Italy in the 1930s, Vasconcelos never gave up his claim on classicism: it is significant that his autobiography, first published in 1935, was entitled *Ulises criollo* (Creole Ulysses), more than implicitly likening its subject to the hero of Homer's *Odyssey*.

In the 1920s the archaeologist Alfonso Caso began his celebrated work on Mexico's indigenous culture, which culminated in *El Pueblo del Sol* (People of the Sun) in 1953. Caso produced a paradigm of academic knowledge that fused with the work of the muralists to reorient entirely conceptions of national culture. His books were brought out not only in Spanish but also in English, tapping into the popular interest in Latin American subjects in the United States which was a reflection of the Pan Americanist sentiments prevalent at the time. In response to this and other work on pre-Columbian civilisation, Reyes, after his definitive return to Mexico in 1939, published several works on Hellenic subjects: *Criticism in the Athenian Age* (1941), *Ancient Rhetoric* (1942) and his 1949 translation of the *Iliad* into Spanish (Reyes, 1982), followed by *Greek Religion* and *Greek Mythology* in the 1950s (Reyes, 1956; 1961).

It was not simply that Reyes was reaching his pinnacle as a Hellenist. He was engaging in a kind of culture war, flooding the public sphere with Greek and Roman knowledge that extended across the disciplines to compete with the budding indigenist intellectual movement which national scholarship connected to pre-Columbian excavation had set into motion. From the perspective of someone outside Mexico, this might not seem unusual, given that classical philology loomed large in the international academy as a legacy of the nineteenth-century German *Altertumswissenschaft*. But Reyes was not only participating in that international scholarly tradition: he was also transplanting it; and he affirmed that for Mexico to be modern, it needed to be able to call itself a home to classical philology.

Classical knowledge was certainly a resource for writers in other Latin American countries who were seeking to position their political projects before their respective publics. Their strategic ways of reading the classics were quite different from those prevalent in Britain and the United States, where knowledge of Greece and Rome has tended to be more specialised and academic in nature. Thus the Bolivian intellectual Franz Tamayo, writing in the 1920s, urged his countrymen to look to classical Greece (as well as northern Europe), and not to Spain for the 'energy' to create a new modern work regime incorporating the nation's vast majority indigenous population as artisans (Tamayo, 1979). Tamayo was taking advantage of the recent foundation of the League of Nations, which Bolivia joined at the outset in the hope that the new organisation could help it regain the ports lost to Chile in the War of the Pacific during 1879-1883.

As a final example of the multiple ways in which classical references were deployed, three very different contexts in which Homer provided a model or parallel can be considered. The Venezuelan essayist Mariano Picón Salas compared the 1935 return to Caracas of his intellectual compatriots (exiled during Juan Vicente Goméz' dictatorship) to the homecoming of Odysseus, as well as to the precursor of independence, Francisco de Miranda, in whose life sea voyages had also been important. In a biography of General José de San Martín, *El santo de la espada* (1933), the Argentine writer and scholar Ricardo Rojas likened his subject to Odysseus, highlighting his heroic decision to give up his career in Spain's army to help lead the Independence movement in Río de la Plata. Lastly, the Cuban writer Alejo Carpentier not only evoked the *Iliad* in his 1953 novel, *Los pasos perdidos* (The Lost Steps), but also in a short story, *Semejante a la noche* (Like the Night), that tells of the ravages and arbitrariness of war from the perspective of the ordinary soldiers obliged to follow the bidding of Agamemnon and other heroes who are heedless of their interests.

Classics and Constructions of the Present in the Mid-Twentieth Century

Interactions with European antiquity in later twentieth-century Latin American literature and thought went beyond ennobling analogies or models for nation-building or individual heroism. Classical knowledge could be framed by the present, with an emphasis on the processes by which it was transmitted. In Jorge Luis Borges' stories from the late 1930s and early 1940s, Greece and Rome appear not as points of origin to be revisited, but as entities generated by systems, texts or translations which came in the wake of the nineteenth century.[1]

El tema del traidor y del héroe (The Theme of the Traitor and the Hero), focuses on the symbolic politics of the nation and of nationalism through the example of a fictionalised Ireland. The narrator discovers that his legendary great-grandfather, the founder of the nation, was in fact a traitor, so that the leaders of the rebellion that brought the nation state into existence had to find a way of punishing his ancestor's treachery, while preserving the integrity of his name – which was synonymous with their movement. Having no time to produce a script of their own to act out for the public, they plagiarise *Julius Caesar* and other plays by William Shakespeare, a figure inimical to the rebels' cause. The archive available to the narrator, which initially seemed to be a coherent tradition, drawing from every epoch, turns out to be incomplete and fragmentary. That is apparently prefigured by a reference early in the text to Oswald Spengler.

Spengler's cosmopolitan vision of different historic sites of culture and civilisation, with the latter in decline, inspired the chaotic version of the ancient world portrayed in *La lotería en Babilonia* (The Lottery in Babylon), which was published in *El jardín de senderos que se bifurcan* (The Garden of Forking Paths) (1941). The narrator, who has at one point been a slave as well as a proconsul, relates the development through successive phases of the menacing Babylonian public lottery, which was instituted by the inscrutable logic of a dictatorial elite, to become internalised by civil society as custom

---

1   Jansen (2018) examines the reconfiguration of modern relations to the classical past in Borges' works.

and tradition. *Las ruinas circulares* (Circular Ruins), which appeared in the same 1941 collection, indicates that classical antiquity might be a construct of the present, by relating the story of the relationship of father and son through two shamanic priests. The condition for adult identity and for moving forward in time is the forgetting of one's origins. The sense of an impossible past in the story is in fact achieved by a fusion of modern, indigenous and classical elements in the narrative, which is relayed in a stylised Latinate prose.

A story by Julio Cortázar, *El ídolo de las Cícladas* (The Idol of the Cyclades) (1956), also frames the classical world in a hermeneutic of the present, involving the black market and sexual intrigue, as it prompts reflection on culture, antiquity and modernity. Somoza, a Latin American archaeologist, and the Morands, a French colleague and his wife, have smuggled into France a valuable statue they have found on an excavation in the Greek islands, hoping to profit from it financially. In the context of an uncertain love triangle, Somoza becomes obsessed with transcending the limits of archaeology, a profession defined by the recognition that the past is inescapably mediated by knowledge acquired in the present: his desire is to embody the time and space of the excavated object. As a 'first-world' Parisian, Morand is dismayed by Somoza's talk about his voyage back in time, which the Frenchman dismisses as the unfounded musing of a typical Latin American whose Romantic imagination has overwhelmed him. The ironic end to the story has Morand stunned to find himself face to face with Somoza, who would seem to have broken apart the institution of archaeology by actually turning into the statue. A form of knowledge that exists outside the reason of the European world thus takes its revenge.

There was a rather different engagement with the classical world in the writing of Octavio Paz (1914-1998), for whom it provided a repository of myths, figures, and narrative devices. Alfonso Reyes' institutionalisation of the Greco-Roman culture had made it into a recognisable, if not a prestigious area of knowledge for Mexicans. As a consequence, Paz was less interested in historicising or placing limits on classicism as a single sphere of activity than he was in deploying it to authorise his own interpretation of Mexican history. Like Vasconcelos, he was also a student of Spengler and Arnold Toynbee (see the introductory chapter to this volume), but he interpreted their narratives of decline and new beginnings in a different way. The essays that make up *El laberinto de la soledad* (The Labyrinth of Solitude) (1950) reconstruct Mexican history as a succession of discrete periods, each responsible for its own decline. In *Conquista y colonia* (Conquest and Colony), for example, Paz held that the end of Aztec culture was the result of self-destruction rather than Spanish intervention, its people betrayed by their gods so that it collapsed under its own weight, much as 'Rome and Byzantium sense the seduction of death at the end of their history': ('Roma y Bizancio sienten la seducción de

la muerte al final de su historia' Paz, 1997: 120). Octavio Paz did not identify colonial society with the Spanish regime either, representing Mexico's
'Catholic period' as one of community and wholeness until it entered into
decline; and finally Mexico, with its liberal reforms of the 1850s and 1860s,
experienced a rupture with its past, prematurely entering modernity.

The consequence of plunging from the old order into the new, was, according to Paz, an ongoing struggle to build institutions to remake a society
which has no more than two subject positions: that of the powerful and
that of the powerless. In *Los hijos de la Malinche* (The Sons of La Malinche),
Paz outlined this idea of a world without moral confines and resorts to
classicism to show that the father who violates – the central thesis in Paz'
socio-psychological account of Mexican history and society – was not unique
to the country, but had its equivalents in male figures from the Greek, Roman
and Judeo-Christian traditions:

> Este aspecto – Jehová colérico, Dios de ira, Saturno, Zeus violador de
> mujeres – es el que aparece casi exclusivamente en las representaciones
> populares que se hace el mexicano del poder viril. (Paz, 1997: 104)

> This aspect – choleric Jehovah, the God of wrath, Saturn, Zeus the vio-
> lator of women – is what appears almost exclusively in popular repre-
> sentations and turns into the powerful Mexican male.

Finally, in his *Critique of the Pyramid* (1969), drawing on previous comparisons
of the ancient culture of Tula in Mexico to that of Greece, Octavio Paz took up
the conventional opposition between the Greek and the Roman. He likened
the Aztec empire to Rome, akin to modern Mexico under the PRI (Institu-
tional Revolutionary Party); while his comparison of the pre-Aztec city states
to ancient Hellenic polities conveyed his desire for a liberal order, defined by
dialogue and openness.

Dislocation of Classicism in the Late Twentieth Century

Even towards the end of the twentieth century, classical references continued
to be highly visible in Latin American literature – not least in two of its most
renowned proponents in the Anglophone world: Roberto Bolaño (1953–2003)
and Gabriel García Márquez (1927–2014). Both those novelists though, much
like Borges and Cortázar, present the Greco-Roman world at a remove.
Bolaño, in his novel *Nocturno de Chile* (By Night in Chile) (2000), provides
his readers with a parodic vision of classicism among Chile's cultural elites
before the military coup of 1973. A versatile, if repressed, Chilean intellectual
who had been a literary critic and priest in the course of his career, speaks in

the highly refined diction of his erudite *persona* as his life draws to its end. In what amounts to a deathbed confession, he reveals everything, including his scorn for the Chilean popular classes. He recounts the personal crisis he experienced in 1970 when Salvador Allende was elected president and Pablo Neruda was honoured with the Nobel Prize for literature and how he coped with it: he returned to the classics, in particular Homer, immersing himself in his reading for three years until his 'nightmare' was ended by the *coup d'état* of 11 September 1973.

There is no general opposition to learning in Bolaño's fiction: the novels are populated by writers and intellectuals who are interested in art and litera-ture, low and high genres alike, and who are far from reactionary. His novel *Estrella distante* (Distant Star) comments on a notable classicising tendency in Latin America – the tradition of using Greek and Roman given names. The narrator, like Bolaño, is an exiled Chilean writer residing in Barcelona. He comments on the propensity of revolutionaries in Central America to adopt the names of Greek gods and heroes. He wonders if the character Stein could have taken a *nom de guerre* like 'Comandante Patroclo' or 'Comandante Héctor' – monikers that strike the narrator as ridiculous and perhaps as vainglorious as the causes for which those who hold them are champions. Yet such revolutionaries were members of the lost generation of the 1960s and 1970s to whom Bolaño pays tribute (1996: 70).

There are moments in *El general en su laberinto* (The General in his Labyrinth) (1989) in which Gabriel García Márquez addresses his fictional Simón Bolívar's relationship to classicism, but his connection to ancient writers is not reified: Bolívar is just presented as a voracious reader with an extraordinary ability to quote from the works he knew, whose scribes checked his citations meticulously, going back to the books he had acquired and read. The story purports to illustrate something of the way in which Bolívar's texts were collectively authored: it is related that if those writings contained any mistakes, he would not speak to the guilty party for days (García Márquez, 2003: 63-64, 99-100). García Márquez does not seem to have attached any foundational value to Bolívar's statements drawing on the classical world, and he certainly took no interest in reviving or addressing the role of classicism in Colombian history: Miguel Antonio Caro, a major conservative thinker and president of Colombia in the late nineteenth century had envisaged a strong centralised Catholic state informed by Bolívarian principles and traditional classical culture (Rodríguez, 2010).

Envoi

It is appropriate that this chapter should end, as it began, with Simón Bolí-var. Many, like Caro, have anchored their projects in Bolívar's statements, and continue to do so. In Venezuela, after the dictatorship of Juan Vicente Gómez, members of the liberal elites trawled through Bolívar's writings for references to Rome and Greece in an attempt to construct a classical tradition. Bolívar's legacy – including his own manipulations of ancient history – has also provided a platform for various agendas involving classicism beyond Latin America. His long engagement with Rome and Greece has enhanced the significance of ancient political models, and continues to provide an arena for Latin America in world history.

The political historian Anthony Pagden, for instance, concluded his *Lords of All the World: Ideologies of Empire in Spain, Britain and France* (1995) by considering Bolívar's classicism in a way which is itself ideological. Pagden set Simón Bolívar and George Washington in opposition, to characterise the contrast between Spanish American history and Anglo-American history respectively. Pagden is critical of Bolívar who, unlike Washington, did not disband his army and who, in his *Angostura Address* of 1819, proposed a social model based on education, virtue and morality (Bolívar, 1942). The Latin American nations of Bolívar's Gran Colombia were thus shaped by concepts that were markedly Roman. Washington, on the other hand, inclined the former British colonies to fashion their union on the multi-state model of Athens – and in relation to commerce. In the 1990s, when Pagden was making this distinction between Anglo-America and Latin America, neo-liberal tendencies were according primary importance to markets, and the privileging of commerce had far more appeal than old regime notions of national virtues and expansion.

But Bolívar did advocate the free market in his *Carta de Jamaica* – that was highlighted for instance by Rufino Fombona Blanco in his attacks on the Venezuelan dictator Gómez in the early 1900s. Simón Bolívar's writings have of course been parsed and interpreted in countless and contradictory ways. Anthony Pagden's particular characterisation is of interest because through classicism it confers a stable value on Bolívar, in order to make a general claim about Latin American identity. A dichotomy between Rome and Greece served Pagden's ends, just as similar dichotomies had served those of Vasconcelos, Paz and many others.

To subscribe to an apparently authoritative application of classicism to Latin America, whether by Anthony Pagden or by Alfonso Reyes (Reyes' works were intended to stand as a repository of classical knowledge), impedes recognition of classicism's wider importance in the region, and makes its protean nature in political discourse much less discernible. Classicism has always been ideological, remaining a malleable resource for cultural and political actors as they conceive and execute their varied projects of state formation and identity definition.

References

Bartosik-Vélez, E. (2016) 'Simón Bolívar's Rome'. *International Journal of the Classical Tradition*. [www document]. URL https://link.springer.com/article/10.1007/s12138-016-0428-0 [accessed 23 June 2018].

Bolaño, R. (1996) *Estrella distante*. Editorial Anagrama: Barcelona.

Bolaño, R. (2000) *Nocturno de Chile*. Editorial Anagrama: Barcelona.

Bolívar, S. (1942) *Carta de Jamaica and Discurso de Angostura in El pensamiento vivo de Simón Bolívar* ed. R. Blanco Fombona. Editorial Losada: Buenos Aires.

Borges, J. L. (1987) *Ficciones*. Alianza Editorial, S.A: Madrid.

Calinescu, M. (1987) *Five Faces of Modernity: Modernism, Avant-Garde, Decadence, Kitsch, Postmodernism*. Duke University Press: Durham.

Carpentier, A. (1958) *Guerra del tiempo*. Compañia General de Ediciones: Mexico.

Caso, A. (1953) *El pueblo del sol*. Fondo de Cultura Económica: Mexico City.

Conn, R. T. (2002) *The Politics of Philology: Alfonso Reyes and the Invention of the Latin American Literary Tradition*. Bucknell University Press: Lewisburg.

Conn, R. T. (2009) 'Vasconcelos as Screenwriter: Bolívar Remembered' in L. Egan and M. Long (eds.) *Mexico Reading the United States*. Vanderbilt University Press: Nashville.

Cortázar, J. (1995) *Final del juego*. Grupo Anaya, S.A: Madrid.

Darío, R. (1931) *Cantos de vida y esperanza*. C. Bouret: Paris.

García Márquez, G. (2003) *El general en su laberinto*. Random House Mondadori: Barcelona.

Gerbi, A. (1973) *The Dispute of the New World: the History of a Polemic, 1750-1900* (trans. J. Moyle). University of Pittsburgh Press: Pittsburgh, [Italian original 1955].

Inés de la Cruz, Sor Juana (2009) *Sor Juana. The Answer/La Respuesta* (ed. and trans. E. Arenal and A. Powell). The Feminist Press at the City University of New York: New York.

Jansen, L. (2018) *Borges' Classics. Global Encounters with the Graeco-Roman Past*. Cambridge: Cambridge University Press.

Larrazábal, F. (1866) *Correspondencia general del libertador Simón Bolívar*. Eduardo O. Jenkins: New York.

Lynch, J. (2006) *Simón Bolívar: A Life*. Yale University Press: New Haven.

Martí, J. (1985) *Nuestra América*. Biblioteca Ayacucho: Caracas.

Pagden, A. (1995) *Lords of All the World: Ideologies of Empire in Spain, Britain and France, c.1500 – c.1800*. Yale University Press: New Haven.

Paz, O. (1997) *El laberinto de la soledad y otras obras*. Penguin Group: New York.

Picón Salas, M. (1983) *Viejos y nuevos mundos*. Caracas: Biblioteca Ayacucho.

Reyes, A. (1956) *Obras completas, II*. Fondo de Cultura Económica: Mexico City.

Reyes, A. (1961) *Obras completas, XIII*. Fondo de Cultura Económica: Mexico City.

Reyes, A. (1964) *Obras completas, XVI*. Fondo de Cultura Económica: México City.

Reyes, A. (1982) *Ilíada* in *Obras completas, XIX*. Fondo de Cultura Económica: México City.

Richard, C. J. (2009) *The Golden Age of the Classics in America: Greece, Rome and the Antebellum United States*. Harvard University Press: Cambridge, MA.

Rochfort, D. (1998) *Mexican Muralists. Orozco, Rivera, Siqueiros*. Chronicle Books: San Francisco.

Rodó, J. E. (1967) *Ariel*. Cambridge University Press: Cambridge.

Rodríguez, J. M. (2010) *The City of Translation: Poetry and Ideology in Nineteenth-Century Colombia*. Palgrave MacMillan: New York.

Rojas, F. (1970) *El santo de la espada*. Campano: Buenos Aires.

Sarmiento, D. F. ([1845] 1981) *Facundo: civilización y barbarie*. Editorial Losada: Buenos Aires.

Sarmiento, D. F. (1850) *Recuerdos de provincia*. No publisher stated: Santiago.

Sarmiento, D. F. (2006) *Facundo: Civilization and Barbarism* (trans. K. Ross). University of California Press: Berkeley CA.

Spengler, O. (1932) *The Decline of the West*. A. A. Knopf: New York.

Tamayo, F. (1979) *Obra escogida*. Biblioteca Ayacucho: Caracas.

Vasconcelos, J. (2015) *La raza cósmica*. Editorial Porrúa: Mexico City.

Winterer, C. (2004) *The Culture of Classicism: Ancient Greece and Rome in American Intellectual Life (1780–1910)*. Johns Hopkins University Press: Baltimore.

10

Classical Motifs in Spanish American Nation-Building: Looking Beyond the Elites

NICOLA MILLER

The historical sources for the wars of Spanish-American independence are steeped in classical references (Taboada, 2014). Public figures of all shades of political opinion deployed examples from the ancient Mediterranean past in order to make comparisons, analogies or contrasts to elucidate their own evolving visions of the American future. Classically styled portraits of the heroes of liberation depicted a direct link between the Americas and classical legacies, which were no longer to be mediated by European representations. In a period of rapid political change, classical culture provided a shared repertoire of knowledge which helped to create the conditions of possibility for debate. Some individuals went so far as to argue that not only the leaders but also the people of the new countries of Spanish America were potentially the equals of their classical forebears. These self-proclaimed moderns in search of ancients attempted to cut through all the competing American myths of origin – whether rooted in the pre-Columbian civilisations, the moment of encounter, or the French and US revolutions. Instead their vision conserved a link to European civilisation but at its earliest phase, in antiquity – long before the colonial connection had been made.

That was why the cleric Francisco Castañeda extravagantly hailed the sons of Argentina as the equals of 'sons of Mars and Minerva', who could have been 'educated by Apollo in the forge of Vulcan' and would become 'the Athenians, the Spartans, the Romans' of the future, 'if we […] form them in the same […] mould' (Castañeda, [1815] 1868: 289–290). Across the continent, the public ceremonies of commemoration held soon after independence adopted versions of classical garb, rhythm and form (Earle, 2002). In the subsequent struggles over how to constitute new political communities, the claim that ancient ideals of virtue could ultimately be realised and renewed in the Spanish-speaking Americas was a rare point of agreement. To borrow a phrase from one of the didactic textbooks of patriotic history known as *catecismos* or 'catechisms', it was as if Cicero and Maecenas were the classical godparents of the modern republic (Sota, 1850).

This founding claim about the relevance of Old World classical civilisations to the potential splendour of the New World continued to resonate in public debates throughout the nineteenth century, even as later generations criticised both the general interest of independence leaders in all things classical and the specifics of many of their precise comparisons. Pre-Columbian civilisations were compared to ancient Greece and Rome by statesmen from all over the Americas; creole writers of *historia patria* sought to 'nationalise' both the classical and the indigenous pasts (Earle, 2007; Laird, 2007, 2010). Through a repertoire of classical references that was shared across political divides, the ruling creoles inserted their new republics into a framework of comparative world history as a means of containing conflicts about potential identities.

Most of the existing work on classical legacies in Spanish American nation-building has focused on the epic poetry, history writing and political thought produced by celebrated individuals such as Simón Bolívar, Andrés Bello or José Martí. Yet it is worth emphasising the sheer range of sites where classical images were visible in nineteenth-century Latin America: on public buildings, monuments and statues; in civic ceremonies from commemorations of independence to school prize-days; in school textbooks of history and grammar; in patriotic poetry and drama; and in the materials for training military officers. Classical forms were woven into the texture of public life. They appeared in popular handbooks of arts, crafts, industry and agriculture that sold in large numbers; and in the widely distributed manuals of good conduct – '*mens sana in corpore sano* (a healthy mind in a healthy body)' and '*aer pabulum vitae* (air is the food of life), (or, more idiomatically, fresh air is good for you), as the ancients used to say' (Constancin, 1900: 10, 20). Classical figures often featured on the covers of illustrated magazines and they were the adornment of choice for the encyclopaedias, albums and almanacs published not only as weighty tomes for the wealthy but also in cheap editions of extracts for everyone else.

This chapter looks beyond elite culture to explore a variety of classical references in popular poetry, sayings and songs. If the full extent of classical presences and their significance to creole nation-building has yet to be understood, it is even more intriguing to explore their role in sources that were not produced by educated creoles. Most of my material is from the second half of the nineteenth century, because more ephemeral printed matter survives from that period than from the early republican years. It was also the age when oral popular culture began to be recorded by linguists and ethnographers using modern techniques. Classical references in these sources tend to be fragmentary or even isolated – a few words here, an image there – but they can only have been introduced in the expectation that they would mean something to their audience. In some cases, they seem to be echoes or adaptations of creole discourse, which in itself is revealing about the success of creole nation-builders in disseminating classical origin myths. In other cases, however, the evidence suggests that marginalised groups deployed classical references both to debate and dispute creole visions of the future of their nations, just as excluded groups sometimes managed to secure legal rights by turning the elites' liberal values against them (Mallon, 1995; Thomson, 1991, 1999). Three themes have emerged: language; liberty; and learning.

Language

Historians have tended to focus on a learned minority who were able to read classical texts, instinctively applying post-Enlightenment canons of interpretation. Far less attention has been paid to an important reality: most people in the Catholic Americas encountered Latin in church liturgy or at Sunday school. The religious orders which ran most of the elementary schools in Latin American countries until at least the late nineteenth century continued to teach Latin. The minority of people attending these schools often did so only intermittently, but they came from more diverse social backgrounds than is always acknowledged. It is also notable that when state schools for artisans were established during the late nineteenth century, basic Latin was included in the syllabus, not least as a means of inculcating the rudiments of grammar. From the mid-nineteenth century onwards, successful textbooks written to help teach children reading and writing included words or short phrases in Latin and used the names of ancient heroes or places as instructive examples. Many people, at least in urban areas, would have thus encountered snippets of Latin in their everyday lives.

A study by the early twentieth-century Chilean ethnographer Ramón A. Laval provides some evidence of the occurrence in popular speech of 'no small number of phrases, expressions and sayings in Latin [that is] more or less macaronic', '*más o menos macarrónico*' (Laval, 1927: 4). He drew on various earlier collections of proverbs, songs and stories dating back to the 1850s, citing examples from Argentina, Brazil, Peru, Cuba, Mexico, and Honduras as well as material he had collected himself in Chile. His stated purpose was to reinforce Sarmiento's claim: 'We have nothing that we can call our own […] Even our vices are European, are Spanish' (1927: 41–42). Laval's work therefore has to be understood as a contribution to the *hispanista* argument that the identity of Chile – and by extension of other Latin American nations – was actually Spanish. However, at least some of the texts he collected indicated the existence of alternative possibilities, not least because he tended to classify 'souvenirs of the colonial period' as Spanish transfers rather than American creations (1927: 4).

Some of his examples must have required a basic knowledge of Latin grammar, but others could have been constructed from phrases familiar from the liturgy. Parodies of, or wordplays on, scripture were common and, as he noted, some of them were probably widely shared across the Spanish-speaking world. Others, he argued, were undeniably Chilean. For example, a parody of a beatitude from the Sermon on the Mount:

> Beati indiani quia manducant charquicanem (Laval, 1927: 6)
>
> Blessed are the Indians because they eat *charquicán*

refers to the *charquicán* stew found only in Chile (1927: 6-7). Similarly, it would be said of someone who took a choice morsel of food without asking:

> – *Aleluya*, dijo el cura
> por comerse las hallullas.
> – El sacristán dijo *amén*
> por ayudarle también. (Laval, 1927: 13)

> 'Hallelujah' said the priest before eating the Communion rolls.
> The sacristan said 'Amen' before helping him [to eat] them too.

Again, this refrain must have been of Chilean derivation, because *hallullas* are a speciality of Chilean baking, rather like a cross between a bread roll and a scone (1927: 13). Laval listed many other cases of liturgical Latin mixed with local Spanish to create plays on words.

Snippets of Latin were often used to signify something difficult to achieve. Another popular saying from Chile:

> Quis vel qui, los burros no pasan de aquí (Laval, 1927: 5)
>
> *Quis* or *qui*, the idiots can go no further

involves a common obstacle for the Latin learner: distinguishing between the interrogative pronoun *quis*, 'who?', and the relative pronoun in its masculine form, *qui* 'he who'. This expression seems to indicate that some people are incapable of advancing beyond a certain point but it may also evoke Christ's dictum in the Gospel that it is easier for a camel to pass through the eye of a needle than for a rich man to enter the kingdom of God (1927: 5).

Latin grammar is directly made an explicit theme in the well-known tale of the bishop and the wine, which is as follows. A bishop renowned for his wisdom went to visit one of the priests in his diocese, who was famous for his fine wine cellar. At lunch, a wine was served that was not at all good, and the bishop, on tasting it, pronounced it *vinum bona*. The priest was taken aback at the bishop's lack of knowledge of Latin adjectival endings, but he pretended not to notice. At dinner, the wine was good, but it was not of the best, and the bishop declared it *vinum bonus*. Again, the priest was astonished at how such a celebrated bishop could be prone to make such an error in Latin. At last, at supper, the wine served was exquisite: *vinum bonum* proclaimed the prelate, congratulating the priest. The next day, as they were saying good-bye, the priest plucked up the courage to ask his bishop why he had said first *vinum bona*, then *vinum bonus*, then finally the correct *vinum bonum*. 'My friend', replied the bishop, '*sicut vinum ita latinum*: as it is with the wine, so it is with the Latin' (1927: 40).

Laval's material, of which I have included only a small, indicative selection here, draws on collections of popular linguistic usage from across Latin America, and Spain. Even so, it suggests that during the late nineteenth century, Latin was still an important element in vernacular Spanish (one element among many others, notably indigenous languages and those of immigrant groups). It reminds us of the persistent presence of the Catholic Church in the everyday experience of many people in the Spanish American republics during the nineteenth century, a presence which is still too often only discussed in terms of formal Church/State relations. It also alerts us to an unexplored aspect of the role of classical languages in the debates about language that were so significant to nation-making during the nineteenth century (Rivas Sacconi, 1949; Deas, 1993; Jaksić, 2001).

Liberty

One intriguing case of the use of classical references to question the nature of the liberty that was so often proclaimed by Republican leaders comes from the work of Gabriel de la Concepción Valdés (1809–1844), a poet of mixed Afro-Cuban and Spanish parentage, who was known as Plácido (the name by which he signed his poems). Plácido became famous throughout Cuba and beyond from the 1830s onwards, with multiple editions and translations of his work printed, in New York, Mexico City and Paris as well as Havana. His poetry ranged widely in theme and purpose – from eulogies commissioned by members of the colonial ruling class to lyrical denunciations of tyranny and oppression.

Few details are known of Plácido's life. He came from a poor background and earned his basic living as a craftsman, but he achieved success as a poet at the age of seventeen and thereafter became part of a lively literary community with transnational connections. As a mixed-race illegitimate child he had little formal education, but that was offset by a succession of apprenticeships, first to an artist's studio and then to one of the printing workshops that served as centres of cultural life in Havana at that time. He probably first learnt about the classical world during his time with the artist Vicente Escobar (1757–1834), a successful portrait-painter trained at the Real Academia de Bellas Artes de San Fernando in Madrid. Indeed, the teaching of drawing, which was a prominent feature of most nineteenth-century education and training in Spanish America, was one of the often overlooked routes by which classical images were disseminated, because the main method was copying from prints, which were often classical or classicised. Plácido had opportunities to extend his knowledge further after moving to the province of Matanzas in 1826, when success in a poetry improvisation contest brought him celebrity and invitations to attend the *tertulias* (gatherings convened to discuss cultural issues) held by a local patron of the arts, Domingo del Monte (1804–1853). The poetry competitions themselves had a markedly classical flavour: participants were dressed up as the nine muses with an Apollo to present the prizes.

Over the next fifteen years, rapidly expanding sugar production, which doubled the slave population in Matanzas, enabled the region to support a thriving cultural scene and Plácido became one of a number of successful Afro-Cuban writers and artists. But in 1844, in the context of accumulating pressures to end slavery and an upsurge in slave revolts, several prominent free black Cubans were targeted by colonial officials, who saw them as the potential leaders of an organised anti-slavery movement. On the pretext of the so-called Escalera Conspiracy, thousands of free blacks and slaves were arrested, hundreds exiled, 78 executed and several hundred more died from torture. Plácido was tried on the charge of joining a conspiracy against white people, sentenced to death despite the lack of evidence against him, and executed (Arias, 2009; Willey, 2010).

The intriguing question about Plácido's work is why so many of his political poems included classical references. The need to evade censorship could be one factor. This could well apply to two powerful complementary sonnets against tyranny: one, 'Muerte de Gesler', the other 'Muerte de César', in which parallels are drawn between William Tell and Brutus as embodiments of the true patriotism that cannot bear to see a homeland deprived of liberty (Concepción Valdés, 1904: 23, 138). But these two examples of heroic assassinations so remote in time and place can be interpreted on another level as a call for contemporary resistance in Cuba to the oppression of slavery and colonial rule. As Plácido did not always date his poems, it is not possible to establish the precise context in which the poem about the death of Caesar was written. There are a few oddities in the text (for example, Brutus is referred to as 'conqueror of Pontus', when it was Pompey who defeated Mithridates), but the general force of it is powerfully clear. Brutus' slaying of Caesar is represented as making it possible for the homeland to break free of its chains by toppling despotic monarchical rule and founding a republic. In the first stanza a personification of Rome issues a desperate lament:

> En cadenas mis palmas se han trocado,
> En pesares mis dichas y en afrentas
> Y nadie osado restaurarme intenta
> […] el esplendor pasado. (Concepción Valdés, 1904: 138)

> My palms have become chains,
> My joys sorrows and insults
> And nobody bold tries to restore me
> To past splendour […].

Brutus then arrives, 'con torvo ceño y ademan airado' (with a grim frown and angry gestures), poised to deliver the fatal blow to the tyrant, and addresses Rome with these words:

> Depon, ¡oh patria! el ominoso luto,
> Un hijo tienes que el acero vibre;
> Hoi muere César, o perece Bruto:
> Mientras exista yo, tú serás libre.

> Shake off, oh fatherland, this dreadful mourning,
> You have a son pulsating with steel;
> Today Caesar dies, or Brutus perishes:
> While I exist, you shall be free.

Plácido's classical references in several poems constitute a symbolic stand against colonialism and slavery. By force of association he lent dignity to the oppressed people of Cuba: a sugar worker was compared to Achilles; a peasant woman to the ancient Greek poet Corinna; a villager to Trajan (Amunátegui, 1858: 532; Concepción Valdés, 1904: 110–112, 160–161, 156). The poet proclaimed that he could tread the length of Greece's shores ('Yo de la Grecia pisaré las playas') without finding heroes equal to the working people of Cuba (Concepción Valdés, 1904: 112). In a poem attacking the poverty of the primary education available on the island, 'La escuela del diablo' ('The Devil's School'), he invoked the mythological judge Rhadaman-thus to refer to the wisdom and judgement that had been abandoned in schools where instead of learning 'artes u oficios', 'useful trades', children were trained only to become 'esbirros y picapleitos', 'minions and crooked lawyers' (Concepción Valdés, 1904: 204–205). In one of his last poems, 'A mi amigo Dóris (en la prisión)', 'To my Friend Dóris (from prison)', he likened his own fate to that of Lucretia, the mythical Roman woman whose rape triggered the revolt that overthrew the monarchy and led to the founding of the Roman republic. He also evoked Zenobia, queen of Palmyra, who led an uprising against the Romans in the third century AD (Concepción Valdés, 1904: 144–146). He repeatedly claimed for himself and his own people, the excluded and repressed blacks and *mulatos* of a slave society, the legitimacy of a horror of tyranny dating back to ancient times:

> Como en las aras del supremo Jove,
> Juró Asdrúbal rencor a los romanos,
> Y los mostró de Marte la fiereza;
> Yo ante el Dios de la gran naturaleza
> Odio eterno he jurado a los tiranos.
> (Concepción Valdés. 1904: 338–341)

> As on the altars of the supreme Jove,
> Hasdrubal swore bitterness towards the Romans,
> And showed them the ferocity of Mars;
> So I, before the great God of Nature,
> Have sworn eternal hatred of tyrants.

Plácido's classical references would have had a particular resonance in Cuba during the 1830s because José María Heredia (1803–1839) had already established Greece as a paradigm for the island's struggle for independence.[1] The Greek War of Independence against the Ottoman Empire (1821–1832) was widely interpreted by Philhellenes across Europe and the Americas as heralding a revival of the greatness of classical culture. In Cuba, where independence movements were repressed with increasing ferocity by a Spanish monarchy determined to hold on to its wealthy colony, many poets adopted a neoclassical style which enhanced parallels with events in Greece (García Marruz, 1978: 20; Miranda Cancela, 2015: 80–81).

Both Concepción Valdés himself and his admirers took steps to locate his work in this tradition where culture and politics converged in quest of liberation. Plácido's first biographer, writing in the midst of the first military struggle for Cuban independence, known as the Ten Years' War (1868–1878), recounted Heredia's legendary meeting with Plácido on his brief return from exile in 1836. Seeking him out in his workshop, Heredia was moved by his poverty, and offered to pay for him to go to Mexico. The tale is deemed improbable by contemporary scholars, but what is beyond doubt is that Plácido dedicated an elegy to Heredia to mark his death in 1839, thereby staking

---

1   See Miranda Cancela's chapter in this volume.

his own claim to the connections between antiquity and modernity forged by the far more privileged, classically educated Heredia (Méndez, 2015: 31–34).

In sum, Plácido's deployment of classical references constitutes a social deepening of their use as a channel for transmitting particular local experience into universal experience and vice versa. In the still colonial, slave economy of Cuba of the 1830s, the classical past provided a popular poet with the tools to communicate his vision of a homeland in which freedom could be for the many not the few.

Learning

The popular poetry of Argentina and Chile from the late nineteenth and early twentieth centuries contains some highly charged classical references. Daniel Meneses (1855–1909), a celebrated popular poet from Chile, and Gabino Ezeiza (1858–1916), an Afro-Argentine balladeer, who composed several famous *milongas*, provide two examples. Both of them introduced classical terms as touchstones for what constituted authentic knowledge for people outside of the learned minority. From being a medium *of* learning, the classics became, in their work, a metaphor *for* learning, with all its contradictory possibilities of inclusion and exclusion.

As had been the case with Plácido, both of these men suffered economic hardship, but secured access to extensive cultural and political networks which offered alternatives to formal education. Meneses, who was from a family of agricultural labourers, seems to have acquired his knowledge of poetry, music and song travelling around the northern mining areas. From the age of fifteen onwards, he sang and recited his poems, which were also distributed *en pliego* (printed on a single sheet of paper) (Navarrete and Palma, 2008). This was during the 1870s and 1880s, when workers' organisations were beginning to support publications, cultural events and educational initiatives. He later settled in the cosmopolitan port of Valparaíso, where he denounced the massacre of dock workers after the strike of 1903. He became a sensation in 1907, when 18,000 copies were printed of his poem about the execution of French-born adventurer, Émile Dubois, a serial murderer and Robin Hood figure who was a hero of popular legend.

Meneses' undated poem 'La ignorancia de populares i Literatos' is an attack on both literary poets and those popular poets who tried to emulate their style. 'In Chile' – the poem opens, establishing the national context right at the start – 'los rimadores' ('rhyme-merchants') were sprouting up everywhere 'como callampas' (like mushrooms) (Navarrete and Palma, 2008: 337). Although they went about assiduously polishing their lyrics, neither they nor the critics in the learned reviews understood anything about poetry, declared the second stanza. Some explicit comments follow about the use of classical allusion by these second-rate *literati*. First, none of them could mention a star without turning it into a classical reference, because otherwise the critics would turn upon them:

> Si uno en versos nombra un astro
> No siendo flor a mi Vesta
> Luego se lo contrarresta
> Con el mismo el criticastro (Navarrete and Palma, 2008: 337).

> If anyone in verse gives a star a name
> Other than 'A Flower to my Vesta',
> Then as an immediate counter
> A fussy critic suggests the very same.

Vesta symbolises an inappropriate use of the classical past as faddish ornamentation grafted onto nationalist sentiment. The poet then complains that an Athenaeum for the people which is supposed to be a centre of wisdom ('centro de sabiduría') has become the very opposite: those that frequent it are fools. Under the illusion that they are the voice of the people, they turn what was beautiful into something ugly. These nationalists thought they were doing their patriotic duty by singing the praises of Chile, but in fact they were undermining the country with their inferior work, to the point where the most enlightened and wise person would lose his mind ('al sabio más ilustrado/Le hace perder la cabeza'). Thus the *Ateneo*, as a symbol of culture for all, echoes independence-era claims of a connection between classical institutions of culture and the potential for full realisation of modern republican ideals in the Americas. Such radical democratic possibilities had long been circumscribed by the practices of the elites but were being revived at the time Meneses was writing by the endeavours of the organised labour movement. Thus, even though there are only two classical words in this poem, its whole force depends upon them.

Finally, there is a contrast in the last stanza, between 'el sabio más ilustrado' ('the most erudite wise man') and 'yo en mi conocimiento' ('I in my knowledge') that seems to be analogous to José Martí's contrast between 'false erudition' and 'nature', that is: understanding derived from experience. Unsurprisingly, Meneses' own patriotic poetry was virtually devoid of classical references (Navarrete and Palma, 2008: 301–316). That enabled him to set his work in contrast to the artificial neoclassicism of the poetasters he opposed.

Gabino Ezeiza, whose father had been killed in 1867 fighting in the war against Paraguay, grew up in the San Telmo district of Buenos Aires, where most of the Afro-Argentine population of the city lived. He began his career as a poet working for one of the periodicals published by Afro-Argentines and continued to work as a literary editor for others. He forged strong connections in Montevideo, where he went to perform in 1884. Like many musicians he was politically active, and expanded his range of contacts throughout the River Plate area.

Classical images are also to be found lodged in the lyrics of Gabino Ezeiza (1893). For example, in 'Gratitud', the poet emphasises that he has never ever profaned the temple of Apollo: the allusion to Horace, *Odes* 3.1 (I hate the profane crowd and keep them far away, I, the Muses' priest …) could imply that he has not sought inspiration from the muses of European culture, but from the triumphs of a friend, to whom the poem is dedicated. It is these experiences that gave him consolation and enabled his inspiration to take flight again. The poet expresses the fear that if he enters the temple he will be so dazzled by glory that he might 'olvidar la historia/Del linaje que yo soy' ('forget the history of the lineage from which I come') and thereby lose sight of his vocation: roaming the world and playing his lute to convey the pain and sorrow of slavery and oppression. While the final stanza recalls the contrast between the Tree of Life and the Tree of Knowledge in the biblical book of Genesis, it also evokes the classical *locus amoenus*, which is rejected in favour of an itinerant lifestyle ending only in the poet's grave. Finally, in his most famous song, 'Saludo a Paysandú' ('My Greeting to Paysandú'), Ezeiza characterised the city in Uruguay 'the American Troy' for heroically withstanding a siege of forces supported by Brazil in 1864.

Conclusion

There has only been space here to examine a few instances of the use of classical references in popular song and poetry, and it would be premature to make any grand claims about their general significance. Even so, the evidence above is suggestive in several ways. None of these examples can convincingly be seen as cases of *resistance*, either to colonial rule or creole domination, but they do point to the presence of a perhaps rather large area of cultural production that lies, both spatially and temporally, in between the conventional poles of opposition and acceptance. Within that field, which is liable to expand and contract with varying social conditions, conventions can be probed, elite culture subjected to scrutiny, a mirror held up to the gaps between rhetoric and reality, and alternative ways of thinking and seeing expressed. This wider field also creates the context from which more overtly oppositional movements may emerge.

When José Martí in 1891 famously called upon Spanish Americans to reject 'the Greece that is not ours', he nonetheless bore witness to the continuing prominence of the classical repertoire in public culture. Martí argued that modern Spanish American cultures should trace their origins back to 'our own Greece' of the ancient indigenous civilisations, but his views would not become prevalent until well into the twentieth century. Other late nineteenth-century intellectuals revived the notion of a culture of the Americas transmitted directly from the classical world, finding inspiration for their struggles against positivism, materialism and US expansionism in Hellenic ideals.

The Uruguayan José Enrique Rodó has remained the most abidingly influential figure in this respect: his essay *Ariel* (1900) promoted the ephebe as the ideal combination of virtue, aestheticism and spirituality represented by 'Latin' America. The ethereal Ariel was contrasted to the base and bestial Caliban, a thinly disguised metaphor for the 'Anglo-Saxon' United States, which had made a colony of Puerto Rico and a neo-colony of Cuba after defeating Spain in 1898. There is no doubting the impact of Rodó's text: *arielismo* was discussed in popular and labour organisations as well as in the various Athenaeums frequented by students and intellectuals. Yet its appeal is hard to understand without appreciating the ubiquity of images of the classical world in Spanish America, not only in the published texts of the learned minority but also in the wider public spaces in which national and supra-national identities were imagined, embodied and contested. Rodó's ideas landed on fertile ground, partly laid by the persistent, diffuse sense of a connection between the modern republics of the Americas and the ancient worlds of Greece and Rome.

References

Academia Cubana de la Lengua (2015) *Plácido en su bicentenario*. Ediciones Boloña: Havana.

Amunátegui, G. V. (1858) 'Gabriel de la Concepcion Valdes (Plácido)'. *Revista del Pacífico (Valparaíso)* **I**: 453–473 and 517–533.

Arias García, S. (2009) 'Prólogo' in *Poesías escogidas [de] Gabriel Concepción Valdés*. Editorial Letras Cubanas: Havana, 5–30.

Castañeda, F. [1815] (1868) 'Alocución ó arenga patriótica' in J. María Gutiérrez (ed.) *Noticias históricas sobre el oríjen y desarrollo de la Enseñanza Pública Superior de Buenos Aires*. Imprenta del Siglo: Buenos Aires, 287–296.

Concepción Valdés, G. de la (1904) *Poesías de Plácido, nueva edición*. Librería de la Vda de Ch. Bouret: Paris and Mexico City.

Constancin, L. A. (1900) *Manual de urbanidad para el uso de los colegios*. Escuela Tipográfica Salesiana: Valparaíso.

Deas, M. (1993) *Del poder y la gramática: y otros ensayos sobre historia, política y literatura colombianas*. Tercer Mundo: Bogotá.

Earle, R. (2002) '"Padres de la Patria" and the Ancestral Past: Commemorations of Independence in Nineteenth-century Latin America'. *Journal of Latin American Studies* **34**(4): 775–806.

Earle, R. (2007) *The Return of the Native: Indians and Myth-Making in Spanish America, 1810–1930.* Duke University Press: Durham.

Ezeiza, G. (1886) *Cantares criollos.* Maucci y Cia: Buenos Aires.

García Marruz, F. (1978) 'Prólogo' in C. Vitier and F. García Marruz (eds.) *Flor oculta de poesía cubana. siglos xviii y xix,* Vol. **20**. Editorial Arte y Literatura: Havana.

Jaksić, I. (2001) *Andrés Bello: Scholarship and Nation-Building in Nineteenth-Century Latin America.* Cambridge University Press: Cambridge and New York.

Laird, A. (2007) 'Latin America' in C. W. Kallendorf (ed.) *A Companion to the Classical Tradition.* Blackwell: Malden, 222–236.

Laird, A. (2010) 'The Cosmic Race and a Heap of Broken Images: Mexico's Classical Past and the Modern Creole Imagination' in S. A. Stephens and P. Vasunia (eds.) *Classics and National Culture.* Oxford University Press: Oxford, 163–181.

Laval, R. A. (1927) *Del Latín en el Folklore Chileno.* Imprenta Cervantes: Santiago.

Mallon, F. (1995) *Peasant and Nation: The Making of Postcolonial Mexico and Peru.* University of California Press: Berkeley and London.

Méndez, R. (2015) 'Plácido y Herrera' in Academia Cubana de la Lengua (2015), 31–48.

Meneses, D. (n.d.) 'La ignorancia de populares i literatos', *Horrible crimen en Gultro: dos ancianos caen bajo el puñal del asesino.* [www document]. URL http://www.memoriachilena.cl/602/w3marticla-68589.html [accessed 23 June 2018] and in Navarrete A. (2008).

Miranda Cancela, E. (2015) 'Plácido y las anacreónticas'. Academia Cubana de la Lengua (2015): 75–92.

Muñoz, D. (ed.) (1968) *Lira popular: una joya bibliográfica que revela la supervivencia de la juglaría medieval en Chile.* F. Bruckmann EG Verlag: Munich.

Navarrete, A. M. and Alvarado, D. P. (2008) *Los diablos son los mortales. La obra del poeta popular Daniel Meneses.* DIBAM: Santiago.

Rivas Sacconi, J. M. (1949) *El latín en Colombia: Bosquejo histórico del humanismo colombiano.* Instituto Caro y Cuervo: Bogotá.

Sota, J. M. de la (1850) *Catecismo geográfico-político é histórico de la República Oriental del Uruguay.* No publisher stated: Montevideo.

Taboada, H. G. H. (2014) 'Centauros y eruditos. Los clásicos en la independencia'. *Latinoamérica* **59**(2): 193–221.

Thomson, G. (1991) 'Popular Aspects of Liberalism in Mexico, 1848-1888'. *Bulletin of Latin American Research* **10**(3): 265–292.

Thomson, G. (1999) *Politics, Patriotism and Popular Liberalism in Mexico: Juan Francisco Lucas and the Puebla Sierra 1854–1917.* SR Books: Wilmington.

Willey, J. V. (2010) Writing and Rebellion in Plácido's Poetry. Master's thesis, Vanderbilt University. [WWW document]. URL https://etd.library.vanderbilt.edu/available/etd-03312010-152757/unrestricted/MasterThesisJackieWilley.pdf [accessed 18 July 2018].

11

Greece and José Martí

ELINA MIRANDA CANCELA

Cuba remained under Spanish rule throughout the nineteenth century, when nearly all of the countries on the Latin American continent had already secured independence. It was as a consequence of this situation that Greek culture, both ancient and modern, acquired a special significance in the colony. Many Cuban thinkers and writers who dreamt of emancipation and hoped for fundamental social change made abundant use of classical quotations and references in their work. This represented much more than a fad for neoclassicism: Greece was the embodiment of these authors' ideals and aspirations and that was due as much to the modern nation's fight for independence as to its classical heritage.

The words of José Martí (1853-1895), the renowned liberator of Cuba, brought out the connection in an 1889 tribute to José María Heredia, 'the first poet of America' (Martí, 1972: 179)[1]:

> ¿Y la América libre, y toda Europa coronándose con la libertad, y Grecia misma resucitando, y Cuba, tan bella como Grecia, tendida así entre hierros, mancha del mundo, presidio rodeado de agua, rémora de América? (Martí, 1972: 188)

> And a free America, all Europe crowning itself with freedom, and Greece herself in revival, while Cuba, beautiful as Greece, [is still] straining like this in shackles, a stain on the world, a prison surrounded by water, an encumbrance on America?

José María Heredia (1803-1839) had agitated for Cuban independence in the 1820s. Martí echoed his call for liberation in the midst of his own preparations for what he called the 'necessary war' for Cuban independence.[2] This chapter aims to explore ways in which José Martí's vision as a liberator was influenced by his classical formation: a brief account of Martí's education in Cuba

---

1 The 'America' to which Martí referred is what he would come to call *Nuestra América*, 'Our America', in later texts.

2 On 'the necessary war' compare the 9 October 1885 letter to J. A. Lucena (Martí, 1975, 1: 184).

and Spain (I) will be followed by an account of the importance he attached to the didactic value of Greek tragedy (II), and to the role of Greek literature in giving expression to a revolutionary American identity (III).

Jose Martí's Classical Education

By the end of the eighteenth century, Cuba saw an increase of wealth from its sugar cane production and coffee plantations. This new prosperity, in conjunction with French migration from Haiti, led to a radical improvement in the quality of education available to the creole bourgeoisie, in spite of Cuba's status as a colony and the comparatively slow progress of literary studies in Spain.[3] Changes in the curricula, teaching methods and materials, and an increased emphasis on the role of classics in moral discourse and in criticism are all evident from a range of essays and articles from the time. In addition, many translations or imitations of Greek and Latin authors were published in magazines and periodicals, and Greek was introduced to private schools in 1831 even before it formed part of the official curriculum.[4]

The young José Martí first encountered classical Greek and Latin when he attended two schools in Havana in the 1860s: San Anacleto and the San Pablo High School. The principal of San Anacleto was Rafael Sixto Casado, author of a Latin grammar, *Compendio de la gramática latina* (1866), and translator and editor of some works of Roman literature. The head of San Pablo was Rafael María de Mendive, a highly regarded poet of pro-independence sympathies. Even as a teenager, Martí had publicised his own objections to Spanish rule, which led to his deportation to Spain for treason in 1870. It was there, during 1871-1874, that he completed his high school studies and obtained a qualification in law before majoring in Philosophy and Letters in the University of Zaragoza.

Zaragoza was no longer a great centre for intellectual life or politics, but local contacts in Aragón drew Martí there from Madrid. Zaragoza was near enough to the capital and offered an affordable and comfortable haven for a student of limited means, who was still in poor health after a period in captivity. According to Martí's friend Fermín Valdés Domínguez, the University of

---

3   Compare Henríquez Ureña (1960: 603): 'After centuries of difficult and inconsistent work, methods that renewed Spanish scholarship emerged from Germany, introduced by the venerable Don Manuel Milá y Fontanals, to be spread by Don Marcelino Menéndez y Pelayo and his brilliant school'.

4   There also indications that there had been private study of Greek from the end of the eighteenth century. Miranda Cancela and Carbón (1985) survey classical education in Cuba at the time; Miranda Cancela (1995a) treats Martí's studies in Spain.

Zaragoza was 'his home, his Athenaeum and a place of emotional fulfilment' (De Quesada y Aróstegui, 1913, 12: 27). The university had a progressive tradition long before Martí's arrival. Braulio Foz, a leading Aragonese intellectual, had reassumed his chair in Greek at Zaragoza in 1835, after being exiled when Spain's progressive interregnum of the *Trienio liberal* had come to an end in 1823. Foz had reflected on teaching of literature in his *Plan y método para la enseñanza de las letras humanas* (1820) but his most popular work was *Literatura griega* (1849), practically the first history of Greek literature to be written in Spain. Foz' legacy would still have left its mark on Zaragoza when Martí was studying there in the 1870s.

An inaugural address given at the university by the Dean of the Faculty of Philosophy and Letters, Martín Villar y García, in 1868, *Sobre la conveniencia del estudio de los escritores clásicos, griegos y latinos* (The Advantages of Studying Classical Greek and Latin Authors), might also help to explain the pivotal role of the classics in Martí's formation. Such orations, much like Renaissance defences of classical literature, reflected a very contemporary preoccupation with protecting the interests of classical learning and promoting humanistic study (Rubio, 1934: 125-140).

José Martí attained the highest grades in classical literature and Greek. He carefully preserved his papers from Zaragoza when he left Spain to settle in Mexico. Along with notes and reflections on his studies, they contain translations of classical fables, passages of Homer and Hesiod, and Spanish versions of verses attributed to the Greek sixth-century BC lyric poet Anacreon. All of these documents throw important light on the distinctive quality of Martí's classical education. His literary prose translation of Anacreon recalls the style of his 1871 essay *El presidio político en Cuba* (The Political Prison in Cuba), which was published upon his arrival in Spain. The innovative disintegration of the rigid boundaries between prose and verse paralleled developments in Cuban letters, and provides important insights into Martí's conception of the role of literature in political transformation.

The Didactic Value of Greek Tragedy

Some ideas about drama which Martí recorded in his notebooks are comparable to those expressed in an inaugural lecture on Greek theatre delivered in Zaragoza for the 1874-1875 academic year by Andrés Cabañero, a professor at the university. Cabañero noted the power of ancient drama as a tool for the manipulation of public opinion and highlighted the political agenda that underpinned the artistic techniques of Aeschylus in particular: the playwright, in his view, sought to preserve the Greek spirit of identity by promoting unity as a way of safeguarding independence (Cabañero, 1874). Martí very probably attended the lecture: Cabañero's name appears in his notes and he was writing his own drama, *Adultera*, at the time.

Martí held in high esteem all three of the great Athenian tragic poets – Euripides and Sophocles as well as Aeschylus – and he recognised the distinctive characteristics of each. But it seems to have been Aeschylus' tragedy which best met his criteria for what drama should be:

> Que sea la escena teatro en forma artística, sin excluir los magníficos tipos eternos de esas espléndidas aspiraciones y soberbios castigos que levantan y fortalecen a los pueblos: Responden a este concepto en Eschylo. (1975, 15: 103)

> A show should be an artistic form of theatre, which must not exclude the great and eternal archetypes of the noble aspirations and severe punishments that can elevate and strengthen a people: offer a counterpart to this concept in Aeschylus.

That sentiment certainly informed Martí's *Abdala*, which he had composed in verse at the age of sixteen in 1869. The tragic dilemma at the heart of the play is the protagonist's obligation to choose between love for his mother and duty to his *patria* or fatherland – clearly recalling the crux of Aeschylus' *Choephoroe*, in which the young Orestes has to kill his mother Clytemnestra in order to avenge her murder of his father Agamemnon. Like the heroes of classical tragedy, Abdala is conscious of taking a decision that risks his life. But above all, the play highlighted the importance of such a decision for national destiny. Its purpose was to incline its audience to civic action, even though it was set in a remote place and time, just as Aeschylus' plays had been set in a mythical realm far removed from the Athens of the tragedian's own day.

It is no coincidence that 'Orestes' was the *nom de plume* José Martí used for his articles in the *Revista Universal* of Mexico. The convergence between Marti's views on theatre and the practice of Aeschylus became more evident in a play he wrote in Guatemala in 1877. This laid bare the problems of *Nuestra América* (Our [Latin] America), whose history is made of 'terrible tragedies with new twists, of historical significance' ('terribles tragedias, con nuevos e históricos resortes') (1975, 7: 175). This work, entitled *Patria y Libertad*, was not primarily intended as a narrative but as a demonstration of the essential forces in conflict as American history developed. Like Aeschylus' tragedies, it served to provoke reflection on the nature of the struggle.

Moreover, just as in Aeschylus' *Persians*, the central theme was the struggle for independence and justice against a proud and oppressive dominant power. The characters embody such forces in a contest which, as in the Greek play, ended with the parade of the defeated – but here the jubilation of the victors was added too. The tragedy of Aeschylus was not a straightforward model, but it provided a revolutionary author with a vehicle for his notion of *Nuestra América* – a conception which appears to have been expressed for the very first time in this work.

Even as he was preparing for the 'necessary war' for Cuban independence, it appears that Martí had not abandoned his interest in developing a new kind of theatre to address the needs of the American situation. His notes from the late 1880s or early 1890s include the outline of a play entitled *Chac-Moc*:

> Tragedia simbólica de los tiempos presentes. Espíritu del país dormido aparentemente, pero capaz por su propia energía, de surgir y obrar en un momento crítico. (1975, 21: 359)

> Symbolic tragedy for the present time. Spirit of a country apparently asleep but capable of arising and acting at a critical moment on its own momentum.

These words recall his notes from Zaragoza which contained earlier reflections on the political nature of Greek tragedy.

The link Martí established between Aeschylus' conception of tragedy and the kind of theatre required to meet the needs of *Nuestra América* provides a good example of how early he sought to integrate classical culture with his interpretation of the American predicament. Martí's reading of the classics was sometimes profoundly transformed by his understanding of his own environment and political context.

Greek Literature and American Identity

Martí's numerous references to Greco-Roman culture in his writing went far beyond literary fashion. It was not without reason that Martí once thought of writing about his way of understanding ancient writers, as he remarked in his draft papers:

> Y por qué no había yo de publicar, con mi propio modo de ver y lenguaje – una especie de discursos, en pequeños libros, sobre cada uno de los clásicos? En el comentario, suavemente y sin causar fatiga, el argumento. Precedida esta colección de mi discurso general sobre los clásicos. (1975, 18: 283)

> And why should not I publish, with my own way of seeing and in my own style – a kind of essay, in small books, about each of the classics? In

the commentary, gently and without causing fatigue, [I would set out] their argument. Preceding this collection, my general discourse on the classics.

Martí was somewhat critical of the philhellenic idealisation of Greece prevalent in his lifetime and distanced himself from those who contemplated ancient Greek culture as an ideal irretrievably lost – something he asserted in an article (1972: 84) on Oscar Wilde: 'The aesthetes err in their search with their peculiar love for the adoration of the past and for the extraordinary quality of past times'. Martí rather identified with the attitude of the Venezuelan Cecilio Acosta, whose vision of antiquity did not involve being oblivious to the present but prompted consideration of the future (Martí, 1972: 61). Thus, rather than searching nostalgically in the ancient past for beauties or values which were lost, José Martí recommended using the classics to gain a better understanding of the present historical moment:

> No desdeñamos lo antiguo porque acontece que lo antiguo refleja de modo perfecto lo presente, puesto que la vida, varia en forma, es perpetua en esencia, y en lo pasado se ve sin esa 'bruma de familiaridad' o de preocupación que la anubla para los que vamos existiendo en ella. (1972: 82)

> We do not disdain the past insofar as it perfectly reflects the present, since life, which is varied in form, is perpetual in essence; and in the past, life can be seen without that 'fog of familiarity' or anxiety that obscure it for those of us who now exist in it.

As the Cuban critic Juan Marinello pointed out, combinations of the old with the new and of the mythological with the everyday were what characterised Martí's appreciation of antiquity and shaped his idea of literature.[5] Awareness of the inevitable rupture between our own time and earlier tradition does not mean that the latter needs to be discarded. As editor of the *Revista Venezolana*, a periodical which provided a programme for Latin American literary study, Martí defined his approach as follows:

> sacará de lo antiguo cuando sea bueno, y creará lo nuevo cuando sea necesario; no hay por qué invalidar vocablos útiles, ni por qué cejar en la faena de dar palabras nuevas a ideas nuevas. (1975, 7: 212)

---

5   Marinello (1964: 34): '[Martí] takes his lucid and exalted passion to such a level that without ridiculous anachronism, he can not only speak of an ancient Greek in familiar terms but also apply classical epithets to someone working alongside him with the same desire to free his *patria*'.

[to] take something out of antiquity when it is good, and create something new when it is necessary. There is no reason to discard old words that are still useful any more than there is a reason to put an end to the business of coining new words for new ideas.

The thousand or so references to the Greco-Roman world in Martí's own works express his particular way of interpreting contemporary situations.[6] The figure of Sisyphus, for example, served to represent exertion and fatigue as a virtuous remedy for the futile sense of mourning for ills American society was then experiencing (1975, 9: 63). In his reworking of the myth, Martí put an end to Zeus' fruitless punishment of Sisyphus, which he saw as a paradigm for the struggle involved in being human. After carrying the heavy boulder to the top of the hill, Sisyphus is not forced to start again but instead sits triumphantly on the stone 'to take in the sunlight and receive offerings from humankind' (1975, 9: 272).

Even when Martí employed classical references in an apparently conventional way, their context could give them a new meaning. The only classical reference in his collection *Ismaelillo* occurs in the poem *Musa Traviesa* (The Mischievous Muse):

> Cual si en mi hombro surgieran
> Fuerzas de Atlante. (1985, 1: 25)

> As if in my shoulder arose
> the strength of Atlas.

Another Titan, Prometheus, is connected to the vocation of poetry, which in its striving for the impossible, at once embracing and devouring, is compared in 'Haschisch' to the 'vulture as well as to lofty Prometheus' ('buitre a la vez que altivo Prometeo') (1985, 2: 92). But Prometheus' true significance emerges when Martí focused on the forceful inner struggle of one who would dare to steal Zeus' fire for the sake of humankind. Prometheus is, he says, an 'idealistic personification – it makes us look into the depths [...] to see a man in conflict with heaven, like an Ishmael of Greece' ('personificación idealista – nos hace mirar a lo hondo [...] que yo amo más ver un hombre en lucha con el cielo, como Ismael de Grecia') (1975, 19: 427).

Martí did not generally quote directly from Greek and Roman literature or make myths or motifs from the classical tradition the primary subject of his

---

6   The figure can be derived from the onomastic and geographical indices in Martí (1975, 26: 13-470, 473-606).

writing. An exception was an article on Homer's *Iliad* published in *La Edad de Oro*, 'The Golden Age', a magazine for children in Spanish America. The first issue contained Martí's contribution on the *Iliad*, written with the professed aim of helping Cuban boys to become 'men of their time, and men of America' ('hombres de su tiempo, y hombres de América') (1975, 20: 147). As well as introducing young readers to Homer's poem, Martí presented the aspects of it which he believed provided a broader understanding of their own circumstances. On *La última página* (The Last Page) of the first issue of *La Edad de Oro*, Martí summarised the import of each of the preceding 31 pages: children should aim to become as nimble as Meñique (a hero akin to Tom Thumb) and as courageous as Simón Bolívar, but not to be poets in the Homeric style: poetry retains similar functions through the ages, but new times impose new requirements to which the children of *Nuestra América* should be prepared to respond. He advocated the importance of becoming familiar with the past as a way of acquiring the strength and the desire to emulate the ancients – without forgetting that 'the earth has lived more' ('la tierra ha vivido más') (1975, 18: 349) and that new values – already prefigured in antiquity itself – have opened up new paths. Ulysses, after all, could secure victory for the Greeks because 'he was a man of talent, who pacified the envious, and could think quickly' ('era hombre de ingenio, y ponía en paz a los envidiosos, y pensaba pronto') (Martí, 1975, 18: 350; Miranda Cancela, 2004).

Appreciation and understanding of poetic value were not obstacles to progress but, for Martí, offered a means to guarantee the fairness and objectivity of the role of letters in Hispanic America. The circumstances of the present provided the basis for the criterion he applied to different classical authors:

> El poeta debe ser Tirteo, no Tíbulo. Los placeres romanos amenazan la vida moral de la patria; los primitivos poetas griegos deben darle el concepto moral. (1975, 6: 457)

> The poet should be Tyrtaeus, not Tibullus. Roman pleasures threaten the moral life of the *Patria*; the primitive Greek poets should supply the concept of morality.

Martí used the term 'Pindaric' (referring to Pindar, the civic poet of archaic Greece) to highlight the quality and character of the verses of José María Heredia, which he believed resonated with nationalist sentiment.

The conviction that a critical approach rooted in the concept of *Nuestra América* was the ideal way to make use of the European tradition far better explains Martí's recommendations for the teaching of the Greco-Roman classics than the hasty, iconoclastic interpretations of his widely quoted remark that 'the history of America, from the Incas up to the present, has to be taught in detail, although the history of the archons of Greece need not be' ('la historia de América, de los incas a acá, ha de enseñarse al dedillo, aunque no se enseñe la de los arcontes de Grecia') (1975 6: 18).

In the debates about education in this period, Martí made a point of supporting the kind of teaching that equipped students for the time in which they lived (1975, 8: 430). He favoured the so-called 'scientific' university as all the more necessary for the difficult and urgent challenges Latin America was facing. However, he saw a place for the teaching of the classics, especially for those with a vocation for literature or an interest in languages, for whom he thought it indispensable (Martí, 1975, 10: 236; Carbón, 1983; Miranda Cancela, 1995b). Of those who said there was no point in learning Latin and Greek, he remarked:

> Ni el Griego ni el Latín han saboreado; ni aquellos capítulos de Homero que parecen primera selva de la tierra, de monstruosos troncos; ni las perfumosas y discretas epístolas del amigo de Mecenas. (1975, 8: 429)

> They have not tasted either Greek or Latin, nor those chapters of Homer that are like the first forest on earth with its enormous tree-trunks, nor do they know the fragrance of the tactful epistles by [Horace] the friend of Maecenas.

But Martí was well aware that a humanistic education could not be limited as it had been in the past to the classical languages, and he believed that modern literature could play the same formative role (1975, 13: 458). He did not make an absolute distinction between a scientific or literary university. Even though an education to meet the needs of time required 'struggling after a yield fruitful for modern life' (1975, 10: 228), Martí insisted that it was not literary education in itself that needed to be eliminated but its exclusive character. A scientific or technical education had to be developed 'without loss of the spiritual elements' (sin merma de los elementos espirituales) (1975, 8: 278). It was a question of promoting the formation of men of ideas as well as men of action (1975, 10: 235).

On the other hand, there was a need for reform in the so-called literary university that would prune 'all the twisted branches and dried leaves so that humanity could flow through broad veins without obstruction' (todas las ramas torcidas y hojas secas que impiden que por las anchas venas corra sin traba el jugo humano) (1975, 9: 445). For those without a literary vocation, the most important thing a classical education could provide was a sense of *lo griego*, 'what is Greek' or 'Greekness'. Martí made clear that such students should read 'some Latin authors; but more Greek than Latin ones' ('algunos latinos; más griegos que latinos') (1975, 21: 398). To make clear that this model of learning did not require everything to be narrowly modelled on ancient precedents, Marti pointed out that *lo griego* – the eternal quality of the Greeks – resided not in whatever information we may have about Attis and Cybele, 'but in the joy and harmony needed to reach the fullness of beauty' (1975, 5: 188):

> Muerta es la vieja Grecia, y todavía colora nuestros sueños juveniles, calienta nuestra literatura y nos cría a sus pechos, madre inmensa, la hermosa Grecia artística. Con la miel de aquella vida nos ungimos los labios aún todos los hombres. (1975, 7: 173)

> The Greece of old is dead, yet she still colours our juvenile dreams, gives warmth to our literature and feeds us at her breast, great mother, the beautiful artistic Greece. With the honey of that life all we men still anoint our lips.

Conclusions

Both Martí's concept of 'magnanimous and thoughtful' revolution and his aesthetics can be attributed to the idea of the beauty he discerned in *lo griego* (Vitier and García Marruz, 1978: 21). It was also the key to his sense of the Promethean challenge of a swift renewal, and to his impulse to recognise 'moderation in judgement and love of freedom as qualities of the man of the Antilles' (1975, 1: 321). This helped set the struggle for the freedom of modern Greece in parallel to the destiny of Cuba.

José Martí thus trawled through classical literature to find the appropriate formula to express the predicament of his particular time. He applied a creative principle of his own to the classical tradition and to the mythical references he employed, transforming them in his poetic praxis to provide a vital historical perspective. The ancient past provided the liberator with the means of understanding the present and envisaging the future – by pairing his Cuban homeland with Greece. In the words of the literary essayist Juan Marinello (1964: 26), a 'hidden closeness that bestrides centuries [...] based not on imitation but on similar realities' was what enabled Martí to appropriate Greek culture for his own profoundly American perspective as a humanist and a revolutionary.

References

Cabañero, A. (1874) *Discurso*. Calisto Ariño: Zaragoza.

Carbón Sierra, A. (1983) 'Algunas ideas de José Martí sobre la enseñanza de las lenguas clásicas'. *Universidad de La Habana* **219**: 176–182.

Henríquez Ureña, P. (1960) *Obra crítica*. Fondo de Cultura Económica: Mexico City.

Marinello, J. (1964) 'Españolidad literaria de José Martí' in *Once ensayos martianos*. Cuban Commission of UNESCO: Havana, 23–50.

Martí, J. (1972) *Ensayos sobre arte y literatura*. Instituto Cubano del Libro: Havana.

Martí, J. (1975) *Obras completas*. Editorial Ciencias Sociales: Havana.

Martí, J. (1985) *Poesía completa*. Editorial Letras Cubanas: Havana.

Miranda Cancela, E. and Carbón, A. (1985) 'La educación clásica de un joven habanero en la segunda mitad del siglo XIX'. *Revista Nacional de la Biblioteca Jose Martí*. **27**(3): 79–94.

Miranda Cancela, E. (1995a) 'Martí, estudiante de Humanidades', in *En un domingo de mucha luz: Cultura, historia y literatura españolas en la obra de José Martí*. Editorial Universidad de Salamanca: Salamanca, 221–130.

Miranda Cancela, E. (1995b) 'José Martí y la polémica en torno a la enseñanza de las humanidades', *Revista Universidad de La Habana* 245.

Miranda Cancela, E. (2004) 'Por qué 'La *Ilíada*, de Homero' en *La Edad de Oro*?' in J. Martí (ed.) *La Ilíada, de Homero*. Centro de Estudios Martianos: Havana, 61–93.

Quesada y Aróstegui, G. de (ed.) (1913-1919) *Martí: obras reunidas*. Vols. 11-15. Imprenta de Rambla, Bouza y Ca: Havana.

Rubio, D. (1934) *Classical Scholarship in Spain*. Catholic University of America: Washington.

Vitier, C. and García Marruz, F. (1978) *Flor oculta de la poesía cubana*. Arte y Literatura: Havana.

12

Pedro Henríquez Ureña's Hellenism and the American Utopia

ROSA ANDÚJAR

The Dominican intellectual Pedro Henríquez Ureña (1884–1946) is widely recognised for his contributions to Hispanic Modernism and the development of pan-Latin American cultural and literary identity, although his role in disseminating ancient Greek literature, culture and philosophy is largely overlooked. In Argentina, for example, he was commissioned to write introductions to Homer's *Odyssey* (1938) and the *Iliad* (1939), Aeschylus' tragedies (1939) and the comedies of Aristophanes (1941) for a popular series, *Las cien obras maestras de la literatura universal*, 'The Hundred Masterpieces of World Literature' (Gutiérrez Girardot, 2014: 241). But most notably, during his time as the 'Socrates' of Mexico's *Ateneo de la Juventud*, Young People's Athenaeum, from 1906 to 1911, he spearheaded a philhellenic cultural programme prior to the Mexican Revolution, introducing fellow members such as Alfonso Reyes and José Vasconcelos to 'la moda griega', 'the Greek way' (Roggiano, 1989; García Morales, 1992: 87–98; Curiel, 1998; Andújar, 2018). That self-conscious turn to Athens and the classical past was aimed at dismantling the positivism which had come to be dominant under the long presidency of Porfirio Díaz, and it became crucial to the larger project of nation-building in Mexico (Brading, 1984: 73–75; Laird, 2010: 174–181).

The present chapter examines the manner in which Henríquez Ureña's deep and comprehensive engagement with the ancient Greeks continued to inform both his broader ideology and his unique vision of a Latin American *magna patria* (Álvarez, 1981; Febres, 1989: 71–84). The focus will be on three influential essays, which were first delivered as public lectures and subsequently published and circulated across Latin America: *La cultura de las humanidades* (National University of Mexico, 1914), *La utopía de América* (La Plata, 1922) and *La patria de la justicia* (Buenos Aires, 1924).[1] These texts are

---

1 *La cultura de las humanidades* was published in Mexico and Havana; *La utopía de América*, excerpted in Argentine newspapers after the event, was later published with *Patria de la Justicia* in 1925 in Argentina and the Dominican Republic (Barcia, 1994: 71–72). The speeches were also summarised in letters to friends (Henríquez Ureña and Reyes, 1981: 214–215).

significant, not only because they were circulated among a wide range of intellectuals in diverse locations from Montevideo to Havana and from Minneapolis to Madrid, but also because they showcase the manner in which Henríquez Ureña combined a Hellenic ideal with a larger utopian vision for a pan-Latin American future.

The first section of this chapter illustrates the manner in which the texts elaborate a specific future for Latin America, guided by an idealised conception of ancient Hellas. The second part traces some of the ways in which Henríquez Ureña transformed ideas about the Greeks found in both José Enrique Rodó and in British Victorian intellectuals into a single utopian vision for the region. The closing discussion considers the larger ideological implications of this idealised Greece both for contemporaneous debates – about Hispanism and about the conflict which had emerged between Latin America and the English-speaking north – and for its ramifications for more recent controversies and racial politics.

A Greek Vision for Latin America

Henríquez Ureña's delivery of *La cultura de las humanidades* in 1914, at the start of the fourth year of classes in the School of Advanced Studies (*Escuela de Altos Estudios*) at Mexico's Universidad Nacional, probably marked the first time in which he argued, publicly and in an official capacity, for the continuing relevance of ancient Greece to modern Latin America – though this argument had already been made to the select membership of the *Ateneo de la Juventud* (Stabb, 1967; Díaz Quiñones, 2006: 76).[2] From 1910 onwards, the group, which included several of post-revolutionary Mexico's future political and intellectual leaders, became involved in the reformation of Mexican universities and began to craft public policy, drawing from the readings and lectures they had previously conducted in private.

Henríquez Ureña begins *La cultura de las humanidades* by providing a brief history of the *Ateneo* as a society of studious young intellectuals eager to improve the condition of their country. Initially they had sought inspiration from Spanish Golden Age writers and from Dante, Shakespeare and Goethe, as well as the Greeks. But Greek texts were deemed to provide the *ateneistas* with first-hand 'spiritual discipline'. There is an anecdotal recollection of how the young men were enraptured by the compelling nature of Plato's *Symposium*:

---

2 Álvarez (1981: 113) notes that this was the first time Henríquez Ureña broached the subject of utopia.

Una vez nos citamos para leer en común el *Banquete* de Platón. Éramos cinco o seis esa noche; nos turnábamos en la lectura, cambiándose el lector para el discurso de cada convidado diferente; y cada quien lo seguía ansioso, no con el deseo de apresurar la llegada de Alcibíades, como los estudiantes de que habla Aulo Gelio, sino con la esperanza de que le tocaran en suerte las milagrosas palabras de Diotima de Mantinea [...] La lectura acaso duró tres horas; nunca hubo mayor olvido del *mundo de la calle*, por más que esto ocurría en un taller de arquitecto, inmediato a la más populosa avenida de la ciudad [...] [C]on esas lecturas renació el espíritu de las humanidades clásicas en México. (Henríquez Ureña, 2004: 266–267)

Once we met to read Plato's *Symposium* together. There were five or six of us that night; we would take turns reading, with a different reader for each symposiast, and each one followed it eagerly, with no desire to rush the arrival of Alcibiades, like the students mentioned by Aulus Gellius, but in the hope that with luck the miraculous words of Diotima of Mantinea would fall to him [...] The reading lasted about three hours; never had there been such disregard for the outside world, despite the fact that this occurred in an architect's workshop, right by the city's busiest avenue [...] With those readings the spirit of the classical humanities was reborn in Mexico.[3]

As well as linking the experience of reading the ancient Greeks to a rebirth of the humanities in Mexico, Henríquez Ureña explains the role of the broader humanities after the Revolution:

Las humanidades [...] han de ejercer sutil influjo espiritual en la reconstrucción que nos espera. Porque ellas son más, mucho más que el esqueleto de las formas intelectuales del mundo antiguo: son la musa portadora de dones y de ventura interior, *fors olavigera* para los secretos de la perfección humana. (Henríquez Ureña, 2004: 267)

The humanities [...] must wield a subtle spiritual influence in the reconstruction that awaits us. Because they are much more than the skeleton of the intellectual forms of the ancient world; they are the muse that brings gifts and inner happiness, the *fors olavigera* [sic] for the secrets of human perfection.

---

3   Translations from Spanish are my own.

John Ruskin's *Fors Clavigera* (1871), an epistolary work addressed to British workmen, had prompted Henríquez Ureña's view that the spiritual awakening and inner peace provided by the humanities enabled men to remain focused on the task at hand, and led him to propose a larger humanistic educational programme for the masses – despite the fact that his own experience of the Greeks was born in an elite setting, reminiscent of a symposium.[4]

The relevance of the Greeks went beyond the philhellenism of the European Romantics. Henríquez Ureña based the 'Greek miracle' on a 'perpetua inquietud de la innovación y la reforma', 'perpetual restlessness for innovation and reform', as he contrasted the Greeks to other 'oriental' civilisations which sought stability rather than progress (2004: 268). His history of the classical humanities illustrated the effect that the 'restlessness' of the Greeks had on various societies from the Renaissance onwards, leading him to conclude that the youth of America should emulate the Greeks, who established perfection as the human ideal (2004: 269).

This vision was elaborated in the two influential speeches delivered in Argentina in the following decade, *La utopía de América* (1922) and *Patria de la Justicia* (1924). Both offer a more concrete articulation of a utopian *Nuestra América* than *La cultura de las humanidades*. In making his case for a Greek renaissance in Latin America, Henríquez Ureña argued for the fundamental relevance of the ancient Greek past to the future of the entire region. Even though *La utopía de América* was addressed to an Argentine audience, it began, like *La cultura de las humanidades*, with the Mexican intellectual landscape: the Dominican scholar was speaking as part of an official educational delegation, led by José Vasconcelos, to advise Argentina's new president of the new cultural and educational changes enacted in Mexico (Roggiano, 1989: 251–257; Barcia, 1994: 67–80).[5]

The speaker moved on from Mexico and political nationalism to address a larger vision of spiritual nationalism that, in his view, united the region and allowed him to broach the subject of a *magna patria* for the first time, as he asserted that Latin American countries after four centuries of history shared 'unity of purpose in political and intellectual life' (Henríquez Ureña,

---

4   García Morales (1992: 237) relates that the members of the *Ateneo* had also established the Universidad Popular Mexicana, whose purpose was to develop the culture of the people of Mexico, especially that of its working class. Compare Curiel (1998: 339-340).

5   For Vasconcelos, see Conn in this volume.

2014: 127).[6] This vision of 'nuestra América' emphasised the youthful audacity which spiritually connected the present-day Americas to classical Greece and the Italian Renaissance:

> Si conserváramos aquella infantil audacia con que nuestros antepasados llamaban Atenas a cualquier ciudad de América, no vacilaría yo en compararnos con los pueblos, políticamente disgregados pero espiritualmente unidos, de la Grecia clásica y la Italia del Renacimiento. (Henríquez Ureña, 2014: 127–128)

> If we were to preserve that youthful audacity with which our forebears called any city in America Athens, I would not hesitate to compare us with the peoples, politically separate but spiritually united, of classical Greece and Renaissance Italy.

The youthful utopia should include universal education for all men, social justice and liberty. Stressing that utopia was one of the great spiritual creations of the Mediterranean, Henríquez Ureña again attributed to the Greeks a particularly Western drive for perfectionism, again built on a notion of restlessness.[7] As in the previous speech, the Greek example was framed in terms of a larger conflict between progress and complacency. And once again the 'Greek miracle' was contrasted with the ancient Near East, in which justice was sacrificed to order, and progress to tranquillity.

Two years later, *Patria de la Justicia* was delivered in Buenos Aires, in honour of Carlos Sánchez Viamonte, an important jurist who later became a leading figure in the Socialist Party of Argentina (Zuleta Álvarez, 1997: 249–251). Again utopianism is attributed to the Greeks, 'our spiritual forefathers from the Mediterranean', and it is opposed to 'Asiatic ideals which only promise man a better life beyond this terrestrial life' (Henríquez Ureña, 2014: 133–134). But there is a significant addition. This Greek vision is a democratic one, for the benefit of all:

> Al diletantismo egoísta, aunque se ampara bajo los nombres de Leonardo o de Goethe, opongamos el nombre de Platón, nuestro primer maestro de utopía, el que entregó al fuego todas sus invenciones de poeta para predicar la verdad y la justicia en nombre de Sócrates. (Henríquez Ureña, 2014: 135)

---

6   Barcia (1994: 69-71) considers a similar speech.

7   Henríquez Ureña (2014: 129): 'el pueblo griego da al mundo occidental la inquietud del perfeccionamento constante', 'the people of Greece give the Western world a restless urge for constant perfection'.

Against selfish dilettantism, though it may shelter under the names of Leonardo or Goethe, let us put forward the name of Plato, our first teacher of utopia, who threw all his poetic inventions into the fire in order to preach truth and justice in the name of Socrates.

This opposition to personal intellectual self-improvement or dilettantism resists precisely the 'Byzantine' tendencies identified in Eric Cullhed's chapter in this volume. Henríquez Ureña's three texts present a vision of Latin America which is unlike other early twentieth-century projections of what the region should be. *Nuestra América* is imagined as an equal society in which a generalised Hellenic conception of art and culture plays as large a role as economic growth in creating social justice. The spirit of a Greek past is directed towards a democratic and collective Latin American future.

New Directions in Utopian Thinking

The three speeches described above were not informed by any particular ancient Greek author or by classical utopian ideas or motifs, such as those found in Hesiod's poetry or Plato's dialogues, though Henríquez Ureña had read those texts and he made mention of Aristophanes and Plato. Nor do they follow engagements with utopian thinking in Latin America or elsewhere, such as Domingo Faustino Sarmiento's *Argirópolis* published in 1850, or Ernst Bloch's *Geist der Utopie* which appeared in 1918 (Febres, 1989: 74; Gutiérrez Girardot, 2014). It will be proposed here that the novelty of Henríquez Ureña's vision for Latin America lay in the conjunction of three main themes – youth, progress and discipline – which he ascribed to the 'restless' ancient Greeks. This dynamic and unique form of Hellenism combined the Uruguayan José Enrique Rodó's conception of a regenerative Greece with that of nineteenth-century British thinkers, notably Matthew Arnold and Walter Pater.

Ideas of ancient Greece as especially youthful and energetic were widespread in the European Hellenic revivalism of the eighteenth and nineteenth centuries (Jenkyns, 1980: 169). These ideas seem to correspond to the youth of the *ateneistas* in the halcyon days when they could stay up all night enraptured by Plato's *Symposium*. Henríquez Ureña certainly advertised the efforts of the *Ateneo de la Juventud* outside Mexico by appealing to the power of youth. In 1907, he stated in an article for Santo Domingo's newspaper *Listín Diario* that Mexico's future literary history would be indebted to these young men, who were 'good sons of Greece' (Henríquez Ureña, 2004: 243). In a letter published the same year in another Dominican journal, *Cuna de América*, Cradle of America, he invited his cousin to join the *ateneistas* in

Mexico as they read Greek literature in an 'atmosphere of intellectual activity and youthful happiness', 'este ambiente de actividad intellectual y alegría juvenil' (Garcia Morales, 1992: 67).

Henríquez Ureña is in fact amplifying connections already made in José Enrique Rodó's *Ariel* (1900). In that groundbreaking essay, dedicated to 'the youth of America', Rodó (1967: 26) affirmed that Latin America's potential hinged precisely on its youthfulness and he linked 'the youthful soul', 'el alma joven', symbolised by ancient Greece to his vision for the future of the region, which he also perceived as another young and emerging civilisation.[8] Rodó made the same case elsewhere: in a letter to Porfirio Parra, the director of the *Escuela Nacional Preparatoria* of Mexico, he stated that his writings 'are and will be property of the youth who will work and fight for the civilization, the culture, and the moral and intellectual elevation of our America' (Rela, 1992: 16). Rodó's new spiritual model of cultural identity for Latin America, which served to differentiate the region from the capitalist north, appealed to its European and Christian heritage. This was in contrast to José Martí's earlier emphasis on indigenous elements.[9] Henríquez Ureña had first facilitated the Uruguayan's acquaintance with Parra; more importantly he introduced Rodó's *Ariel* to a Mexican readership, having arranged for it to be published in Monterrey (Henríquez Ureña, 1989: 61; Rela, 1992: 10–16).

But where Rodó found evidence of the same Greek youthfulness in Christianity, Pedro Henríquez Ureña was promoting a more secular vision, explicitly intended to fight utilitarian and pragmatist educational trends. What is more, Henríquez Ureña was amalgamating his knowledge of English authors and intellectual trends in Victorian Britain with Rodó's conception of a youthful Hellas.[10] Henríquez Ureña's ideas of Greece as a source of

---

8   Compare Van Delden (1990: 304). The association of youth with ancient Greece was made in Europe, but in the context of historical theories that the present represented a deterioration in relation to the past period of childhood which Greece represented (Jenkyns, 1980: 168–170).

9   Martí (2012: 17): 'The European university has to give way to the American one. The history of America, from the Incas until now, has to be taught in detail, even if the history of the archons of Greece is not. Our Greece is preferable to the Greece that is not our own' ('La Universidad europea ha de ceder a la universidad americana. La Historia de América, de los Incas a acá, ha de enseñarse al dedillo, aunque no se enseñe la de los arcontes de Grecia. Nuestra Grecia es preferible a la Grecia que no es nuestra'). Miller (2008: 44-45) examines Martí's and Rodó's competing visions of *Nuestra América*; Martí's Hellenism is treated by Miranda Cancela in this volume.

10 Brading (1984: 73), Díaz Quiñones (2006: 178, 228–230), Laird (2010: 175). Henríquez revealed in a letter to Alfonso Reyes (25 March 1914) that John Sandy's *A History of Classical Scholarship* (1903) was a source for his *La cultura de las*

spiritual discipline and reasoned learning for the improvement of humanity were inspired by Matthew Arnold, who defined culture as a 'study of perfection' (Arnold, 1993: 59, 66). The ideas of Walter Pater were also of critical importance: indeed Pater and Plato are named as the two individuals responsible for Henríquez Ureña's conversion to Hellenism and in Mexico he had made the only translation into Spanish of Walter Pater's *Greek Studies* for *Revista Moderna* (Andújar, 2018). Pater's *Studies in the History of the Renaissance* proposed a new understanding of the period, which was centred on notions of renewal and progress (Pater, 1873: 21; Evangelista, 2015: 643–644). This is epitomised by the quotation that appeared at the end of the work:

> Heraclitus somewhere says that everything moves and nothing is at rest. (Evangelista, 2015: 644)[11]

Other Victorian writers connected progress to the ancient Greeks, but maintained that the modern world lacked the same discipline and innovation, so that each generation had to reclaim and revive Hellenic values. That was to propose a more dynamic conception of 'evolutionary humanistic Hellenism' and its value to modernity (Turner, 1981: 61–76). John Addington Symonds, for example, claimed in the concluding chapter to *Studies of the Greek Poets* that the notion of progress was characteristic of ancient Greece and that advances in later times could be measured in terms of a society's contact with the Greeks: all modern civilised nations could thus be regarded as 'colonies of Hellas' (Symonds, 1893: 397–398). But for Symonds this Greek past was especially difficult to recover in the British industrial world of his time. The values of Greece were not universal, as others had believed, because they were lacking to modern man (Symonds, 1893: 362).

Henríquez Ureña's claims for a Latin American exception, built on an intrinsic spiritual affinity to the Greeks, are a novel departure from these reflections. In this manner, the Dominican intellectual not only extends Rodó's thinking on the importance of the youthful Greece to the equally youthful Spanish America, but he also marries these to current debates about Hellenic progress and whether it is achievable in modernity.

Humanidades. The same letter quoted George Saintsbury and Matthew Arnold in English (Henríquez Ureña and Reyes, 1981: 215).

11   Plato, *Cratylus* 402a, attributed this remark to Heraclitus.

The Greeks: A New Paradigm for Latin America

Pedro Henríquez Ureña was by no means the first intellectual to invoke idealised notions of ancient Greece for Latin America, but his thinking brought a fresh perspective to the 'culture wars' over 'Hispanism' and peninsular Spain's legacy for the twentieth century (Gutiérrez Girardot, 2014: 233–234). By seeking to establish their direct spiritual link to the ancient Greeks, Henríquez Ureña sought to free the new Latin American nations from the claims of an imperialist Spanish literary tradition. *La cultura de las humanidades*, presented in 1914, had been conceived in the wake of Marcelino Menéndez Pelayo's formidable *Historia de la poesia hispano-americana* which was first published three years before. Scholars such as Arcadio Díaz-Quinoñes have shown how Menéndez Pelayo's work was part of a larger attempt by Spain to re-assert a kind of control over its former colonies by laying claim to their literature:

> El erudito español quería restaurar la autoridad espiritual del imperio y el prestige del Libro, asegurando así un lugar protagónico a la España vencida […] Era una Guerra por la autoridad de la tradición. (Díaz Quiñones, 2006: 28)

> The erudite Spaniard wanted to restore the spiritual authority of the empire and the prestige of the Book, thus assuring the defeated Spain of the position of protagonist […] It was a war over the authority of tradition.

The very notion of language and literature was part of the imperial project for Menéndez Pelayo, who cited the example of Greece and then Rome to show how the ancients extended their empire through distant regions (Menéndez Pelayo, 1911: 11). It is no coincidence that Henríquez Ureña's pan-American *magna patria* was being formulated during this period. Having spent a significant amount of time in Spain, he was familiar with the efforts of Menéndez Pelayo and others to re-establish Spain's authority in the domain of Latin American literature (Zuleta Álvarez, 1997: 125–158). For the Dominican intellectual, ancient Greece, I would like to suggest, afforded a new beginning for Latin America: by creating a direct link with Spanish America's 'Mediterranean forefathers' ('nuestros abuelos del Mediterráneo'), Henríquez Ureña could bypass the influence of peninsular Spain, in order to define a Latin American essence that did not depend on Rome, which had always been invoked as an important forebear for Spain.

Additionally, the Greeks afford a new perspective in light of the other imperial power that haunted Latin America at the time: the United States.

For the new Latin American republics to achieve progress, capitalism was a prominent choice. The spectre of the North American labour and economic system had been tackled both by José Martí and José Enrique Rodó. Henríquez Ureña did not address the question of the United States so directly. Nonetheless, it is highly likely that his invocations of the ancient Greeks were also aimed against the northern power at a time when it began to expand beyond its continental borders, with the acquisition of Puerto Rico and the Philippines following the Spanish-American war.[12] The United States began to cast itself as a new Rome in celebration of its new empire, wealth and power (Malamud, 2009: 150–185; Wyke, 2012). Henríquez Ureña's construction of a Latin American affinity with the Greeks conferred a certain degree of autonomy and even cultural superiority on the region, offering it an opportunity to align itself with a different cultural model.

The Hellenic model was, furthermore, attractive as a means of unification. In the speeches analysed above, Henríquez Ureña continually appeals to the joint history, language and experience of Latin America as a basis for utopia. However, the effacing of important considerations on the ground would ultimately doom the vision to failure. In his personal recollections of Henríquez Ureña, Jorge Luis Borges addresses the larger issues of race and nationalism:

> Yo tengo el mejor recuerdo de Pedro [...] bueno, él era un hombre tímido y creo que muchos países fueron injustos con él. En España, claro, lo consideraban, digamos, un mero indiano; un mero centroamericano. Y aquí en Buenos Aires, creo que no le perdonamos el ser dominicano, el ser, quizá, mestizo; el ser ciertamente judío – el apellido Henríquez, bueno, como el mío, es judeo-portugués. Y aquí él fue profesor adjunto de un señor, de cuyo nombre no quiero acordarme; que no sabía absolutamente nada de la materia, y Henríquez – que sabía muchísimo – tuvo que ser su adjunto, porque, finalmente, un mero extranjero [...] el otro, claro, tenía esa inestimable virtud de ser argentino [...] la gente nunca se portó bien con él; la República Argentina no se portó bien con él. España tampoco [...] nunca lo reconocieron del todo. (Borges, 1985: 182)

> I have the best of memories of Pedro [...] well, he was a shy man and I think that many countries were unjust towards him. In Spain, of course, they considered him, well, a mere Indian, a mere Central American. And here in Buenos Aires, I don't think that we ever forgave him for

---

12   'Patria de la Justicia' rejected the North American utopia because the US is 'one of the least free countries in the world' – despite the US often having been conceived as an archetype of liberty (Henríquez Ureña, 2014: 134).

being Dominican, being, perhaps, *mestizo*; certainly being Jewish – the surname Henríquez, well, like mine, is Judeo-Portuguese. And here he was the adjunct professor to a gentleman, whose name I do not wish to remember, who knew absolutely nothing about the subject, and Henríquez – who knew so much – he had to be his adjunct, because in the end he was a mere foreigner […] the former, of course, had the inestimable virtue of being an Argentine […] the people never treated him well; the Argentine Republic did not treat him well. Neither did Spain […] they never fully acknowledged him.

Pedro Henríquez Ureña was thus dismissed for being a colonial of mixed race, and potentially a Jew.[13] This accentuates the narrow view upon which his utopia was ultimately founded: a *Nuestra América* constructed as the spiritual heir of Mediterranean forefathers but which excluded any mention of elements crucial to Latin America: the indigenous, Afro-Latinos and women. Even in Mexico, where Henríquez Ureña was celebrated as a founder of the renowned *Ateneo*, he encountered resistance for being a foreigner: newspaper headlines reported that student strikes were incited by his status as a foreigner in a *Mexican* university (Roggiano, 1989: 154–155). In the end, the vision of a Latin American utopia inspired by Greece was unrealisable in a fragmented post-imperial world in which nationalism would reign supreme.

References

Álvarez, S. (1981) *La magna patria de Pedro Henríquez Ureña*. Taller: Santo Domingo.

Andújar, R. (2018) 'The Caribbean Socrates: Pedro Henríquez Ureña and the Mexican Ateneo de la Juventud' in E. Richardson (ed.) *Classics in Extremis*. Bloomsbury Academic: London, 101–114.

Arnold, M. (1993) *Culture and Anarchy and Other Writings*, ed. S. Collini. Cambridge University Press: Cambridge.

Barcia, P. L. (1994) *Pedro Henríquez Ureña y la Argentina*. Secretaría de Estado de Educación, Bellas Artes y Cultos: Santo Domingo.

Borges, J. L. (1985) *Borges en diálogo: conversaciones de Jorge Luis Borges con Osvaldo Ferrari*. Ediciones Grijalbo: Barcelona.

Brading, D. A. (1984) *Prophecy and Myth in Mexican History*. Centre of Latin American Studies, University of Cambridge: Cambridge.

Conn, R. (2002) *The Politics of Philology: Alfonso Reyes and the Invention of the Latin American Literary Tradition*. Bucknell University Press: Lewisburg.

---

13   Compare Díaz Quiñones (2006: 178). Henríquez Ureña only rarely and obliquely discussed his physical appearance: in a letter to Reyes of 13 March 1908 (Henríquez Ureña and Reyes, 1981) he attributed his decision not to relocate to New York to the evidence of prejudice he experienced on a daily basis because he was not a white north American.

Curiel, F. (1998) *La revuelta: interpretación del Ateneo de la Juventud, 1906–1929*. Universidad Nacional Autónoma de México: Mexico.

Díaz-Quiñones, A. (2006) *Sobre los principios: los intelectuales caribeños y la tradición*. Universidad Nacional de Quilmes: Buenos Aires.

Evangelista, S. (2015) 'Towards the *Fin de Siècle*: Walter Pater and John Addington Symonds' in N. Vance and J. Wallace (eds.) *The Oxford History of Classical Reception in English Literature, Volume 4*. Oxford University Press: Oxford, 643–668.

Febres, L. (1989) *Pedro Henríquez Ureña: crítico de América*. Ediciones La Casa de Bello: Caracas.

García Morales, A. (1992) *El Ateneo de México, 1906–1914: orígenes de la cultura mexicana contemporánea*. Publicaciones de la Escuela de Estudios Hispano-Americanos de Sevilla: Seville.

Gónzalez Echevarría, R. (1985) *The Voice of the Masters: Writing and Authority in Modern Latin American Literature*. University of Texas Press: Austin.

Gutiérrez Girardot, R. (2014) *Ensayos sobre Alfonso Reyes y Pedro Henríquez Ureña*. El Colegio de México: Mexico.

Henríquez Ureña, P. (1945) *Literary Currents in Hispanic America*. Harvard University Press: Cambridge.

Henríquez Ureña, P. (1989) *Memorias, diario*, ed. E. Zuleta Álvarez. Academia Argentina de Letras: Buenos Aires.

Henríquez Ureña, P. (2004) *Estudios mexicanos*, ed. J. L. Martínez. Fondo de Cultura Económica: Mexico City.

Henríquez Ureña, P. (2008) *Estudios griegos de Walter Pater. Traducción y notas de Pedro Henríquez Ureña*. 2nd edn. Cielonaranja: Santo Domingo.

Henríquez Ureña, P. (2014) *Obras completas Vol. 7: 1921–1928*. Cielonaranja: Santo Domingo.

Henríquez Ureña, P. and Reyes, A. (1981) *Epistolario íntimo (1906–1946)*. Vol. 1. UNPHU: Santo Domingo.

Jenkyns, R. (1980) *The Victorians and Ancient Greece*. Blackwell: Oxford.

Laird, A. (2010) 'The Cosmic Race and a Heap of Broken Images: Mexico's Classical Past and the Modern Creole Imagination' in S. A. Stephens and P. Vasunia (eds.) *Classics and National Cultures*. Oxford University Press: Oxford, 163–181.

Malamud, M. (2009) *Ancient Rome and Modern America*. Wiley-Blackwell: London.

Martí, J. (2012) *Nuestra América*, ed. C. Vitier. Centro de Estudios Martianos: Havana.

Menéndez Pelayo, M. (1911) *Historia de la poesia hispano-americana*. Vol. 1. Suárez: Madrid.

Miller, N. (2008) *Reinventing Modernity in Latin America: Intellectuals Imagine the Future, 1900–1930*. Palgrave Macmillan: New York.

Pater, W. (1873) *Studies in the History of the Renaissance*. Macmillan: London.

Pater, W. (1895) *Greek Studies: A Series of Essays*. Macmillan: London.

Rela, W. (1992) *Rodó en la crítica de Pedro Henríquez Ureña*. Ediciones El Galeón: Montevideo.

Rodó, J. E. (1967) *Ariel*, ed. G. Brotherston: Cambridge University Press.

Roggiano, A. (1961) *Pedro Henríquez Ureña en los Estados Unidos*. Casa Editorial Cultura: Mexico.

Roggiano, A. (1989) *Pedro Henríquez Ureña en México*. Colección Cátedras: Mexico.

Stabb, M. S. (1967) *In Quest of Identity; Patterns in the Spanish American Essay of Ideas, 1890–1960.* University of North Carolina Press: Chapel Hill.

Symonds, J. A. (1893) *Studies of the Greek Poets (Vol. II)*, 3rd edn. Adam and Charles Black: London.

Turner, F. M. (1981) *The Greek Heritage in Victorian Britain.* Yale University Press: New Haven.

Van Delden, M. (1990) 'The Banquets of Civilization: The Idea of Ancient Greece in Rodó, Reyes and Fuentes'. *Annals of Scholarship* **7**.3: 303–322.

Wyke, M. (2012) *Caesar in the USA.* University of California Press: Berkeley.

Zuleta Álvarez, E. (1997) *Pedro Henríquez Ureña y su tiempo: vida de un hispanoamericano universal.* Catálogos: Buenos Aires.

13

Born with the Wrinkles of Byzantium: Unclassical Traditions in Spanish America, 1815–1925

ERIC CULLHED

In *Bolívar: A Greek Poem* (1944) the Greek surrealist poet Nikos Engonopoulos evokes an unlikely first encounter with the South American Liberator. As a young boy wandering the Phanar district of Constantinople, he suddenly caught Simón Bolívar's gaze in a lamp-lit orthodox icon. Could Bolívar have been, the poet wonders, yet another reincarnation of the marble emperor Constantine Palaiologos? Bolívar is now 'a deserted chapel on an Attic beach', then the whole of Mesoamerica and the South American continent. When the hero speaks, volcanoes erupt in Peru, while orthodox icons tremble in Kastoriá. Bolívar was there with the poet on the front, from Colombia to Peru to Albania. He is 'beauteous as a Greek' (Stabakis, 2008: 109).

This double exposure of Greece and South America in *Bolívar* has understandably been characterised as a typical surrealist paradox (Stabakis, 2008: 348; Rentzou, 2010: 129). Yet Engonopoulos' automatism captures a mental oscillation between the two worlds that had been very real for early nineteenth-century revolutionary idealists like Lord Byron. Before he finally set sail to the Balkans, Byron wrote to Thomas Moore on 27 August 1820: 'I had, and still have, thought of South America, but am fluctuating between it and Greece' (Marchand, 1979: 198).[1] The two wars of independence were contemporary reverberations of the French and North American revolutions; both imported the European Enlightenment's neoclassical vision of Greece as a symbol of liberty. Patriotic poets such as the Ecuadorian José Joaquín de Olmedo did indeed hail Bolívar for being as beauteous as a Greek, representing him and his brothers in arms as Olympian gods or Homeric heroes (Blanco-Fombona, 1921: 332; Briceño Perozo, 1992; Hernández Muñoz, 2000).

But the liberator himself famously criticised such analogies: Achaean wagons, Bolívar pointed out, never rolled over the Andean battlefields of Junín and Ayacucho. At the same time, Bolívar was certainly no stranger to analogies with pre-modern Europe. In his *Letter from Jamaica* of 1815, he conjectured that on the Isthmus of Panama, with its potential to connect

---

1 Compare Marchand (1979: 173, 215), Beaton (2013: 112).

Europe, Asia and America, the capital of the world could one day arise, 'as Constantine wished Byzantium to be [the capital] of the ancient hemisphere': 'como pretendió Constantino que fuese Bizancio la del antiguo hemisferio.' (Bolívar, 1964, 8: 119; compare Taboada, 2011: 45). The comparison with Constantinople to convey a city's wealth owing to its strategic geographical position is natural enough; it could just as well have been Alexandria or Tyre (Bolívar, 1964, 8: 206).[2] Yet, it is difficult not to see connections to other sections of the same letter where Bolívar rejects the notion of Spanish America as 'young' and prefers to liken the continent's situation to that of Rome after its fall (1964, 8: 107-108r). He fights not for a heroic or classical world rising to its first glory, but for a late antique transitional age in which new unknown futures are shaped from the ruins of a magnificent past. The psychological motivation for this dash of medievalism appears to be the same complication that made Bolívar repudiate Olmedo's mythological excesses. It was the complication that over a century later, in 1943, made Pablo Neruda pray:

> Muera la mitología griega: más terriblemente hermosa que una columna corintia es una anaconda de quince metros saliendo del lodo de la selva. (Neruda, 1943)

> Let Greek mythology die; more terribly beautiful than a Corinthian column is an anaconda, fifteen meters long, emerging from the jungle mud.

It was what made Engonopoulos, also in 1943, turn less to the classical than to the Byzantine world and even to America when assembling the surreal hero that could liberate him from swastikas swaying before the colonnade of the Parthenon. Classicism may have become the international idiom of revolution, but it was also the vehicle of Europe's old utopian interpretations of the American continent as well as Greece, which had proved so oblivious to their respective realities.

Identifying something as unclassical is, of course, more often a form of disparagement. Byzantium was seen as the antithesis of Enlightenment ideals, Edward Gibbon's 'tedious and uniform tale of weakness and misery' (Gibbon, 1788: 2). In 1845, the French historian Edgar Quinet used the same analogy as Bolívar had done in order to describe Spanish America as culturally and intellectually pinioned by the Catholic Church during the preceding three centuries in words which have been recalled by several Spanish American writers (Luco, 1878: 280; González Prada, 1933: 164; Tejeras, 1970: 180):

> Le souffle matinal de l'univers passe sur le front de l'homme, et ne peut raviver ce vieillard. Que sont ces berceaux d'empire, Mexico, Rio Janeiro,

---

2   Sarmiento (1854: 97) configured Rio de Janeiro as Constantinople.

Buenos-Ayres, Lima, qui, dès le premier jour, ont les rides de Byzance?
(Quinet, 1845, 296)

The morning breeze of the universe sweeps over the forehead of the
human race, but it cannot awake this old man. What are those cradles
of empire – Mexico, Rio de Janeiro, Buenos Aires, Lima – which, from
their very first day, bore the wrinkles of Byzantium?

Byzantium can mean many things: decrepitude, maturity, decadence and cos-
mopolitanism; but it is almost always a converse, a relational antonym to the
classical. Tracing its conceptual history might help us to circumscribe and,
conceivably, to relativise the importance of the classical tradition alongside
other pre-modern narratives.[3] The following account reiterates a well-known
story, the dramatic evolution of Spanish American literature in the late nineteenth and early twentieth century, but with a focus on favourable or hostile
receptions of the Byzantine.

The interest in Byzantium among Spanish American romantics was limited. Philhellenic meditations on the Greek War of Independence, obliquely
commenting on the situation at home, tended to focus on antiquity. A common scheme was to connect the recent struggle against the Ottomans to the
ancient Greco-Persian wars.[4] But occasionally the gaze fell instead on 1453
and the fall of Constantinople to the Ottomans, as in the Mexican intellectual
Manuel Carpio's sonnet 'Mahomet II', or the Cuban poet Plácido's 'To Greece'
(Carpio, 1874: 305; Concepción Valdés, 1856: 160–161).

This changed during the last decades of the century as the increasing
stream of French influences invested Byzantium with new significations.
A predilection for the post-classical and medieval had always been central
to the European Decadent movement and its rejection of Enlightenment
progressivism (David-de Palacio, 2001; Delouis, 2003: 110). The Parnassians
and Symbolists, from Baudelaire to Huysmans, adopted the concept of
cyclical time and acknowledged that just as Rome had risen and fallen, so
must France, having passed its ages of youth and maturity, now embrace
its imminent fall. Charles Baudelaire praised 'the language of the last Latin

---

3 Medievalists and classicists alike claim pivotal roles for their respective periods in
   modern imperialism without showing much awareness of one another (Warren,
   2012).
4 Typical examples are Heredia's *Ode to the Uprising of Greece 1820* [sic] (Latorre Broto,
   2013) and Joaquín Lorenzo Luaces' *La caída de Misolonghi* (1856) (Fischer, 2004:
   98–100; Taboada, 2008: 29–30), as well as Martí (1991, 5: 168): Miranda Cancela
   in this volume.

decadence – the final sigh of a robust person, already transformed and pre-pared for spiritual life': 'la langue de la dernière décadence latine – suprême soupir d'une personne robuste, déjà transformée et préparée pour la vie spir-ituelle' (Baudelaire, 1857: 125). In his introduction to the posthumous edition of *Les fleurs du mal*, Théophile Gautier emphasised Baudelaire's preference for Tertullian's style, which was like black ebony, over that of Virgil or Cicero (1868: 18). This devotion to the late antique is shared by the protagonist in the 'bible of decadence', Joris-Karl Huysmans' *À rebours*, 'Against the Grain', published in 1884. In the same year, Paul Verlaine opened his famous 'Langueur' with the words 'Je suis l'Empire à la fin de la décadence': 'I am the empire at the end of its decadence' (Verlaine, 1884: 104). Byzantium was more than one of the many exotic subjects that the symbolists drew from different phases of European, African and Asian history and mythology. Rome fallen, medievalised, orientalised and lost became a hieroglyph for Parisian life towards the end of the century, for aestheticism and a strong preoccupation with the musical qualities of verse.

The first traces of this brand of decadent Byzantinism in Spanish American literature can be detected in the Puerto Rican poet José de Jesús Domínguez. His poem *Las huríes blancas* ('The White Houris') from 1886 is a captivating tale about the final dreams and death of the Ottoman 'Osmalín, poet of Byzantium'. The year after, the Nicaraguan poet Rubén Darío opened his *Rimas* by announcing the lapidary exquisiteness of his work as 'Byzantine mosaics and rare enamels': 'bizantinos mosaicos, pulidos y raros esmaltes' (Darío, 1887: 186). Byzantium played no prominent role in Darío's next collection, *Azul* (1888), which marked the beginning of *modernismo*. But for our purposes it is worth repeating the well-known fact that critics had great difficulties in accepting its decadentist spirit. 'Is Rubén Darío decadent?' Eduardo de la Barra asked himself. 'He thinks that it is so, but I deny it': '¿Es Rubén Darío *decadente*? Él lo cree así; yo lo niego' (Darío, 1888: xv; Olivares, 1980).

The same uneasiness with decadence transplanted to American soil was expressed in Byzantine terms in the work and reception of Augusto de Armas. This young Cuban poet moved to Paris in 1888 and published his only collec-tion of poems, *Rimes Byzantines*, a few years later. In the introductory sonnet the poet closely imitates Verlaine's *Langueur* and proclaims himself 'a degen-erate child of the Late Empire […] lost in this city of perfect luxuries': 'enfant dégénéré du dernier Bas-Empire […] perdu dans cette Ville aux luxures par-faits' (Armas, 1891: xiii). But back home in Cuba this seemed unacceptable. The writer Diego Vicente Tejéra could not bear this proud *mestizo* characteris-ing himself as a Byzantine 'with the dark color that is specific to his new race, and a body healthy and robust': 'con el color trigueño propio de la raza nueva á que pertenece, sano y robusto de cuerpo' (Tejera, 1895: 109–113).[5] Cuba was 'a nation without a past, but a nation of the future': 'un pueblo sin pasado, pero de porvenir'. The young poet's fascination for Byzantium was nothing but an illusion (Tejera, 1895: 112).

De Armas died in Paris two years later, and Darío included him in *Los raros* (1896a), a collection of presentations of *modernista* idols. Here he appears as a decadent Byzantine hero, young, fragile and nervous, who 'arrived in Paris as somebody who arrives at an enchanted Orient': 'llegó a París, como quien llega a un Oriente encantado' (1896a: 143). Darío's *Prosas profanas* from the same year included a great deal of Byzantinising, if not strictly Byzantine, scenery. In the preface he discusses his proclivity for 'princesses, kings, imperial things and visions of distant or impossible lands': 'princesas, reyes, cosas imperiales, visiones de países lejanos o imposibles'. Alluding to a post-classical motif of Poe and Baudelaire, he exclaimed:

> á un presidente de República no podré saludarle en el idioma en que te cantaría á ti, oh Halagabal! de cuya corte – oro, seda, mármol – me acuerdo en sueños. (Darío, 1896b: xi)

> A president of the Republic I could never salute in the language that I would sing for you, Heliogabalus, whose court – gold, silk, marble – I recall in dreams.

The motif of Byzantium became one out of the many exotic pre-modern story worlds employed by the *modernistas* of the 1890s (Cullhed, 2014: 230–231). Medieval and ancient Greece became almost interchangeable in the poetic imagination, as Greek antiquity was, to borrow Darío's famous phrase, not the 'Greece of the Greeks' but the 'Greece of France' (1896b: 14), a vague Rococo or Gothic Greece, populated by Dionysian mythological characters and where it did not matter whether it was Achilles' or Odysseus' crew who had covered their ears with wax (Darío, 1901: 155).[6] But Byzantium, for all of its escapist allure, could never be divested of its negative semantics, and this fuelled its fecundity as *modernismo* entered its later phases, marked by an ambition to step down from the ivory tower and address more explicitly the sociocultural problems facing Spanish America.

In 1894, the Colombian poet José Asunción Silva (1865–1896) parodied Darío's symbolist synaesthesia in his 'Symphony the colour of strawberries

---

5   The review was originally published in *América en París* 6, 31 March 1891.

6   There are similar intentional misquotations in Caribbean literature (Greenwood, 2010).

in milk', addressing the 'Byzantines of our literature', 'los bizantinos de nuestras letras'.[7] Moreover, the Colombian poet Guillermo Valencia (1873–1943) alluded to Darío's 'The White Page' and declared:

> ¡Bebed dolor en ellas, flautistas de Bizancio!,
> que amáis pulir el dáctilo al son de las cadenas.
> (Valencia, 1898: 18)

> Drink pain from them, flautists of Byzantium!
> You who love polishing the dactyl to the sound of chains.

The gold, silk and marble of aestheticism delivered not the freedom that it had promised but chains and servitude to any artist who had been drawn to its court.

The same critique was launched more vigorously by José Santos Chocano (1875–1934), an explosive, larger-than-life figure who strove to become the 'Whitman of the South' by drawing on any moment of grandeur in the history of the American continent: the pre-Columbian past, the Greco-Roman legacy, the Spanish conquest or the wars of independence. His poetic ideal was epic and patriotic, and in many poems he asks his muse to rip off her costly attire, clearly referring to *modernista* aestheticism (Chocano, 1899: 15).

One such poem is 'In the Forge', written in 1897 and included in Chocano's collection *The Virgin Rainforest* from 1901. The poem alludes to a section of Olmedo's *Victory in Junín,* dubbed one of his rare moments of astonishing brilliance and beauty by Menéndez Pelayo (1894: cxxiv-cxxvi). At a decisive moment in the battle of Ayacucho, the soft and dainty youths of Peru suddenly come to the rescue and save the day. Olmedo likens them to young Achilles hiding on Scyros dressed as a woman in order avoid his fate at Troy. Odysseus also disguised himself – as a merchant – and tricked Achilles into revealing his identity by showing him exceptionally well-forged weapons, which the hero could not resist grabbing. Similarly, the young Peruvians have turned from passivity to activity and thrown off the chains of servitude in order to fulfil their destiny in the struggle for freedom. In this Peruvian *aristeia,* Chocano found a prophetic allegory of what had to happen in the literary culture of his day. In his poem 'In the Forge' Achilles has returned to Scyros:

> Arte caritativo que futilezas labra
> y asicála los trajes, y los descuidos peina,

---

7   'Sinfonía color de fresas en leche' was originally published in *El Heraldo* in Bogotá on 10 April 1894 (Asunción Silva, 1996: 118–119).

finge piadosa mano que bruñe la palabra
como un espejo intacto para una faz de reina.

Proscrita de Bizancio, la excelsitud de mi arte
no es dar fiesta al oído con frase amartelada:
si quieres un espejo para narcisearte,
mírate en la ancha hoja de mi radiante espada.

Aquiles qué, entre tocas, en la extranjera corte,
pone al músculo férreo disímulos de raso,
es pueril comediante, que nunca alcanza el porte
del que en la Iliada cruza con resonante paso.

Las enguantadas manos no son para las lanzas,
ni los nítidos verbos les dan alma a las cosas …
No me deis pies hercúleos tejiendo muelles danzas,
ni me deis bravas frentes coronadas de rosas.
(Chocano, 1901: 84-85).

Charitable art that labours on futilities
and decks out costumes and combs out oversights,
it fakes, the pious hand that polishes the word
as an intact mirror for a queen's face.

Exiled from Byzantium, the supremacy of my art
is not to please the ear with infatuated phrases:
If you desire a mirror to narcissise yourself,
behold your reflection in the broad blade of my shining sword!

Achilles, wearing a headdress at the unfamiliar court
placing satin deception on his iron muscle,
is a ridiculous comedian who never attains the size
of the man who marches in the *Iliad* with resounding steps.

The gloved hands are not meant for lances,
and cowardly words cannot give soul to things …
Give me no Herculean feet knitting mild dances
give me no brave brows crowned with roses.

The American poet dressed in French garb is a cowardly Achilles in drag; a narcissistic, luxurious and stagnant 'Byzantine' Greek. But like cunning Odysseus, Chocano holds up a broad sword in his poetry and hopes that his generation will tear off the silk and wake up from the decadent dream.

The culmination of these critiques came in the works of the Uruguayan essayist José Enrique Rodó. Here too, Byzantium had a prominent role to play.

In reviews and essays written during the 1890s, before his big breakthrough, Rodó often complained that the young world of America had become a Byzantium prematurely:

> La artificiosidad decadente ha vertido, además, en nuestro vaso, aún no bien cincelado por el tiempo, algunas gotas del filtro mágico y sobreexcitador que viejos pueblos beben en copa bizantinamente trabajada. (Rodó, [1896] 1967: 826)[8]

> The decadent artificiality has poured into our cup a few tiny drops of the magic potion that ancient cities drink in a cup Byzantinely produced; but our cup has not yet been chiselled out by time.

The idea was more fully developed in Rodó's pamphlet *Rubén Darío: su personalidad literaria* from 1899. It opened with the statement that Darío is not the Whitman of the South; not the poet of *América*. His verse belongs not in the Forum but 'in a palace of spiritual princes and conversationalists': 'en un palacio de príncipes espirituales y conversadores' (Rodó, 1967: 171). This was far away from the Greece that is pure, which for Rodó was the Greece of Apollo, 'luminous and serene' (1967: 182). The youth and idealism that it stood for were crucial to his vision of Latin America achieving autonomy through a new humanism – a humanism that would employ Parnassian means for Enlightenment ends. Writers had to reawaken the idealistic Hellenism of the early nineteenth century and isolate the vein of marble that runs uninterpreted 'amidst the Gothic stones of Romanticism' and Oriental imagery (1967: 182–183). The first humanism had seen how 'larvae in the medieval codices suddenly turned into attic butterflies and spread out over an awe-stricken world': 'vio propagarse sobre el mundo asombrado las mariposas áticas salidas de las larvas de los códices' (1967: 210). Postclassicism was the nemesis of the revolutionary spirit of Greece in its eternal struggle, and Darío had let the former oppress the latter.

This perspective also pervades Rodó's epoch-making essay *Ariel* written a year later. Here, an idealised ancient Greece is offered as a source of internal youth and energy that can never be extinguished, only diminished or increased. The decrepitude of imperial Rome, the Middle Ages and the Orient had invaded his own century and turned the heroes of romanticism into a decadent Huysmans. As Latin America was now facing the Caliban of the north, in the United States' military and cultural expansion, the countries of the southern continent had to guard the sacred chain that connected them to ancient Greece at the one end and to a glorious future at the other.

---

8   See also Rodó ([1898] 1967: 987). On Rodó and Greece, see Taboada (2007).

Chocano's epic spirit was appreciated by Rodó, who praised the Peruvian poet's ambition to 'return the arms of combat' to poetry: 'se propone devolver a la poesía sus armas de combate' (1903). As for Darío, his use of Byzantium changed in the direction of his overall evolution. The existential anguish that beset many of his later works is strongly present in the sonnet dedicated to his son, 'To Phocas the farmer'. Here, the tenth-century emperor, born in Cappadocia on the eastern frontier, becomes the child lying in the poet's arms, born to this life of pain without 'azure and fresh roses'. The impossibility of escaping to Byzantium was now more important to the Nicaraguan poet.

As decadentist identifications with Byzantium faded away, it became more firmly a negative term for social stagnation. We often find it in historical characterisations of Lima's colonial past as a wealthy commercial metropolis. Rodó looked back on this 'Byzantine' society as the epitome of the unnatural mixing of young and old (1967: 737). Similarly, the Peruvian historian José de la Riva-Agüero noted that Lima under the Habsburg dynasty 'was like a new Byzantium – a pale and quiet Byzantium without heresies or military revolutions': 'Lima era como una nueva Bizancio – una Bizancio pálida y quieta, sin herejías ni revoluciones militares' (Riva Agüero, 1910: 292).

Polemicists could declare that nothing had really changed since then, as did the Peruvian anarchist Manuel González Prada, who had called for the young to rise up and sweep away the old, long before the appearance of Rodó's *Ariel*. As in the case of Rodó, the free spirit symbolised by Greece and paganism was an eternal source of youth and vigour, always struggling against the medieval and imperial. In the prelude to the collection of poems *Exóticas* (1911), Prada lamented the moment when the race of Solon and Aeschylus had to put on 'the iron yoke of Byzantium':

> Pudo la raza de Solón y Esquilo
> rendirse al férreo yugo de Bizancio.
> (González Prada, 1911: 8)

In Peru's situation at the time, this translated as an opposition between the provinces and the capital for González Prada. In the essay 'The festering core' (1914), he described Lima as the ailment that kept the whole Peruvian organism in the state of a sickly Byzantium (González Prada, 1933: 164). He invoked Edgar Quinet's wrinkled youth and complained that nothing had changed over the course of the last century:

> Todo viejo, todo rancio;
> el joven lleva en su frente
> las arrugas de Bizancio.
> (González Prada, 1938: 47)

Everything old, everything putrid;

the young man bears on his forehead
the wrinkles of Byzantium.

Culturally, Lima was a swamp where 'the man prepared to breathe the air of
modernity is asphyxiated': 'Aquí se asfixia el hombre organizado para respi-
rar un ambiente moderno' (González Prada, 1933: 162).

   The very same Byzantine asphyxiation is described by another Peruvian
poet, César Vallejo, who had himself moved from the province to the capital.
At the age of 24, still living in his university city of Trujillo, he published
an Andean pastoral which was first printed in *La Reforma* on 27 May 1916
entitled 'Mayo azul':

> Hoz al hombro calmoso,
> acre el gesto brioso,
> va un joven labrador a Irichugo.
> Y en cada brazo que parece yugo
> se encrespa el férreo jugo palpitante
> que en creador esfuerzo cuotidiano
> chispea, como trágico diamante,
> a través de los poros de la mano
> que no ha bizantinado aún el guante.
> Bajo un arco que forma verde aliso,
> oh cruzada fecunda del andrajo!
> pasa el perfil macizo
> de este Aquiles incaico del trabajo.
> (Vallejo, 1996: 68–69, lines 19–31)

> Sickle on sluggish shoulder,
> his lively countenance bitter,
> a young farm-hand goes to Irichugo.
> And in each yoke-like arm
> the iron juice agitates, throbbing,
> and in a daily creative effort
> sparkles, like a tragic diamond,
> through the pores of a hand
> no glove has ever byzantinised.
> Under an archway formed by green alder
> – oh fecund crossing of a man in rags! –
> the massive profile
> of this Incan Achilles of labour passes.
> (Vallejo, 2007: 93)

The farmer from Irichugo is still an Incan Achilles, still an ungloved hero of an archaic world who has not yet suffered his inevitable 'decline and fall'. He works the soil and his recompense is sweat sparkling 'like a diamond' where it passes through his hands unchecked by the decadence and passivity symbolised by the Byzantine glove, alluding to Chocano's image of a daintily gloved Byzantine Achilles. Vallejo even appears to have been aware of the larger intertextual web to which his poem belonged, as he had discussed Olmedo's simile of the Peruvian youth as Achilles on Scyros in his BA thesis on Hispanic romanticism at the University of Trujillo from the year before *Mayo* was published. But in contrast to Olmedo's neoclassical heroism or Chocano's poetic call-to-arms, Vallejo's Peruvian Achilles has no thought of Troy but lives out his days on the farm. His heroism is not one of epic grandeur but pastoral withdrawal.

A few years later the poet left Trujillo for Lima. Finding himself at the heart of the González Prada's 'festering core', he wrote yet another bucolic poem, but this time one that has lost its spark of life: the *Idilio muerto* which was first printed in *Los heraldos negros* in 1918. Trapped in an urban setting, the speaker remembers his beloved Rita and life in the mountains:

> Qué estará haciendo esta hora mi andina y dulce Rita
> de junco y capulí;
> ahora que me asfixia Bizancio, y que dormita
> la sangre, como flojo cognac, dentro de mí.
>
> Dónde estarán sus manos que en actitud contrita
> planchaban en las tardes blancuras por venir;
> ahora, en esta lluvia que me quita
> las ganas de vivir.
>
> Qué será de su falda de franela; de sus
> afanes; de su andar;
> de su sabor a cañas de mayo del lugar. (Vallejo, 1996: 72, lines 1–11)

> What would she be doing at this very hour, my sweet, Andean Rita
> of the wild reed and the dusk berry;
> now that Byzantium asphyxiates me, and that blood dozes,
> like insipid cognac, inside me.
>
> Where would her hands be, which used to contritely
> iron in the evenings whitenesses to come,
> now that this rain takes away
> my will to live.
>
> What has become of her flannel skirt, of her

worries, of her walking,
of her taste of local May sugar canes?

The activity of the farmer in 'Mayo azul' has now been replaced by the total passivity of the urban poet, inebriated and asphyxiated by the capital. Taken together, the two poems appear to foreshadow Vallejo's later well-known critique of Chocano's 'barato americanismo' or 'cheap Americanism' and his touristic imagery of condors and Andean flutes or *quenas* (Vallejo, 1927). If there is a Greece and Arcadia to be found in America, these early poems seem to imply, it is in the quiet life of the Andean village; not in the mishmash *criollo* fantasies of American grandeur. The Byzantium rejected by Chocano is identified with the culture in Lima that this poet dominated and that mistook his superficial Americanism for the true voice of the continent.

This was not the last time that Chocano was implicitly accused of the Byzantinism he had rejected. During the 1920s as his popularity increased so too did his passion for grandeur, not least in the form of dictatorships. In 1924, he performed at the centenary of the battle in Ayacucho as one of several poets who voiced their support for the American dictatorships of Augusto B. Leguía in Peru and Juan Vicente Gómez in Venezuela. This made him incur the censure of the Mexican philosopher and ex-minister of education José Vasconcelos. In the article 'Poets and Buffoons', Vasconcelos (1926: 11–18) lamented the Peruvian poet's recent development and decision to serve as a jester at the dictator's court. Chocano published an enraged reply, which reached Vasconcelos during his stay in Istanbul (1926: 19–47). Vasconcelos' response, entitled 'Democracy and Tyranny', invokes the life and death of the Byzantine empire to illustrate his main point:

> Todo lo tenía Bizancio: el territorio extenso y fértil, los puertos abrigados y numerosos, el eje del mundo antiguo como base, las razas mejores del planeta, la lucidez del griego, el genio sagrado del sirio, la organización del estado romano, la riqueza, la tradición, el poderío. Todo lo tenía Bizancio. Pero todos esos poderes reunidos los puso Bizancio en manos de un hombre, en manos de un déspota. (1926: 61)

> Byzantium had everything: a wide-ranging and fertile territory; harbours, numerous and safe; the axis of the ancient world as its base; the best races on the planet; the lucidity of the Greek; the sacred spirit of the Syrian; the organization of the Roman state; the riches, the tradition and the power. Byzantium had everything. But Byzantium placed all of those strengths together in the hands of one man, the hands of a despot.

Far from being a decrepit, doomed society, the Byzantine empire started off with the perfect conditions for progress but with one tragic flaw: its autocratic rule. The system rendered the civilisation a dysfunctional one as the common good was repeatedly compromised by rulers and generals looking out for their own interests.

But more importantly, the description of these favourable conditions is strongly reminiscent of Vasconcelos' grand vision for Spanish America's future as the fifth race of humanity, formulated the very same year in *La raza cósmica* (1925): the mixture of European and the Asian races; the spirituality of Christian and other Eastern traditions; the Roman heritage of state organisation via Spain; and the intellectual lucidity of Hellas. Byzantium is not mentioned in this influential treatise, but in other works of Vasconcelos and in his practice of cultural politics, the impact of Byzantium, not least of the church of Holy Wisdom, *Hagia Sophia*, as an emblem of racial and cultural hybridity is clear.[9] America was to succeed where Byzantium had failed.

*

In most cases considered here, Byzantium is an historical concept virtually empty of historiographical data. It was defined, rather, through its relationship with other entities: after antiquity, before modernity; east of the Western and west of the Oriental. Its association with decline and Christian eschatology made it virtually synonymous with the biological metaphor of decline and old age. Thus, as was also the case elsewhere, it was embraced by decadentism and rejected by progressivism. But it also engendered a rather fatalistic scheme of thought that is quite specific to the postcolonial situation: that of being somehow out of tune with a natural biological order. America was a new world, but asphyxiated by old habits from the very start; its youthful energy was checked by a Byzantine glove and marked by wrinkles that never seemed to fade. But we have also seen an approach that stayed clear of this problem: one that reconstructed a Byzantium as counterfactual and idealistic as classical Hellenism by freezing the medieval empire at its birth. Bolívar returned to Constantine's vision, and Vasconcelos to the age of Justinian and the church of *Hagia Sophia* that had swept him off his feet during his stay in Istanbul. The allure of this narrative is clear: it is one about building a future from the ruins of a glorious past, from a long and heterogeneous prehistory, where the classical Greece is neutralised to become just one of many elements.

References

Armas, A. de (1891) *Rimes byzantines*. Bibliothèque de la Europa y América: Paris.

---

9   See especially the letter to Marcelino Valencia from 1932 (Vasconcelos, 1950: 156).

Asunción Silva, J. (1996) *Obra completa*, ed. H. H. Orjuela. Colección Archivos: Madrid.

Baudelaire, C. (1857) *Les fleurs du mal*. Poulet-Malassis et De Broise: Paris.

Beaton, R. (2013) *Byron's War: Romantic Rebellion, Greek Revolution*. Cambridge University Press: Cambridge.

Blanco-Fombona, R. (1921) *Cartas de Bolívar 1823–1824-1825*. Editorial-América: Madrid.

Bolívar, S. (1964) *Escritos del Libertador*. Sociedad Bolivariana de Venezuela: Caracas.

Briceño Perozo, M. (1992) *Reminiscencias griegas y latinas en las obras del Libertador*. Editorial Texto: Caracas.

Carpio, M. (1874) *Poesías*. M. Murguia: Mexico City.

Concepcion Valdes, G. de la (1856) *Poesias completas de Plácido*. C. Denné Schmitz: Paris.

Chocano, J. S. (1899) *La epopeya del Morro: poema americano*. J. R. Sánchez: Lima.

Chocano, J. S. (1901) *La selva virgen*. Garnier: Paris.

Cullhed, E. (2014) 'From Byzantium to the Andes' in I. Nilsson and P. Stephenson (eds.) *Wanted, Byzantium: The Desire for a Lost Empire*. Acta Universitatis Upsaliensis: Uppsala, 217–236.

Darío, R. (1887) *'Rimas'* in *Certámen Varela* (vol. 1). Imprenta Cervantes: Santiago de Chile, 186–196.

Darío, R. (1888) *Azul …* Excelsior: Valparaiso.

Darío, R. (1896a) *Los raros*. Tipografía La Vasconia: Buenos Aires.

Darío, R. (1896b) *Prosas profanas y otros poemas*. Pablo E. Coni e Hijos: Buenos Aires.

Darío, R. (1901) *Prosas profanas y otros poemas*. Charles Bouret: Paris and Mexico City.

David-de Palacio, M.-F. (2001) 'Les "nacres de la perle et de la pourriture": Byzance' in A. Montandon (ed.) *Mythes de la decadence*. Presses Universitaires Blaise Pascal: Clermont-Ferrand, 163–175.

Delouis, O. (2003) 'Byzance sur la scène littéraire française (1870–1920)' in M.-F. Auzépy (ed.) *Byzance en Europe*. Presses Universitaires de Vincennes: Saint-Denis, 101–151.

Engonopoulos, N. (1944) *Mpolibar: ena Ellēniko poiēma*. Ikaros: Athens.

Fischer, S. (2004) *Modernity Disavowed: Haiti and the Cultures of Slavery in the Age of Revolution*. Duke University Press: Durham.

Gautier, T. (1868) 'Charles Baudelaire' in *Charles Baudelaire: Les fleurs du mal, précédées d'une notice par Théophile Gautier*. Michel Lévy frères: Paris.

Gibbon, E. (1788a) *The History of the Decline and Fall of the Roman Empire*, Vol. **5**. Strahan and Cadell: London.

Gibbon, E. (1788b) *The History of the Decline and Fall of the Roman Empire*, Vol. **6**. Strahan and Cadell: London.

González Prada, M. (1911) *Exóticas*. Tipografía de 'El Lucero': Lima.

González Prada, M. (1933) *Bajo el oprobio*. Tipografía de Louis Bellenand et Fils: Paris.

González Prada, M. (1938) *Antología poética*. Editorial Cultura: Mexico City.

Greenwood, E. (2010) *Afro-Greeks: Dialogues between Anglophone Caribbean Literature and Classics in the Twentieth Century*. Oxford University Press: Oxford.

Hernández Muñoz, F. G. H. (2000) 'Encanto y desencanto griego en la obra bolivariana'. *Praesentia: Revista Venezolana de Estudios Clásicos* **2-3**: 127–139.

Latorre Broto, E. (2013) 'Grecia como camino hacia la libertad: el filohelenismo de José María Heredia'. *Anales de Literatura Hispanoamericana* **42**: 279–296.

Marchand, L. A. (1979) *Byron's Letters and Journals, Volume IX: 'In the Wind's Eye'*: *1821–1822*. Harvard University Press: Cambridge.

Martí, J. (1991) *José Martí: obras completas*. Editorial de ciencias sociales: Havana.

Menéndez Pelayo, M. (1894) *Antología de poetas Hispano-Americanos*, Vol. **3**. Sucesores de Rivadeneyra: Madrid.

Neruda, P. (1943) 'Concepto breve de Pablo Neruda sobre la obra de Pedro Nel Gómez'. *El Diario* (Medellín) (8 October).

Olivares, J. (1980) 'La recepción del decadentismo en Hispanoamérica'. *Hispanic Review* **48**: 57–76.

Orrego Luco, A. (1878) 'El Padre Lopez. (Estudio sobre la poesía colonial)'. *Revista chilena* **11**: 274–306.

Quinet, E. (1845) *Le christianisme et la révolution française*. Comptoir des imprimeurs unis: Paris.

Rentzou, E. (2010) *Littérature malgré elle: le surréalisme et la transformation du littéraire*. Pleine Marge: Paris.

de la Riva Agüero, J. (1910) *La historia en el Perú*. Imprenta Nacional de Federico Barrionuevo: Lima.

Rodó, J. E. (1903) 'Carta a J. S. Chocano'. *Actualidades* **34** (14 September), Lima.

Rodó, J. E. (1967) *Obras completas*. Aguilar: Madrid.

Sarmiento, D. F. (1854) *Viajes en Europa, África i América*. Imprenta de Mayo: Buenos Aires.

Stabakis, N. (2008) *Surrealism in Greece: An Anthology*. University of Texas Press: Austin.

Taboada, H. G. H. (2007) 'José Enrique Rodó: el oriental y la Hélade'. *Anuario del Colegio de Estudios Latinoamericanos* **2**: 89–95.

Taboada, H. G. H. (2008) 'La sombra del Oriente en la independencia americana' in S. Nagy-Zekmi (ed.) *Moros en la costa: orientalismo en Latinoamérica*. Iberoamericana Editorial: Madrid, 25–40.

Taboada, H. G. H. (2011) 'De la España africana a la América teocrática: notas sobre el ideario de Simón Bolívar'. *Cuyo. Anuario de Filosofía Argentina y Americana* **28**: 35–59.

Tejera, D. V. (1895) *Un poco de prosa: crítica, biografía, cuentos etc. 1883–1896*. El Fígaro: Havana.

Tejeras, J. D. (1970) *Hojas de analectas*. Archivo General de la Nación: Caracas.

Vallejo, C. (1927) 'Contra el secreto profesional: a propósito de Pablo Abril de Vivero'. *Variedades* (Lima) (7 May).

Vallejo, C. (1996) *Poesía completa*. Akal: Madrid.

Vallejo, C. (2007) *The Complete Poetry: A Bilingual Edition* ed. C. Eshleman. University of California Press: Berkeley, Los Angeles, London.

Valencia, G. (1898) *Poesías*. Papelería de Samper Matiz: Bogotá.

Vasconcelos, J. (1926) *Poetas y bufones: polémica Vasconcelos-Chocano; el asesinato de Edwin Elmore*. Agencia Mundial de Librería: Madrid.

Vasconcelos, J. (1950) *Discursos 1920–1950*. Ediciones Botas: Mexico City.

Verlaine, P. (1884) *Nadis et naguère: poésies*. Léon Vanier: Paris.

Warren, M. R. (2012) 'Classicism, Medievalism, and the Postcolonial'. *Exemplaria* **24**: 282–292.

14

Envoi: Whose Classical Traditions?

JORGE CAÑIZARES-ESGUERRA

What are 'classical traditions'? To whom do they belong? Both of these questions are more than implicit in the preceding chapters which investigate different ways in which classical traditions endured in a region rarely associated with Greco-Roman antiquity. Classical studies originated in the Renaissance, but modern conceptions of the 'classical' are the more direct product of the northern European legacy of *Altertumswissenschaft*, established by Friedrich August Wolf towards the end of the eighteenth century (Grafton, 1999). That 'science of antiquity' not only excluded the Egyptians, Persians, Jews, Arabs and other peoples from consideration, but also removed Roman late antiquity, Byzantine Greece and the European Middle Ages from its purview. The practitioners of this science also played down the achievements of earlier antiquarians in Iberia as well as in Italy – at the same time as they made full use of their work. Wolf's narrower definition of the ancient world is still prevalent, causing many of its legacies to disappear altogether.

It is worth asking whether the Christian productions of late antiquity, at least, should count as classical traditions. And if so, do systems of education based on those works that gave centre place to Augustine, Jerome and Eusebius qualify as rightful heirs to the intellectual traditions of classical Rome and Greece? Do the Franciscan, Augustinian, Dominican and Jesuit inheritors of the radical Aristotelianism of Aquinas, Duns Scotus and William of Ockham qualify as rightful heirs? And what about the tens of thousands of youths trained for 300 years in the scholastic legacies of Greek academic philosophy and in the Justinian code of Roman law at universities, academies and courts in Lima and Mexico, and throughout Spanish America?

In addition to the historical authors and protagonists already mentioned in this book, some better known than others, there are several further forgotten figures, who could be the subjects of future studies. There was Juan Suárez de Mendoza from Cartagena de Indias, author of one of the most influential European texts in classical Roman tort and property law of the seventeenth century (Suárez de Mendoza, 1640). Entitled *Commentarii ad Legem Aquiliam*, it was dedicated to the Count of Castrillo, President of the Council of the Indies. First published in Salamanca, this work was reissued in Lyon and Antwerp, and would remain in print into the late 1700s. One could point out that Suárez de Mendoza's emulation of the legislators of antiquity in effect enabled him to help administer an empire even larger than Rome's. The

Professor of Theology at the Royal University of Mexico in the mid-1600s, Juan Díaz de Arce, was another important figure, now unjustly forgotten, who produced a magisterial study of Scripture: the *Opus Sacrorum Bibliorum* (Díaz de Arce, 1648). The book was reprinted in Rome in 1750, when it became influential with the Papal Curia at the height of the Catholic Enlightenment. Its author boldly advanced an epistemology of popular prophecy and affirmed the central role of the illiterate in biblical interpretation.

Fray Alonso de la Vera Cruz and the Jesuit Antonio Rubio are still known for the course books they produced on Aristotle in sixteenth-century Mexico (Burrus 1968; Osorio Romero, 1988; Beuchot, 1998: 71–79, 83–90). But while both those authors had been educated in peninsular Spain, there were scholars in New Granada and Peru who were trained or taught at local American universities. Their Latin works on theology and jurisprudence became standard texts – from central and eastern Europe to Asia and the Philippines. Gabriel Álvarez Velasco, for instance, addressed from the small college town of Tunja the rights of widows, orphans and the downtrodden in his *De privilegiis pauperum* and in other Latin works which sold widely in Europe for the best part of a century (Álvarez Velasco, 1630, 1662). Two brothers from Riobamba in Peru, Alonso and Leonardo Peñafiel, were influential logicians who could compete with their great Jesuit confrère, the philosopher Francisco Suárez (Alonso Peñafiel, 1653–1655, 1678; Leonardo Peñafiel, 1663–1666, 1678; Gracia, 1982). Numerous works by the Peñafiels which issued from the printing presses of Antwerp, Cologne and Lyon were read in the colleges of Goa and Manila as well as Rome and Prague. Diego de Avendaño, who was educated in Cuzco to become one of the most innovative canon lawyers of his generation and celebrated for his *Thesaurus indicus* (1668), was also a leading scholar of Aristotle and interpreter of Scripture. His careful commentaries on Psalm 44 and on Psalm 88 were respectively given provocative titles: *Epithalamium Christi et sancta sponsae*, 'The Wedding of Christ and Rites of his Betrothed', and *Amphitheatrum misericordiae*, 'World Theatre of Christ's Mercy' (Avendaño, 1653, 1668).

The Augustinian Gaspar de Villarroel was another formidable linguist and biblical scholar at the University of San Marcos in Lima: his typological and literal interpretation of the Book of Judges, *Ivdices Commentariis* which was published in Madrid, collated the Hebrew and Aramaic versions of the text as well as the Greek of the Septuagint and Jerome's Latin Vulgate (Villaroel, 1636). The fact that Villaroel's endeavours were repaid with a series of bishoprics, first Chile, then Arequipa, and finally Charcas, the seat of the silver mines, is ample demonstration of the extent to which the society in which he received his formation was investing in scholarship. Huge sums of money were directed into sustaining institutions of humanist learning like the University of San Marcos: a revenue that came straight from the forced labour of miners in Potosí and Huancavelica. By the mid-seventeenth century, San Marcos had a roster of 150 Masters and 100 *doctorados* educating a community of 1,500 students in the liberal arts, theology, jurisprudence, and medicine. The image of such a society, in which an academy of hundreds of philosophers could thrive on the work of armies of Andean labourers who were virtually unpaid, in itself recalls the extent to which the cultural glory and intellectual greatness of Greece and Rome depended on the inequity and cruelty of imperialism and slavery.

Further thinkers made more direct use of their learning to engage with European classical humanists – in order to challenge their assumptions about the deficiency of nature in the New World and to refute their allegations about the dearth of erudition in the Indies. Just as the jurist Juan Solórzano de Pereira had rejected Scaliger's disparaging account of American geography, members of the University of San Marcos like Fray Buenaventura de Salinas y Córdova created genealogies of local academic excellence to address the Flemish humanist Justus Lipsius' failure even to consider Spanish American institutions of learning (Solórzano de Pereira, 1629; Cañizares-Esguerra, 1999). Diego de León Pinelo's 1648 *Hypomnema apologeticum pro regali Academia Limensi*, 'A Reminder and Defence of the Royal Academy of Lima', for instance, promoted the intellectual achievements of his milieu – long before José de Eguiara y Eguren set about compiling his celebrated *Bibliotheca Mexicana* (1755) to counter Manuel Martí's patronising account of the state of education in the Americas (Gerbi, 1946; Eguiara y Eguren, 1996).

These and other examples, such as those highlighted in this volume by Stuart McManus and Desiree Arbo, illustrate the variety of ways in which classical traditions were pervasive among colonial elites. Elina Miranda Cancela and Rosa Andújar describe how, with the onset of independence, intellectuals appealed to ancient Greek political ideals as a way of endowing their *patrias* and nations with potent moral genealogies. Nicola Miller has argued that the idioms of Roman republican resistance to tyranny allowed marginalised but popular black poets like Gabriel de la Concepción Valdés, or 'Plácido', to inveigh against the oppression of racism in Cuba during the mid-1800s. Eric Cullhed maintains that the language of decadent imperial Byzantium enabled later nineteenth-century poets, like the Puerto Rican José de Jesús Domínguez, the Cuban Augusto de Armas and the Nicaraguan Rubén Darío, to invent a pan-Latin culture appealing to French as well as Hispanic literary modernism. Ranging from popular to elite culture, from the Caribbean and Central America to the Andes and the Southern Cone, and from the 1500s to the 1900s, the evidence taken together is overwhelming: there were many, vibrant classical traditions all over Spanish America.

Standard scholarship on early modern humanism has painstakingly explored the impact of encounters with the indigenous peoples of the

Americas on the creation of the Renaissance, itself a kaleidoscope of many possible classical traditions. There have been studies of how Columbus, Luther and so many others brought worlds which were new to theology as well as geography into the glossaries, commentaries, and exegeses of ancient books (Elliott, 1970; Pagden, 1982; Ordahl Kupperman, 1995). Here it is the Indian, projected as either a demonic or noble savage, who is always summoned as a heuristic device. The learned creole authors and Latinists of colonial Spanish America are never mentioned. And, needless to say, there is never any inkling in this type of scholarship of those 'Indians' who were themselves scholars – whose endeavours overthrow longstanding conceptions about who was entitled to possess, transmit and manipulate European classical traditions.

In their contributions to this collection Byron Hamann and Alejandra Rojas make clear that, soon after the Spanish conquest of Mexico, native artists were swift to enhance traditional pictorial language with classical themes and motifs. The same was true of indigenous and *mestizo* writers: Andrew Laird reveals that Alva Ixtlilxochitl's presentation of his ancestral world of pre-Hispanic Aculhua, its theology and architecture – a world historians had long assumed was authentically Mexican – was really constructed by this seventeenth-century historian from his readings of Ficino's Latin works on Plato; while the Nahua chronicler Chimalpahin, though he knew his Mesoamerican chronology and calendars, is also shown to have studied Isidore's *Etymologies,* Caelius Rhodiginus' *Antiquae lectiones,* and Ambrogio Traversari's Latin translation of Diogenes Laertius' *Lives.* Erika Valdivieso introduces us to an Inca Garcilaso de la Vega who was familiar with Medici Florence and the Venetian Jewish ghetto. Garcilaso was also an avid reader of Ficino, and a masterful translator of León Hebreo's *Dialoghi d'amore.* Valdivieso indicates that Garcilaso used Hebreo to construct an Inca monarchy of Platonists who understood the proper hierarchies of wisdom and creation. One might also consider another celebrated noble Quechua chronicler, Felipe Guaman Poma (1535–1616), who made use of his extensive European learning to win influence as a *letrado* and to devise honourable genealogies for himself and his family (Adorno, 2002).

Such examples take us beyond merely asserting that there were 'indigenous intellectuals': these examples help to crush the curse of an orientalism which has long impeded Latin Americanist scholarship. The Indians who wrote sprawling histories and chronicles make nonsense of the assumption that Indians are meant to have been authentic and organic, and to have written only by painting pictures and weaving quipus. For all the talk of hybridity, current ideas of the 'colonial' all too often involve facile Manichean dualities: just as orality is set in opposition to writing, local to the global, and peripheries to centres, so what is indigenous is set against what is European, and native belief is set in opposition to the instrumental reason of an imperialist Enlightenment. For anyone who has taken on board Ángel Rama's *La ciudad letrada* (1984), Magdalena Chocano's *La Fortaleza docta* (2000) or, worse, Walter Mignolo's *The Darker Side of the Renaissance* (1994), it is as if Chimalpahin ought to have been ashamed of reading the Italian humanist publications he found in the bookstores and libraries of Mexico City.

However that may be, there should now at least be no question about whether there have long been muscular classical traditions in Latin America. Indeed, I, for one, find that the conceptions of time, space, hierarchy, labour, family, the sacred, and community current in Quito, my home town, make it far more convergent with the legacy of classical Rome than London or several other European cities. We should instead ask why these traditions in the Americas, distinctive as they were, are not held to be as deep and as significant as those of, say, early modern France, Germany or Britain? A further related question is also raised by the chapters in this book: why have intellectual historians (and historians of the classical tradition in particular) never even thought of looking at the global South to consider the extent to which learned communities of Latin America might have influenced or surpassed the achievements of those in Europe?

References

Adorno, R. (2000) *Guaman Poma: Writing and Resistance in Colonial Peru*. University of Texas Press: Austin.

Álvarez Velasco, G. (1630) *De privilegiis pauperum et miserabilium personarum*. Madrid.

Álvarez Velasco, G. (1662) *Epitome de Legis humanae mundique fictione, veritate divinae*. Boissat: Lyon.

Avendaño, Diego de (1653) *Epithalamium Christi et sacrae sponsae: seu explanatio psalmi quadragesimiquarti*. Laurentius Anisson: Lyon.

Avendaño, D. d. (1666) 'Amphitheatrum misericordiae' in *Expositio psalmo LXXXVIII*. Horace Boissat and George Remeus: Lyon.

Avendaño, Diego de (1668) *Thesaurus indicus seu generalis instructor pro regimine conscientiae, in iis quae ad Indias spectant*. Jacobus Meursius: Antwerp.

Beuchot, M. (1998) *The History of Philosophy in Colonial Mexico*. Catholic University Press of America: Washington.

Burrus, E. J. (1968-1972) *The Writings of Alonso de la Vera Cruz. The original texts with English translation*. (5 vols.). Jesuit Historical Institute and St Louis University: Rome and St Louis.

Cañizares-Esguerra, J. (1999) 'New World, New Stars: Patriotic Astrology and the Invention of Indian and Creole Bodies in Colonial Spanish America, 1600-1650'. *American Historical Review* **104**(1): 33–68.

Chocano Mena, M. (2000) *La fortaleza docta. Elite letrada y dominación social en México colonial (siglos XVI-XVII)*. Bellaterra: Barcelona.

Díaz de Arce, Juan (1648) *Expositivi quaestionarii libri XLIX de studio Bibliorum.* Madrid (reprinted *Opus de studioso Sacrorum Bibliorum authore D. Johanne Diaz de Arce.* Antonius de Rubeis: Rome).

Eguiara y Eguren, J. J. de (1996) *Prólogos a la Biblioteca Mexicana* (trans. A. Millares Carlo). Fondo de Cultura Económica: Mexico City.

Elliott, J. H. (1970) *The Old World and the New 1492–1650.* Cambridge University Press: Cambridge.

Gerbi, A. (1946) *Diego de Leon Pinelo contra Justo Lipsio: una de las primeras polémicas sobre el nuevo mundo.* Editorial Lumen: Lima.

Gracia, J. J. E. (1982) *Suárez on Individuation.* Marquette University Press: Milwaukee.

Grafton, A. (1999) 'Juden und Griechen bei Friedrich August Wolf' in R. Markner and G. Veltri (eds.) *Friedrich August Wolf: Studien, Dokumente, Bibliographie. Palingenesia.* Franz Steiner Verlag: Stuttgart. Vol. **67**, 9–31.

León Pinelo, Diego (1648) *Hypomnema apologeticum pro regali Academia Limensi.* Julian de los Santos et Saldaña: Lima.

Mignolo, W. (1994) *The Darker Side of the Renaissance: Literacy, Territoriality and Colonization.* University of Michigan Press: Ann Arbor.

Ordahl Kupperman, K. (ed.) (1995) *America in European Consciousness 1493–1750.* University of North Carolina Press: Chapel Hill and London.

Osorio Romero, I. (1988) *Antonio Rubio en la filosofía novohispana.* Universidad Nacional Autónoma de México: Mexico.

Pagden, A. (1982) *The Fall of Natural Man: The American Indian and the Origins of Comparative Ethnology.* Cambridge University Press: Cambridge.

Peñafiel, A. (1653-1655) *Cursus Integer Philosophicus.* Borde, Arnaud and Rigaud: Lyon.

Peñafiel, A. (1678a) *Theologia Scholastica Naturalis.* Huguetan: Lyon.

Peñafiel, L. (1663-1666) *De Deo uno.* Boissat and Remeus: Lyon.

Peñafiel, L. (1678b) *Disputationes Scholasticae.* Huguetan: Lyon.

Rama, Á. (1984) *La ciudad letrada.* Ediciones del Norte: Hanover.

Solórzano de Pereira, J. (1629) *De Indianorum jure disputatio siue de justa Indiarum Occidentalium inquisitione.* Francisco Martinez: Madrid.

Suárez de Mendoza, Juan (1640) *Commentarii ad Legem Aquiliam.* Tabernier: Salamanca.

Villarroel, Gaspar de (1636) *Iudices commentariis literalibus cum moralibus aphorismis illustrati.* P. Taço: Madrid.

Contributors

ROSA ANDÚJAR is Lecturer and Deputy Director of the new Department of Liberal Arts at King's College London. She has published several articles on various aspects of ancient Greek tragedy as well as its modern reception in Latin America, and is the editor of *Paths of Song: The Lyric Dimension of Greek Tragedy* (De Gruyter 2018). She is completing two book-length projects: the first examining the various roles and capabilities of the fifth-century Greek tragic chorus beyond the choral ode, and the second on twentieth-century re-imaginings of ancient Greek drama in the Hispanic Caribbean.

DESIREE ARBO is a Fellow at the Warwick University Institute of Advanced Study. She obtained her PhD in Classics in 2017 and is working on the uses of classical learning in the Río de la Plata, analysing the functions of Jesuit humanism in literature and in the political discourse of Paraguayan independence. She has co-authored an essay on José Manuel Peramás' *De Invento Novo Orbe*, an eighteenth-century Latin epic about Christopher Columbus (*Dieciocho* 38.1, 2015).

JORGE CAÑIZARES-ESGUERRA is the Alice Drysdale Sheffield Professor of History at UT-Austin. His award-winning books include: *How to Write the History of the New World: Histories, Epistemologies, and Identities in the Eighteenth Century Atlantic World* (Stanford University Press 2001); *Puritan Conquistadors* (Stanford U.P. 2006); and *Nature, Empire, and Nation: Explorations of the History of Science in the Iberian World* (Stanford U.P. 2007). He is editor of *Entangled Empires: The Anglo-Iberian Atlantic, 1500–1830* (University of Pennsylvania Press 2018), and co-editor of *The Black Urban Atlantic in the Age of the Slave Trade* (University of Pennsylvania 2013); the *Princeton Handbook to Atlantic History* (Princeton University Press 2014); *The Atlantic in Global History*, 1500–2000 (2nd ed.) (Routledge 2017); and *As Américas na Primeira Modernidade (1492–1750)* (vol. 1) (Editora Prismas 2017).

ROBERT T. CONN is Associate Professor of Romance Languages and Literatures and chair of the Latin American Studies Program at Wesleyan University in Connecticut. He has written on Mexico, publishing *The Politics of Philology: Alfonso Reyes and the Invention of the Latin American Literary Tradition* (2002) and he has a forthcoming book on Simón Bolívar and public discourse in the Americas.

ERIC CULLHED is Associate Professor in Greek Philology at Uppsala University, working on Greek, Latin, Swedish and Latin American literary and intellectual history. He is producing a critical edition of the twelfth-century orator Eustathios of Thessalonike's *Commentary on Homer's Odyssey* (Studia Byzantina Upsaliensia; first volume published in 2016) and investigating metaphorical aesthetic descriptors in India, Greece and Rome.

BYRON ELLSWORTH HAMANN holds a dual PhD in Anthropology and History from the University of Chicago. His research focuses on the art and writing of pre-Hispanic Mesoamerica and the connections linking the Americas and Europe in the early modern Mediterratlantic world. He is an editor of *Grey Room* (www.greyroom.org); co-director (with Liza Bakewell) of *Mesolore: Exploring Mesoamerican Culture* (www.mesolore.org); project manager (for Dana Leibsohn and Barbara Mundy) of *Vistas: Visual Culture in Spanish America, 1520–1820* (http://vistas-visual-culture.net); and author of *The Translations of Nebrija: Language, Culture, and Circulation in the Early Modern World* (University of Massachusetts Press 2015).

ANDREW LAIRD moved in 2016 from the United Kingdom to Brown University, Rhode Island, where he is John Rowe Workman Distinguished Professor of Classics and Humanities and Professor of Hispanic Studies. His publications on classical literature, humanism and history of scholarship in Europe and the Americas include: *Powers of Expression, Expressions of Power* (Oxford University Press 1999), *Ancient Literary Criticism* (Oxford University Press 2006), *The Epic of America* (Duckworth 2006), *Italy and the Classical Tradition: Language, Thought and Poetry 1300–1600* (Duckworth 2009), and the first comprehensive surveys of Latin writing from colonial Spanish America and Brazil for *Brill's Encyclopaedia of the Neo-Latin World* (Brill 2014) and for *The Oxford Handbook of Neo-Latin* (Oxford University Press 2015).

NATALIA MAILLARD ÁLVAREZ, PhD in History (2007), is currently Ramón y Cajal researcher at the Pablo de Olavide University in Seville. Among other positions, she has been Marie Curie Fellow at the European University Institute in Florence (2010–2012). She has published several articles and essays on the history of the book trade and the history of reading in the Hispanic monarchy during the sixteenth and seventeenth centuries. She is author of *Lectores y libros en la ciudad de Sevilla, 1550–1600* (2011) and editor of *Books in the Catholic World during the Early Modern Period* (2014).

NICOLA MILLER is Professor of Latin American History in the History Department of University College London. She has recently held a Leverhulme Trust Research Fellowship to work on a history of nation-building knowledge in Spanish America during the century after independence. Her findings will be published as *Republics of Knowledge* (Princeton University Press 2018 forthcoming). She has also worked on the intellectual and cultural histories of Latin American countries from a transnational perspective, for example in *America Imagined: Explaining the United States in Nineteenth-Century Europe and Latin America* (ed. with Axel Körner and Adam I. P. Smith, 2012), and 'Reading Rousseau in Spanish America during the wars of independence (1808-1826)', in *Engaging with Rousseau* (ed. Avi Lifschitz, 2016).

ELINA MIRANDA CANCELA holds a PhD in Philological Sciences from the University of Havana where she is a Distinguished Professor in Classical Philology and the Classical Tradition in the Faculty of Arts and Letters. She has written and edited various books, and published articles in European and American academic journals. Her authored works include *La tradición helénica en Cuba* (Havana 2003), a critical edition of José Martí's *La Ilíada de Homero* (Havana 2004), *Calzar el coturno americano* (Havana 2006), *Laura Mestre* (Madrid 2010), and two further books in press, *Poesía griega* and *Dionisos en las Antillas*.

STUART M. McMANUS is a cultural historian of global early modernity. He received his PhD from Harvard University in 2016 and is currently a post-doctoral fellow at the Stevanovich Institute on the Formation of Knowledge at the University of Chicago. He has published widely on Mexican, Roman, Renaissance, European, colonial US and Filipino history, and is currently completing a monograph on the global history of the classical rhetorical tradition and its relationship to early modern European expansion.

ALEJANDRA ROJAS SILVA investigates the role of the production and use of images in the negotiation of identity in colonial Latin America. She has been working on botanical images in the colonial period in the wake of her PhD research at Harvard University in History of Art. In 2013–2014 she was a Dumbarton Oaks junior fellow in pre-Columbian Studies in Washington, DC.

ERIKA VALDIVIESO is a classical philologist with interests in the history of education and humanism in the Americas, especially colonial Peru. She is completing her doctoral dissertation at Brown University on the Virgilian tradition in colonial Latin America, with a particular focus on Latin poetry written in New Spain and Brazil.

Index